D0049012

The Pastoral Novel

Michael Squires

THE
PASTORAL NOVEL

Studies in George Eliot,
Thomas Hardy,
and D. H. Lawrence

University Press of Virginia

Charlottesville

The publication of this volume is sponsored
by the VPI Educational Foundation, Inc.

THE UNIVERSITY PRESS OF VIRGINIA
Copyright © 1974 by the Rector and Visitors
of the University of Virginia

Second printing 1975

Frontispiece: Samuel Palmer's *The Shearers*.
(Private collection; photograph courtesy of
the Courtauld Institute of Art, London)

ISBN: 0-8139-0530-3
Library of Congress Catalog Card Number: 74-75793
Printed in the United States of America

To

Sylvia, Kelly, and Cameron

Acknowledgments

I gratefully acknowledge the help and encouragement of many friends and colleagues who assisted me in writing this book, especially George A. Panichas, Eleanor T. Lincoln, Russel E. Kacher, Wilson C. Snipes, and John P. Broderick. I owe a particular intellectual debt to the criticism of Renato Poggioli, Dorothy Van Ghent, F. R. Leavis, J. Hillis Miller, and Ian Gregor. I also want to thank Keith Cushman of the University of Chicago for his superb reader's report. My wife and sons, with good cheer, have done much to sustain my work, and the dedication expresses my gratitude.

In another form, parts of this study have appeared in *Studies in English Literature, Nineteenth-Century Fiction, Texas Studies in Literature and Language*, and *ELH*. I wish to thank the copyright holders for permission to reprint "*Far from the Madding Crowd* as Modified Pastoral," © 1970 by The Regents of the University of California, in *Nineteenth-Century Fiction*, 25 (1970), 299–326; "Lawrence's *The White Peacock*: A Mutation of Pastoral," © 1970 by The University of Texas Press, in *Texas Studies in Literature and Language*, 12 (1970), 263–83; "Pastoral Patterns and Pastoral Variants in *Lady Chatterley's Lover*," © 1972 by The Johns Hopkins University Press, in *ELH*, 39 (1972), 129–46; and "*Adam Bede* and the *Locus Amoenus*," © 1973 by William Marsh Rice University, in *Studies in English Literature*, 13 (1973), 670–76.

For kind permission to quote from *The White Peacock* and *Lady Chatterley's Lover* by D. H. Lawrence, I wish to thank the Estate of the late Mrs. Frieda Lawrence, Laurence Pollinger Ltd., and William Heinemann, Ltd.

Permission to quote from works protected by copyright has been generously granted by:

Harold Matson Company, Inc., for quotations from *The Eclogues of Virgil* translated by C. Day Lewis (Copyright 1963 by C. Day Lewis) and for quotations from *The Georgics of Virgil* translated by C. Day Lewis (Copyright 1968 by C. Day Lewis).

Macmillan Publishing Co., Inc., and Weidenfeld and Nicolson, for quotations from *Thomas Hardy* by Irving Howe (Copyright © 1966

Irving Howe. Copyright © 1967 by Macmillan Publishing Co., Inc. Copyright © 1968 by Weidenfeld and Nicolson).

The Trustees of the Hardy Estate, The Macmillan Company of Canada, and Macmillan, London and Basingstroke, for quotations from *Under the Greenwood Tree*, *Far from the Madding Crowd*, and *The Woodlanders* by Thomas Hardy.

The Viking Press, Inc., for quotations from *The Collected Letters of D. H. Lawrence*, edited by Harry T. Moore (Copyright © 1962 by Angelo Ravagli and C. M. Weekley, Executors of the Estate of Frieda Lawrence Ravagli. All rights reserved).

Southern Illinois University Press, for quotations from *The White Peacock* by D. H. Lawrence (Copyright © 1966 by Southern Illinois University Press).

Grove Press, Inc., for quotations from *Lady Chatterley's Lover* by D. H. Lawrence (Copyright © 1957 and 1959 by Grove Press, Inc.).

Contents

The Pastoral Novel

The Nature of
the Pastoral Novel

THE PASTORAL NOVELS of George Eliot, Thomas Hardy, and D. H. Lawrence have aroused surprisingly similar remarks from a wide range of scholars. Thomas Hardy is "our greatest master in the old pastoral tradition." His Dorsetshire novels are "modern pastoral romances." George Eliot, writing "pastoral fiction," became "the great novelist . . . of pastoral England," and *Adam Bede* is "the finest pastoral novel in English," "our supreme novel of pastoral life." If *Silas Marner* reflects a "quiet pastoralism," *Under the Greenwood Tree* is "a pastoral . . . idyll of English country life," Hardy's "finest pastoral." *Far from the Madding Crowd*, termed also "a pastoral idyll," creates a "pastoral world of antique simplicity" and is a "composition of pastoral elements very consciously designed." *The Woodlanders*, a late novel by Hardy, is "a charming idyll laid in a remote Arcadia"—a "traditional pastoral." Finally, if *The White Peacock* features "the loving evocation of a pastoral setting," *Lady Chatterley's Lover* takes the form of "a pastoral romance."[1] These quotations represent a sampling of critical remarks about the seven novels and three novelists chosen for discussion. The use of the word *pastoral* in these quotations illustrates the need for a

[1] Works cited are listed *seriatim*: Thomas Hardy is "our greatest master in the old pastoral tradition" (G. M. Young, "Thomas Hardy," *Victorian Essays* [London: Oxford Univ. Press, 1962], p. 187). His Dorsetshire novels are "modern pastoral romances" (E[dmund] G[osse], *The Encyclopaedia Britannica*, 11th ed., s.v. "Pastoral"). George Eliot, writing "pastoral fiction" (Irving Howe, *Thomas Hardy* [London: Weidenfeld & Nicolson, 1968], p. 177), became "the great novelist . . . of pastoral England" (Graham Hough, *The Last Romantics* [New York: Gerald Duckworth, 1947], p. xi), and *Adam Bede* is "the finest pastoral novel in English" (Walter Allen, *George Eliot* [1964; rpt. New York: Collier, 1967], p. 105), "our supreme novel of pastoral life" (V. S. Pritchett, *The Living Novel* [New York: Reynal & Hitchcock, 1947], p. 91). If *Silas Marner* reflects a "quiet pastoralism" (John Holloway, *The Victorian Sage* [1953; rpt. New York: Norton, 1965], p. 152), *Under the Greenwood Tree* is "a pastoral . . . idyll of English country life," Hardy's "finest pastoral" (Howe, pp. 45, 102). *Far from the Madding Crowd*, termed also "a pastoral idyll" (Joseph Warren Beach, *The Technique of Thomas Hardy* [1922; rpt. New York: Russell & Russell, 1962], p. 50), creates a "pastoral world of antique simplicity" (Albert J. Guerard, *Thomas Hardy* [1949; rpt. Norfolk, Conn.: New Directions, 1964], p. 74) and is a "composition of pastoral elements very consciously designed" (Beach, pp. 50–51). *The Woodlanders*, a late novel by Hardy,

term that will identify these novels as a group, as a subgenre of the novel. Because of the patent need for a category to include rural fiction that is more than simply "rural," I have employed the term *pastoral novel*. The pastoral novel as a subgenre has not been studied. Although commentators have frequently remarked that relatively modern novels may be pastoral—the above quotations are proof—no one has substantiated the belief by a detailed analysis of a group of related novels.

We are accustomed to associating the words *pastoral* or *pastoralism* with artificiality, stylization, simplification, idealization, convention, idyll, romance. Such associations are often legitimate responses to traditional pastoral. In Arden we were permitted to "fleet the time carelessly, as they did in the golden world." But we must regard the pastoral novel as a variation or version—a mutation—of traditional pastoral. It is a form which combines realism with the pastoral impulse. Not only is the world of the pastoral novel a precise geographical spot, which the Arcadian landscape of tradition rarely was, but the delight in rural landscape and figures no longer kneels before the conventions of pastoral. The bower of Theocritus and Vergil expands, in the pastoral novel, into the small rural community, where work blends with pleasure and where shepherds may become farmers or woodsmen or gamekeepers. The imagined landscape of the pastoral novel may also show signs of photographic reality. Love may become problematic, and allegory may disappear.

The pastoral novelist differs from the traditional pastoralist in still more important ways. Whereas the traditional pastoralist works consciously within a frame of generic expectations, the pastoral novelist works within the genre only as it expresses naturally his aim of dealing with rural life; that is, the novelist's pastoral feeling *precedes* the attempt to write within a traditional genre. The pastoral novelist, we might say, *uses* the genre—its potential for expressing complex attitudes toward human experience—rather than allows the genre as traditionally conceived to dictate the form of his fiction. This difference is a function of the pastoralist's distance from his rural material. If traditionally the distance was great, in the nineteenth and twentieth centuries distance has shrunk and has encouraged actuality to enter the genre. The his-

is "a charming idyll laid in a remote Arcadia"—a "traditional pastoral" (Robert Y. Drake, " 'The Woodlanders' as Traditional Pastoral," *Modern Fiction Studies*, 5 [1959], 251–52). Finally, if *The White Peacock* features "the loving evocation of a pastoral setting" (George H. Ford, *Double Measure* [New York: Holt, Rinehart, & Winston, 1965], p. 47), *Lady Chatterley's Lover* takes the form of "a pastoral romance" (David Cavitch, *D. H. Lawrence and the New World* [New York: Oxford Univ. Press, 1969], p. 200).

torical development of pastoral parallels the development of the literary hero as analyzed by Northrop Frye—progressing from a point of view above rural life, as in much traditional pastoral, to a point of view almost on a level with rural life, as in fiction of the nineteenth and early twentieth centuries. This possibility of sustained identification with rural life has encouraged full exploration of rural material, and pastoral has thus expanded from a miniature form such as an eclogue, or from an interlude in a longer work, to a full-scale novel. These various changes in the nature and form of pastoral have resulted in part from changing assumptions about man and reality, in part from the demands of complexity and variety made by the longer form of the novel.

The seven novels that comprise this study—*Adam Bede* and *Silas Marner* by George Eliot, *Under the Greenwood Tree*, *Far from the Madding Crowd*, and *The Woodlanders* by Thomas Hardy, and *The White Peacock* and *Lady Chatterley's Lover* by D. H. Lawrence—are usually thought of as realistic or regional, and the claim that they are pastoral may be questioned for two reasons: first, many pastoral conventions—song matches, piping shepherds, love-sick swains, mourning nature, the refined Arcadian atmosphere—often disappear from these novels; and second, their realism may appear to negate or dissolve their idyllic qualities. Yet as John F. Lynen has pointed out, the conventions of pastoral, though typical of the genre, do not define its essential nature but grow out of some more fundamental impulse buried in the human psyche.[2] I think of pastoral, then, as a body of literature distinguished by its capacity to dress attractively in three different costumes, each costume representing one way that men have linked their experience to the countryside as it represents an ideal way of life: the "pure" pastoral lyric, the allegorical or Christian pastoral, and the fusion of pastoral with other genres such as the romance, the drama, or the novel. In this study I am primarily interested in the last "costume" (see chapter 2). My conception of the pastoral novel leans heavily on the fusion of pastoral and realism found both in the earliest examples of the genre—in the tenth idyll of Theocritus and the first and ninth eclogues of Vergil —and then again in later examples such as Spenser's "August" and Sidney's *Arcadia*. I maintain that the pastoral novel, though it blends realism with pastoral, has always been implicit in the pastoral genre, and my discussion concentrates on this realistic outgrowth or version of pastoral.

Since traditional pastoral, strictly defined, appears to have lost its vitality sometime in the eighteenth century, critics such as William

[2] *The Pastoral Art of Robert Frost* (New Haven: Yale Univ. Press, 1964), pp. 13–14.

Empson and Renato Poggioli have taken up the challenge of discovering in what ways and in what forms the pastoral ideal—the vision of a life of contentment located in the rural past—has survived into the nineteenth and twentieth centuries. It is my thesis that the pastoral novel is one form of survival. The pastoral novels of George Eliot, Hardy, and Lawrence do not continue the pastoral tradition without adapting it: Wordsworth uncovered for artistic treatment new segments of the rural community; and the drift toward individual, nonshared values set in motion by the Romantic revolt has made it difficult for post-Romantic writers to imitate directly the forms of any traditional genre, whether epic, tragedy, georgic, or pastoral. Nonetheless, the pastoral novel, lying on the banks of the genre's mainstream, represents a manifestation of the pastoral impulse, along with diverse other nineteenth- and twentieth-century works—*Alice in Wonderland*, the poetry of Robert Frost, Jewett's *The Country of the Pointed Firs*, Dickens' *Oliver Twist*, Malamud's *The Assistant*, and James's *The Bostonians*.[3] All of these works depend for their pastoral designation upon the definition of pastoral their critics have elected to use. In this study I deal with only one of the modern manifestations that have developed out of the old pastoral tradition, a manifestation however that seems very close in spirit and mood to the pastoral tradition of earlier ages.

It may be argued that other terms or designations could with equal propriety be used to categorize this group of seven novels by George Eliot, Hardy, and Lawrence. Such terms as *rural novel, regional novel, provincial novel, bucolic novel, georgic novel*, or *lyrical rural novel* might supply alternatives. Although they partly describe the novels as a group, such terms are either too broad (*rural novel*) to permit fruitful discussion of a small group of novels, or else they inaccurately describe (*georgic novel*) the characteristic quality that the novels achieve as a group. The problem with *regional novel*, for example, is its breadth and consequent lack of exclusion, which makes possible Walter Allen's

---

[3] Works cited are listed *seriatim*: *Alice in Wonderland* (see William Empson, *Some Versions of Pastoral* [1935; rpt. Norfolk, Conn.: New Directions, 1960], pp. 241 ff.), the poetry of Robert Frost (Lynen, see n. 2), Jewett's *The Country of the Pointed Firs* (Robin Magowan, "Pastoral and the Art of Landscape in *The Country of the Pointed Firs*," *New England Quarterly*, 36 [1963], 229–40), Dickens' *Oliver Twist* (Joseph M. Duffy, Jr., "Another Version of Pastoral: *Oliver Twist*," *ELH*, 35 [1968], 403–21), Malamud's *The Assistant* (James M. Mellard, "Malamud's *The Assistant*: The City Novel as Pastoral," *Studies in Short Fiction*, 5 [1967], 1–11), James's *The Bostonians* (Robert C. McLean, "*The Bostonians*: New England Pastoral," *Papers on Language and Literature*, 7 [1971], 374–81). See also Howard Anderson, "A Version of Pastoral: Class and Society in *Tristram Shandy*," *Studies in English Literature*, 7 (1967), 509–29, and Neil Schmitz, "Richard Brautigan and the Modern Pastoral," *Modern Fiction Studies*, 19 (1973), 109–25.

statement that Arnold Bennett is "entirely a regional novelist" in his portrayal of the industrial community of the Potteries.[4] Because none of the terms mentioned above sufficiently accounts for the connection these novels show with the pastoral tradition, the term *pastoral novel* alone satisfactorily describes the novels as a group. W. W. Greg aptly remarks in his classic study of the pastoral genre: "we have a perfect right to adopt whatever classification suits our purpose best, provided always that we have a clear notion what it is we are discussing."[5]

In the twentieth century a number of critics have attempted to provide us with a "clear notion" of pastoral. As a result of their attempts at definition, the term *pastoral* has been used to describe a surprising variety of literary works. "In fact, one might claim that there are as many definitions as there are critics of pastoral," laments one writer.[6] A survey of the significant twentieth-century discussions of pastoral will persuade us to accept his conclusion and finally to adopt our own definition, although Rosenmeyer's reluctance in 1969 to settle upon a firm definition of pastoral should put us on our guard.[7] Yet a definition of the way the term is employed in this study—to mean, in its simplest form, the novel that fuses pastoral attitudes with realistic subject matter —has seemed a necessity in order to suspend a kind of fixed lantern of meaning above each of the succeeding chapters.

W. W. Greg, in his standard historical study *Pastoral Poetry and Pastoral Drama* (1906), defines pastoral in terms of its city-country contrast: "What does appear to be a constant element in the pastoral as known to literature is the recognition of a contrast, implicit or expressed, between pastoral life and some more complex type of civilization" (p. 4). From this sense of contrast between town and country arises the idea, universal in pastoral, of the Golden Age, a fictitious age of innocence and simplicity set deep in the past. In *Some Versions of*

[4] *The English Novel* (New York: Dutton, 1954), p. 382. For a good discussion of regionalism in the novel, see Henry Auster, *Local Habitations* (Cambridge: Harvard Univ. Press, 1970), esp. ch. 2.

[5] *Pastoral Poetry and Pastoral Drama* (1906; rpt. New York: Russell & Russell, 1959), p. 370.

[6] Robin Magowan, "Fromentin and Jewett: Pastoral Narrative in the Nineteenth Century," *Comparative Literature*, 16 (1964), 331. Donald Cheney remarks similarly that "each critic must determine for himself the point at which the term [*pastoral*] best combines breadth of relevance with depth of focus" (*Spenser's Image of Nature* [New Haven: Yale Univ. Press, 1966], pp. 3–4).

[7] Thomas G. Rosenmeyer, *The Green Cabinet: Theocritus and the European Pastoral Lyric* (Berkeley and Los Angeles: Univ. of California Press, 1969): "In all probability a tidy definition of what is pastoral about the pastoral tradition is beyond our reach. The tradition is extraordinarily rich and flexible" (p. 3). "A definition of the genre and its limits is likely to run counter to much accumulated experience" (p. 6).

Pastoral (1935), William Empson considerably modifies Greg's basic definition of traditional pastoral—tension between city and country, the concept of the Golden Age. Empson is the first to demonstrate that the pastoral of tradition survives in various "versions" beyond its brilliant Renaissance heyday. In works as diverse as *The Beggar's Opera* and *Alice in Wonderland*, Empson shows how "the pastoral process of putting the complex into the simple" has been used in English literature.[8] Although he reduces the essence of pastoral to this loose and simple formula that can be applied to numerous works, he does succeed in breaking through the limits of the old term and enlarging our conception of pastoral.

The year 1952 produced three discussions of pastoral: Frank Kermode's anthology *English Pastoral Poetry*, Hallett Smith's chapter in *Elizabethan Poetry*, and J. E. Congleton's *Theories of Pastoral Poetry in England, 1684–1798*. Kermode's essay expands earlier ideas about pastoral. Offering a sociological explanation of the genre, Kermode says that pastoral flourishes with urbanization, when the dialogue between metropolis and village can still be heard. Like Greg, he stresses the city-country contrast as essential to the genre: Pastoral poetry should reveal "a sharp difference between two ways of life, the rustic and the urban."[9] Justifiably, he says, critics have described as pastoral any work which contrasts simple and complicated ways of living. Shifting his focus from that of earlier critics, Hallett Smith argues that Renaissance pastoral offered a criticism of life. In its effort to represent an ideal life, Renaissance pastoral absorbed the traditional idea of a Golden Age by identifying pastoral life with its conditions: Whereas the Golden Age criticized the present by describing an ideal past, its complement—pastoral—"was a criticism of life by means of adopting the point of view of its simplest and purest elements."[10] Pastoral makes this criticism by contrasting "the simple, natural goodness of the pastoral ideal, self-contained and unaspiring, to the vanity and ambition of

[8] *Some Versions of Pastoral*, p. 23. Three recent studies also approach pastoral from an Empsonian point of view: Laurence Lerner, *The Uses of Nostalgia: Studies in Pastoral Poetry* (New York: Schocken Books, 1972); Julian Moynahan, "Pastoralism as Culture and Counter-Culture in English Fiction, 1800–1928," *Novel*, 6 (1972), 20–35; and John Bayley, *Tolstoy and the Novel* (New York: Viking, 1966), pp. 147–63. Bayley argues that a pastoral novel imposes a frame on its material in order to see only what is *characteristic*, "to enfold a total complexity in terms of itself." His argument is very stimulating, though it came to my attention too late to be of use.

[9] *English Pastoral Poetry: From the Beginnings to Marvell* (London: Harrap, 1952), p. 14.

[10] *Elizabethan Poetry* (Cambridge: Harvard Univ. Press, 1952), p. 14. The quotation that follows is from p. 56.

the world." This contrast, in its rejection of the aspiring mind, affirms the life of peaceful withdrawal. The pastoral novel, also withdrawing into the rural past, makes a similar criticism of urban life.

Thomas G. Rosenmeyer has recently suggested that social criticism is not an essential element in pastoral, found almost never in the *Idylls* of Theocritus. Social criticism may not enter the genre until Vergil's *Eclogues*, but it appears saliently in the pastoral novel. Rosenmeyer's study *The Green Cabinet* (1969) is a distinguished piece of scholarship, filled with insights into the pastoral genre. But his approach has the defect, despite his disclaimer (p. 30), of judging all post-Theocritean pastoral on the practice of Theocritus, of assuming that features of pastoral not found in Theocritus are illegitimate.[11] Hence his comments on social criticism (pp. 5–6), the city-country contrast (pp. 207–14), the Golden Age (pp. 214–24), and figurative language (pp. 254–64), among others. I incline to the view that the enduring themes and forms and uses of pastoral represent the purity of the tradition, and not the work of a single poet, and so I have discussed the stable and recurrent features of pastoral, some of which do not appear in the *Idylls*. I agree, however, that definition is essential to a meaningful discussion of pastoral, especially since excesses have been frequent; but I find it dangerous to insist on too narrow a conception of the pastoral genre or of its "characteristic and analyzable pastoral forms." Room for expansion and development is necessary to any genre.

Congleton, in his useful study of eighteenth-century pastoral theory, relies on Greg and to some extent Empson for his conception of the genre, and little alters our basic idea of pastoral. An excellent and influential study of the genre has been made by Renato Poggioli, principally in "The Oaten Flute" (1957).[12] Poggioli discusses traditional pastoral poetry and the pastoral ideal, and their survivals in modern culture. Though never directly stated, his definition of the traditional genre can yet be summarized: pastoral, appearing whenever metropolitan life grows hard to bear, rejects ambition, opposes wealth, urges a self-contained community, and tends to create an economic idyll of favorable weather, bountiful nature, and freedom from work. Poggioli

[11] An argument similar in import could be advanced about the novel, though it is an argument few will find tenable. For example: *Don Quixote*, our first novel (or perhaps *Moll Flanders*, our first English novel), does not feature psychological analysis, selective omniscient narration, symbolic setting, or interior monologues. Therefore these features are not properly part of the genre. Or reversed: It is a perversion of the genre not to moralize explicitly since the earliest workers in the field did so.

[12] "The Oaten Flute," *Harvard Library Bulletin*, 11 (1957), 147–84. See also his "The Pastoral of the Self," *Daedalus*, 88 (1959), 687–99; "Naboth's Vineyard or the Pastoral View of the Social Order," *Journal of the History of Ideas*, 24 (1963), 3–24; and "Zampogna e cornamusa," *Inventario*, 8 (1956), 216–47.

also categorizes, rather loosely, various kinds of pastoral into useful subgroups: the pastoral of innocence, the pastoral of happiness or love, the Christian pastoral, the pastorals of mirth and melancholy, the pastoral of the self, the pastoral of solitude, and the political pastoral. Although his categories sometimes overlap (as self and solitude) and although they are not always clearly defined (as mirth and melancholy), Poggioli nonetheless successfully divides pastoral into various types and so helps to prepare the way for a study like this one. Most important, Poggioli concludes that the pastoral ideal has survived in varied metamorphoses which are "almost always written in prose: and break all traditional patterns and attitudes."[13] One of these modern versions is of course the pastoral novel.

In 1960 appeared John F. Lynen's fine book *The Pastoral Art of Robert Frost*. Building on the studies of Greg, Empson, and Poggioli, Lynen succeeds in extending the boundaries of the old pastoral tradition by showing how much of the poetry of a modern writer develops from traditional pastoral. To define pastoral, Lynen—rightly objecting to the breadth of Empson's definition—argues for rural life as the essential subject matter of pastoral: "I shall take the term pastoralism," he says, "to denote that mode of viewing common experience through the medium of the rural world."[14] Every critic of pastoral, because of the protean nature of the genre, wishes to give special emphasis to those aspects of pastoral which support his point of view or, if he is not tendentious, to emphasize what he thinks are the fundamental elements of the genre. Lynen's emphasis falls on the idea, derived from Empson, that at bottom pastoral is not an escape from, but an oblique exploration of, the world. Pastoral plays urban against rural values, exploiting the tension and emotional ambiguity that result from the contrast.

Pastoral comes to life whenever the poet . . . casts himself in the role of the country dweller and writes about life in terms of the contrast between the rural world, with its rustic scenery and naive, humble folk, and the great outer world of the powerful, the wealthy, and the sophisticated. Though rural life is the subject of pastoral, it is not seen in and for itself; the poet always tends to view it with reference to the more sophisticated plane of experience upon which both he and his audience live.[15]

Lynen, by stressing that the pastoral poet views rural life as representative of human life, can support his claim that Frost is a major poet who deals (if obliquely) with the problems of his time, can justify the omission of pastoral conventions in Frost's verse, and can call him a "pas-

13 "The Oaten Flute," pp. 176–77.
14 Lynen, pp. 8–9.
15 Lynen, p. 9.

toral" poet without diminishing his stature. The pastoral novel, however, insists considerably less than does a pastoral poet like Frost on the allegorical dimension, by which I mean the dimension of some more-than-implicit correspondence between rural and urban planes. In the pastoral novel such planes of opposing experience tend not to run parallel, like flat roof to floor, but to intersect along a single central axis, the axis of love, pain, hope, and other universal emotions; the details that remain largely differ. In *The Woodlanders*, for example, points of intersection between rural and urban do not extend to asexual love, stoical outlook, harmony with nature, ambition, or intellectual and social sophistication. The pastoral novel, one might say, is not insistently literal nor is it in any meaningful sense allegorical. Rather, it is allusive: the reader senses another dimension of experience only by implication and not by direct clues that lead to a system of correspondences.

Because his interpretation of pastoral derives largely from earlier critics, we may simply cite Leo Marx's interesting *The Machine in the Garden: Technology and the Pastoral Ideal in America* (1964) and then consider the approach of Robin Magowan. In "Fromentin and Jewett: Pastoral Narrative in the Nineteenth Century" (1964), Magowan extends the boundaries of the genre to include nineteenth-century prose fiction. Although Magowan's definition of pastoral combines ideas expressed by Smith and Poggioli ("pastoral is a narrative form seeking to project within certain arbitrary limits [of time and space] a vision of the good life"),[16] Magowan successfully analyzes as pastoral some works of nineteenth-century fiction. To analyze as pastoral a group of novels by George Eliot, Hardy, and Lawrence is to modify and extend his approach.

More recently the structure of some longer works of traditional pastoral has been reinterpreted by Walter R. Davis in "Masking in Arden" (1965) or *A Map of Arcadia* (1965)[17] and Harold E. Toliver in *Marvell's Ironic Vision* (1965). These critics argue that many pastoral works have a three-part form: a withdrawal to a place apart that

[16] "Fromentin and Jewett," p. 333. Like Lynen, Magowan interprets pastoral in the way that illuminates the novels he chooses to analyze. Thus he stresses the idea that pastoral is fundamentally "an art of perspective" ("Fromentin and Jewett," p. 334), or, an art demanding a proper distance between the pastoral retreat and the urban narrator's vision of this retreat, so that the narrator's vision of the good life is meaningful only for himself. To define perspective in this way is, however, to offer a refined variation of the fundamental city-country contrast, in which critical distance is assumed in order for meaningful contrast to exist.

[17] "Masking in Arden: The Histrionics of Lodge's *Rosalynde*," *Studies in English Literature*, 5 (1965), 151–63. *A Map of Arcadia: Sidney's Romance in Its Tradition* (New Haven: Yale Univ. Press, 1965).

offers a perspective on sophisticated life, a reassessment of values and a reorientation toward society, followed by a return to the complex and active world. "In poems of pastoral success," says Toliver, the general pattern varies but is "remarkably persistent."[18] In his study of Renaissance pastoral, Davis found that the plot of pastoral romance often traced the hero's experience of two differing worlds: "his entrance into 'Arcady' full of the pain and turmoil he contracted in the actual world, his experience of calm self-analysis in the inner pastoral circle, and his return to the outer world in harmony with himself."[19] Such structures appear in the pastoral novel; however, the pastoral novel, poised atop the rapidly shifting balance between rural and urban, prefers to generate narrative tension by using a sophisticated intruder rather than by alternating one world with another.

The purpose of adducing these various twentieth-century attempts to define pastoral is not only to identify some of the important critical concepts in discussions of pastoral but also to show how the term has lost its originally narrow focus.[20] The term *pastoral*, used loosely, can function as nothing more than a synonym for peaceful rural life; it can indicate all forms of idealized country life; it can signify only the conventions of traditional pastoral; it can suggest any literature about shepherds; or it can apply to literature revealing a single dominant feature of pastoral, as it has most frequently in recent critical usage. Modern critics have used the term to signify city-country contrast; complexity viewed as simplicity; criticism of life; an economic idyll; universal experience seen through the medium of the rural world; perspective; or a pattern of escape, illumination, and return. Because the definitions of the term are diverse and because each reveals a different emphasis, a definition that will apply to novels by George Eliot, Hardy, and Lawrence is essential, and a single idea (such as "putting the complex into the simple") should not be permitted to monopolize our understanding of the genre.

A dominant feature of both traditional pastoral and the pastoral novels of George Eliot, Hardy, and Lawrence is the sharp city-country con-

[18] *Marvell's Ironic Vision* (New Haven: Yale Univ. Press, 1965), p. 88.

[19] "Masking in Arden," p. 152. Examples of the pattern include Sannazaro's *Arcadia*, Montemayor's *Diana*, *As You Like It*, *The Winter's Tale*, Sidney's *Arcadia*, Greene's *Pandosto*, and Book VI of *The Faerie Queene*.

[20] After my study was essentially completed, Harold E. Toliver's *Pastoral Forms and Attitudes* (Berkeley and Los Angeles: Univ. of California Press, 1971) appeared. Although our fundamental ideas are similar (e.g., selection of constant elements in pastoral literature), his approach to Hardy's pastoralism is in general very different from mine, and he does not discuss George Eliot or D. H. Lawrence.

trast—with all the nuances and complexities this contrast implies—in which country life, seen as best revealing man's essential nature, is praised at the expense of the urban world. Critics generally agree that an important element of pastoral is this rural-urban contrast,[21] which also takes the subordinate forms of nature versus art, past versus present, and simplicity versus refinement and complexity. All of the novels we will study greatly heighten this contrast. When, for example, Silas and Eppie Marner return to Lantern Yard—"a dark ugly place"—they are greeted by noise and a "multitude of strange indifferent faces" peering from gloomy doorways: " 'O father, I'm like as if I was stifled,' " says Eppie. " 'I couldn't ha' thought as any folks lived i' this way, so close together. How pretty the Stone-pits 'ull look when we get back!' "[22] The city-country contrast is exploited not so much to reveal in simplified form the urban world to itself—the way it functions for Empson or Lynen—as to reveal the peace and the sense of an integrated community outside the industrial and cultural centers of nineteenth-century England. The pastoral novelist writes sympathetically about the virtues of peasant life and offers the rural world as the best place to locate value because of its unity and simplicity, its intimate communion with nature, and its freedom from sophistication. In part, we might say, the pastoral novel seeks to create a feeling of wholeness in those whose lives have been fragmented in urban centers. The wedding party "under the greenwood tree" is in Hardy's novel a metaphor for the unfragmented existence that the pastoral novelist aims to portray. Because the fictional re-creation of such an existence shows a marked contrast between both rural and urban and past and present, a strong sense of tension is always felt in the pastoral novel. The same kind of tension through contrast had vitalized much traditional pastoral—Vergil's *Eclogues* or Ben Jonson's *Sad Shepherd*, for example. In pastoral, Lynen has said, the ambiguity of feeling between two sets of values is exploited. Though rural values are consistently preferred in the pastoral novel, urban values attract many of the characters: Hetty Sorrel, Dick Dewy, Bathsheba Everdene, Grace Melbury, George Saxton, and the Beardsalls. The sense of tension in the pastoral novel is used to illuminate both rural and urban worlds, to cause the reader to see both in perspective, with the values of one pitted against the values of the other, and thus the more clearly to reveal human nature to the reader.

Closely related to the rural-urban contrast is the reader's frequent

[21] On the matter of whether the rural-urban contrast is essential to pastoral, I side of course with Greg (p. 4) and Kermode (pp. 13–14) against Rosenmeyer (pp. 207–14).

[22] George Eliot, *Silas Marner*, vol. IX in *The Works of George Eliot*, Standard Edition (Edinburgh and London: William Blackwood, n.d. [1868]), pp. 266–67.

sense in the pastoral novel of both rural and urban points of view. Although the pastoral novelist is intimately and genuinely acquainted with the rural world, he is or has been urbanized. George Eliot, Hardy, and Lawrence were, during later parts of their lives, urban dwellers familiar with great cities. In this respect they differ from other major Victorian or early modern novelists such as Dickens, Thackeray, Emily Brontë, Conrad, Virginia Woolf, or Joyce. In 1851 George Eliot, age 31, left her native Warwickshire and, with the exception of her travels, remained in or near London until her death. As a young architect, Hardy lived in London from 1862 to 1867 and made regular visits thereafter. Lawrence, though he earned a lasting intimacy with rural life by his vacations and weekly visits to the Haggs farm near Eastwood, was town-born and town-bred; and in 1908 he went to London where he remained until 1911, traveling thereafter. All three novelists, like Theocritus and Vergil and Renaissance writers of pastoral, have urban ties but rural roots, a fact that accounts for their monopoly on the pastoral novel in England. They look back with nostalgia on their early rural experiences. Unlike merely regional writers, they see rural life (because of their urban experience) from a perspective other than that of the innocent rural present. As Lynen has remarked, "to yearn for the rustic life one must first know the great world from which it offers an escape" (p. 13). It is therefore not surprising that the action of the pastoral novel often extends beyond the scope of the rural world and that urban characters and urban life are introduced to heighten the sense of contrast and thus of perspective. We think immediately of Hardy's Sergeant Troy or Mrs. Charmond, the pastoral picnickers in *The White Peacock*, Clifford in *Lady Chatterley's Lover*. In each novel to be discussed we are consistently aware of both rural and urban values.

Now, the urban point of view does not exist to the degree that the rural scene merely provides the scaffolding for an allegory, a humorous and charming disguise of courtly friends (as in more than a few pastoral poems of Theocritus, Vergil, Mantuan, Boccaccio, or Spenser). What does exist in these seven novels is a felt tension between the values inherent in two modes of life—one refined and urban, the other simple and rural—without our feeling any direct correspondences. In the pastoral novel, country life is *interpreted* for an urban audience. As one writer remarks, Hardy did not write for country people "but about them, to a mainly metropolitan and unconnected literary public."[23] The portrait of country life functions partly, it is true, to charm the reader for charm's sake, but it functions also to awaken and illumi-

[23] Raymond Williams, "Thomas Hardy," *Victorian Literature: Selected Essays,* ed. Robert O. Preyer (New York: Harper, 1966), p. 212.

nate the reader's sense of contrast between city and country in order that man's ambition, grown too powerful, can be seen from the perspective of both the cycles of nature and the simpler, more fundamental life of the country. In this way ambition, illustrated by the actions of William Dane, Troy, Mrs. Charmond, or Clifford, is shown to be destructive rather than honorific or glorious. The urban reader does not see himself in the mirror that the pastoral novelist holds up to rural life, but senses acutely the virtues of another way of life and so tends to evaluate critically the values of his own urban culture—in short, to make a criticism of his sophisticated world. Throughout *The White Peacock*, for instance, Lawrence creates in his reader an awareness of the rural values of the Saxtons as they oppose the cultured values of the Beardsalls and the Tempests. By his juxtaposition of modes of life, we see the strengths in both—the vitality and innocence of the one, and the grace and elegance of the other.

In the pastoral novel we find, growing out of this double viewpoint, an intense nostalgia for a Golden-Age past, for what is distant in time and space. To look for what is distant in time and space is to search, like the chronological primitivist, for an earlier form of social organization when human life is believed to have attained its happiest condition. By focusing on a specific geographical region in the rural past, the pastoral novelist creates a microcosmic world that recaptures what was, for him, a recent version of the Golden Age. When the poet of traditional pastoral looks back to the shepherd's life, he sees simplicity, leisure, and happiness; he sees man and nature in harmony. Similarly, although his sense of the Golden Age is more vital, the pastoral novelist envisions a life of harmony existing in an actual past and in a believable setting that is sequestered yet concrete. The pastoral novel provides a retreat through time and space, a journey through memory to rediscover the lost unity of human and natural worlds. Sometimes this journey is represented in the novel concretely (in *Silas Marner*, *Far from the Madding Crowd*, and *Lady Chatterley's Lover*) or hypothetically (at the opening of both *Adam Bede* and *The Woodlanders*) or ironically (near the close of *The White Peacock*). Whether it is within the novelist's memory or within the fictional world, the journey in the pastoral novel represents not only a search for the good life in a remote and peaceful world but for its complement, a retreat from ugly industrialism and artificial urban life symbolized by London, satellites of London, and Paris. The pastoral life that is depicted, though modified and imperfect, serves as an ideal of contentment by which the world outside its boundaries may be viewed.

The pastoral novels of George Eliot, Hardy, and Lawrence reveal, then, the withdrawal from complexity and power typical of pastoral.

Silas Marner withdraws from Lantern Yard, *The White Peacock* from Nottingham, and all three of Hardy's novels from urban refinement and deception. By withdrawing from the present to the past as well as from urban to rural, the pastoral novel can, as Smith has said of Renaissance pastoral, evaluate and criticize the complex industrial present by comparing it with the simpler past. Though such criticism is always implicit in the re-creation of rural life, it often breaks upon the narrative surface explicitly. "Ingenious philosophers tell you, perhaps," says George Eliot in *Adam Bede*, "that the great work of the steam engine is to create leisure for mankind. Do not believe them: it only creates a vacuum for eager thought to rush in." [24] When the sheepshearing season began in June, writes Hardy in *Far from the Madding Crowd*, "God was palpably present in the country, and the devil had gone with the world to town." [25] From the "insentient iron world . . . of mechanized greed" Constance Chatterley and her lover will make their escape. [26] The pastoral novel, sometimes obliquely and sometimes openly, registers a critical reaction to the loss of beauty and to the depersonalization of modern industrial life. Irving Howe has commented on the element of critical perspective in pastoral when he speaks of the nostalgia triggering the fiction of Eliot or Hardy or Faulkner, a nostalgia that makes possible "an interplay between past and present in which each becomes a premise for the criticism of the other. This nostalgia, so different from the indulgence usually passing under that name, is available to the writer only upon reaching the point of sophistication at which he can surrender the fantasy of returning home. It is as if some deracination in real life were necessary for enabling him to summon the remembered homeland in literature." [27] Yet George Eliot, Hardy, and Lawrence commit themselves to a definite moral position; they have, it is true, achieved critical distance from their material, thus obviating the easy regionalism of lesser writers such as William Barnes or Anne Manning. But the scale weighing past and present, innocence and sophistication, country and city, is in the pastoral novel less evenly balanced than it is—to cite an example—in the Scottish novels of Sir Walter Scott, in which the narrative is related from a neutral position located between the extremes of tradition and progress. At the close of *Waverley*, one is in doubt about the relative value of opposed cultures. If Scott is neutral, Hardy

[24] *Adam Bede*, ed. John Paterson, Riverside Edition (Boston: Houghton Mifflin, 1968), pp. 428–29.

[25] *Far from the Madding Crowd*, Wessex Edition (London: Macmillan, 1912), p. 163.

[26] D. H. Lawrence, *Lady Chatterley's Lover*, Modern Library Edition (New York: Random House, n.d.), p. 134.

[27] Howe, *Thomas Hardy*, p. 2.

(for one) is not. In his essay "The Dorsetshire Labourer" (1883), Hardy reflects upon the rapid migration of people from country to city that resulted partly from the disastrous decline of agriculture after 1874 and partly from the lure of the city. Such depopulation, Hardy says, "is truly alarming. . . . The poignant regret of those who are thus obliged to forsake the old nest can only be realised by people who have witnessed it." [28] But the pastoral novelist, in spite of his firm stand (perhaps because of it) succeeds in illustrating human nature much more often than he permits himself the easy job of illustrating the picturesque differences that distinguish one age from another.

On the surface of the narrative, however, the pastoral novelist is involved less in appraising the urban present than he is in creating patiently—with concrete incident and descriptive detail—a small, remote, circumscribed pastoral world. In such a creation lies his artistic achievement. To build such a pastoral world the methods he uses are various, and include so traditional a *topos* as the *locus amoenus* and so modern a *topos* as the secluded hut, both of which announce rhetorically the initiation of physical or spiritual change. High on the list is the manipulation of nature to correspond to human character (see, e.g., chapter 6) or to create the image of a remote and circumscribed world. Thus the pastoral novelist usually describes his pastoral haven as a place set apart in space from the great world beyond, isolated by thick trees or imposing hills that function as agents of circumscription. Dense trees are, for example, insistently mentioned at the opening of *Silas Marner, Under the Greenwood Tree*, and *The Woodlanders*; in Fir-tree Grove the lovers find the *locus amoenus* of *Adam Bede*; and in Wragby Wood lies hidden the *locus amoenus* of *Lady Chatterley's Lover*. The pastoral haven is not only circumscribed but, within, is recognized for its remarkable beauty and its close correspondence between mind and setting. All of the novels bear lush and lyrical descriptions of landscape, flowers, and the harmonious interaction of man and nature. The natural world in the pastoral novel is usually portrayed as intensely sympathetic to the pastoral characters of the novel; and the pastoral characters demonstrate a similar sympathy for nature. We think of Adam Bede and his trees, Eppie and her garden, Gabriel Oak and his sheep, Giles and Marty and their trees, the Beardsalls and their flowers, Constance Chatterley and Wragby Wood. We are asked to envision man organically related to his environment and defined by his physical setting. The moral functions of nature in Hardy's novels provide an example. Within the pastoral retreat the lives of the characters, spent in oneness with their natural sur-

---

[28] Thomas Hardy, *Life and Art*, ed. Ernest Brennecke, Jr. (1925; rpt. New York: Haskell House, 1966), pp. 45–46.

roundings, attain simplicity. The characters, because they reflect the pastoral ideal of the contented life, appropriately extend the lyrical atmosphere that imbues the pastoral haven. The pastoral characters in these seven novels—e.g., Adam, Eppie, Dick Dewy, Oak, Winterborne, Marty, George Saxton—tend to be limited in their insights, especially in relation to their implied authors; their simplicity preserves their organic bond with their environment and preserves them from the corruption of acrobatic creeds. Like Theocritean herdsmen, the pastoral characters are youthful; they tend not to be thinkers but perceivers of concrete sensations or beauties of landscape, admirers of human vitality and even of an intuitive morality. And as in pastoral romance—in works such as *Daphnis and Chloe, Rosalynde, As You Like It, Hymen's Triumph*, Sidney's *Arcadia*, or *The Winter's Tale*—the marriages that close *Adam Bede, Silas Marner, Under the Greenwood Tree, Far from the Madding Crowd*, and (in an unconventional form) *The Woodlanders* and *Lady Chatterley's Lover*, grow naturally out of the pastoral atmosphere already created in the novel. Providing one of the few formal elements of the pastoral novel, they are the suitable idyllic conclusion, restoring to the pastoral haven a mood of peaceful harmony, providing an analogue to the integration of landscape and character, and illustrating the novelists' interest in ceremonial scenes. Within the circumscribed pastoral world, such ceremonial scenes as marriages, suppers, parties, dances, church services, picnics, or erotic rituals—common to all the novels—regularly punctuate the narrative line. They function to set the individual into a larger social context, to relax narrative tensions (generally romantic) by introducing humor or spontaneity into the sequence of events, and to create a pastoral effect of joy and harmony.

Although the harmony within the pastoral world is central, perhaps the best way to define the total impression of the pastoral novel is to use the term *sympathetic realism.* Such a term has the advantage of accounting for both the idealization and the realism clearly at work in these novels.[29] The intense nostalgia, already mentioned, has as one of its effects the tendency to idealize country life and, like traditional pastoral, to make country life palatable to urban society. Since a transcript of real rural life might be disturbing and unpleasant, as it is in Zola's *La Terre* (1886), the pastoral novelist makes rural life palatable by softening or omitting its coarseness. Thus the characters in the pastoral novel lie somewhere between the refined, idealized creations of traditional pastoral and coarse or gross transcripts from country life. William J. Hyde concludes in his study of Hardy's peasants that Hardy usually omits

[29] Generally I intend the term *realism* to suggest a literary focus on the actual, the observable, the verifiable; the ordinary, the everyday, the typical, the representative; .he truthful; the normal in human experience.

"the animal nature of the peasant and the economic suffering of his lot."[30] Albert J. Guerard believes similarly that the Wessex novels "leave an idealized impression of an ancient and stable world rather than an accurate almanac of Dorset."[31] We find, it is true, some sense of pastoral simplification, though the degree varies. Hardy's rustics, for instance, sometimes appear stylized and conventional: we think of *Under the Greenwood Tree*. And some critics (Barbara Hardy or David Cavitch, e.g.) have found *Lady Chatterley's Lover* schematic in its simplification. But none of the novels is purely idyllic; and none places its landscape and characters in Arcadia. The advent of science and the habit of looking at rural life sharply and squarely that we find in Crabbe or Cobbett or Richard Jefferies sufficiently affected the general outlook on rural life to prevent a pure idyll from being written by novelists of the first rank.

If the country life re-created in these novels is simple, and perhaps "simplified," it is in no way remote from the life of the fields. We discover realism in numerous ways: plausible characterization, accurate and detailed rendering of an actual locality, the use of dialect to achieve verisimilitude, and an honest acknowledgment of human suffering. If we find neither graceful shepherds, dressed with artificial language and populating an Arcadian landscape, nor a masquerade of disguised poets, we do find rural life treated with intense sympathy and idealized only to the point where realism of character and accuracy of landscape still shape our response to the novel's fictional world and qualify its idyllic atmosphere. Here a modification of traditional pastoral occurs. We should not look for stylized artificiality or for the ironic stance found often in traditional pastoral (in Montanus' lyrics from *Rosalynde*, e.g.): the figures and setting in these seven novels are for the most part taken literally rather than emblematically. And because the heroes of these novels are not sojourners but natives of the pastoral world, we should not, except in *The White Peacock*, look for the return to active involvement in the sophisticated world that we find in pastoral romance. And though many can be found, we should not look for heavy emphasis on the conventions of traditional pastoral. The point to be stressed is that these novelists maintained an organic rather than a mechanical relationship to the conventions. Whereas earlier pastoralists generally used the conventions because their audience expected them to adhere to generic requirements, George Eliot, Hardy, and Lawrence used the conventions because the conventions helped them to express crucial aspects of their experience that could not be expressed as well by other means

[30] "Hardy's View of Realism: A Key to the Rustic Characters," *Victorian Studies*, 2 (1958), 48.

[31] *Thomas Hardy* (Norfolk, Conn.: New Directions, 1964), p. 33.

—deep affection for country people, identification with country life, nostalgia for its sense of community, regret at its demise, dislike of cities, and mistrust of modernism. In other words, George Eliot, Hardy, and Lawrence found pastoral forms and attitudes not imitative but viable, not expected but needed.

We should then, to summarize, define the pastoral novel as the sub-genre of the novel, developing out of the pastoral tradition, which idealizes country life by using many of the elements and techniques of traditional pastoral—principally, the contrast between city and country; the re-creation of rural life from both urban and rural viewpoints; the implied withdrawal from complexity to simplicity; the nostalgia for a Golden-Age past of peace and satisfaction; the implied criticism of modern life; and the creation of a circumscribed and remote pastoral world. This remote pastoral world features harmony between man and nature, idyllic contentment, and a sympathetic realism which combines elements of idealization and realism and by means of which country life, stripped of its coarsest features, is made palatable to urban society. The term *pastoral novel* thus defined is, I have said, the most useful available term to describe the group of related novels which cluster around this term and its definition, but which have not before been studied as such. Each of the seven novels does not necessarily reveal all of the specified characteristics (though several do), but the aim has been to isolate those novels in which most of these characteristics can be found.

A final word about my approach. Because I have wished to emphasize the novels themselves as coherent imaginative wholes, believing that formal criticism would most fully illuminate the novels selected, my emphasis has been primarily but not exclusively critical. Questions about the historical development of the period and about the biographies of the three novelists—and the way these relate to the novels—are very useful to ask; but I have taken up such matters only to the extent that they allow my focus to remain steadily on the novels as pastoral.

In the chapters that follow, two procedures in particular have guided the study. First, in each chapter I try to show briefly some specific connections of a particular novel to traditional pastoral, then to show the way that a modified pastoral world is created within that novel. Pastoral contrasts, the development of a circumscribed pastoral world, and the correspondence between landscape and character are features especially salient and stable in both the pastoral tradition and the pastoral novel, and are therefore stressed in my analyses. I try to focus on the artistic means, the techniques, that each novelist uses to create a pastoral world, and I employ (to use David Lodge's terms) both textural and structural approaches to study the language of the novel, attempting to isolate the moral threads that establish its design.[32] In order to show the artistic creation of such a world, the approach of studying a single novel in each chapter proved more advantageous than a topical approach, although the extended discussion in one place of common techniques or patterns of thought was necessarily sacrificed. But in studying individual novels, I hope to gain the greater advantages of observing a writer's development and of seeing a work in its artistic wholeness.

Second, my intention has not been to discuss those novels which reveal only brief pastoral interludes, such as *Tess of the d'Urbervilles* or *The Rainbow* (or for that matter *Joseph Andrews* or *The Vicar of Wakefield*), but to discuss those novels that seem to be largely pastoral. The seven novels under discussion were selected because they form a conveniently limited group for study and because they fall with one exception into a late Victorian period, 1859 to World War I, a period battered by a series of rapid changes—of migration from villages to towns and cities, of increasing industrialization and ailing agriculture, of peace shattered by the Boer War and then by the Great War, of a weakening of Christian morality, of the spread of democracy (especially after the Reform Bill of 1867), of compulsory education in 1870, of artistic realism narrowing to naturalism and then experimentation, and of increasing specialization in all art forms.[33] Because of these rapid changes, the pastoral impulse ignited the imaginations of some of our best writers. Although these seven novels are not the only novels that might be included in a complete study of the pastoral novel, readings suggested for the novels that are discussed would hopefully make sense

[32] Because the novel-critic "is compelled to select more drastically than the critic of poetry . . . the alternative procedures open to him are (1) to isolate, deliberately or at random, one or more passages, and submit them to close and exhaustive analysis, or (2) to trace significant threads through the language of an entire novel. One might label these approaches 'textural' and 'structural' respectively" (David Lodge, *Language of Fiction* [London: Routledge & Kegan Paul, 1966], p. 78).

[33] Perhaps the year 1859 inaugurated this period, Asa Briggs has written in *Victorian People* ([1955; rpt. New York: Harper & Row, 1963], p. 298). In 1859 and 1860, says G. M. Young, we approach a frontier and begin to hear "the voices of a new world. . . . The late Victorian age is opening" (*Victorian England: Portrait of an Age*, 2d ed. [London: Oxford Univ. Press, 1953], p. 102). To know precisely when the late Victorian period ended is difficult: a variety of dates has been suggested. But in the words of G. Kitson Clark, "Since . . . the Queen herself survived into the next century, and much else that must be considered as being typically Victorian went on after that, a twentieth-century date might seem to be suitable . . . the evening of August 4th 1914 when so many of the lights of Europe were put out never to be lighted again" (*The Making of Victorian England* [Cambridge: Univ. Press, 1962], p. 32).

for those excluded. In some novels, for example, the creation of a pastoral world is subordinated to the need for full representation of a nonpastoral world. In *The Mill on the Floss* or *The Return of the Native* or *Tess of the d'Urbervilles* or *Sons and Lovers*, unlike *The Woodlanders*, the partial pastoral world that is created collapses before it makes a dominant impression on the reader. The sense of collapse overshadows the pastoral atmosphere of peaceful and harmonious rural life. *The Mill on the Floss* focuses on the town rather than on agricultural life, and in *The Return of the Native* the malignancy of the heath denies the possibility of a pastoral world.[34] Though artistically more mature, *Sons and Lovers* treats with less detail and less atmosphere of idyll roughly the same rural experiences as *The White Peacock*; much of *Sons and Lovers* does not treat rural life at all. The difference between the novels is one not only of emphasis but of treatment as well. To extend the term *pastoral* to such novels as these would be to strip it of the specialized meaning which, despite its recent broadening, the term should retain to be critically useful.[35] Some recent critics of pastoral, while expanding our awareness of potential pastoral works, have allowed themselves to reduce pastoral to a single feature of the genre, which is like calling a work of prose a novel on the basis of its moral vision or its length. But to interpret pastoral too broadly is, in its inclusiveness, as harmful to the concept of genre as to interpret pastoral too rigidly and thus to miss seeing the continuity of the pastoral tradition.

Still, if they sustain the tradition, the seven novels I have selected are not entirely detachable from their authors' literary careers, and the pastoral perspective can to some extent be used to talk about all of their fiction. The three novelists do not, in their other novels, quite reject pastoral; instead, they alter their emphasis and use pastoral in less salient ways. In general, the shift in their perspective parallels the larger shift, especially after 1850, from rural to urban. George Eliot, for example, reveals her inclination toward pastoral as early as "Mr. Gilfil's Love-Story." But after *Silas Marner* she tends to fix her interest not so much upon memories of village life as upon the intersection of historical process and country estates, as in *Felix Holt* or *Middlemarch*

34 "The country environment of *The Return of the Native*," writes Douglas Brown, "is not attractive, in the way that woods and farmlands and hills and fields are. The heath is formidably antagonistic to human society and human ways. This is the other side of the scene that dominates *Under the Greenwood Tree, Far from the Madding Crowd, The Trumpet-Major* and *The Woodlanders*" (*Thomas Hardy*, 2d ed. [London: Longmans, 1961], p. 55).

35 Rosalie L. Colie writes in 1972: "these days, when Empson's vagaries are ignored and the looseness of Poggioli and Snell are challenged, the tendency is rather to limit than to extend the term *pastoral*" (Review of Harold E. Toliver's *Pastoral Forms and Attitudes* in *JEGP*, 71 [1972], 447–48).

or *Daniel Deronda*, where a more sophisticated level of experience can be represented. Her sphere of interest gradually synthesizes—with increasing objectivity—her provincial experience, her knowledge of urban culture, and her awareness of historical change. Although Hardy's confidence does wane in the admixture of rural and urban modes, it is well known that he faithfully uses rural material throughout the span of his fiction. However quickly it can decay into the meanness of Casterbridge or the ugliness of Marygreen, pastoralism runs like a stream through all his major novels, taking simply a marginal position, as in *The Return of the Native*. The ironic title, "Saturday Night in Arcady," which Hardy gave to the scene of Tess's betrayal when he first published it, reveals his distance from pastoral yet also his consciousness of working within the tradition. As Poussin's famous inscription "Et in Arcadia ego" suggests, change is the enemy of Arcadia; and so it is in Hardy's novels. As his nostalgia gave way to social criticism and despair, he increasingly focused on what, for him as artist, reduced the vitality of the pastoral mode and extinguished the idyllic flame from his fiction.

Lawrence too shows a strong predilection for pastoral in novels as different as *Sons and Lovers*, *The Rainbow*, *The Lost Girl*, *The Fox*, and *The Plumed Serpent*. If Marsh farm is a pastoral haven to the early Brangwens, Alvina retreats from a sterile English town to the mountains of Italy, March and Banford to an isolated farm, and Kate from the sophistication of Europe to the Aztec rituals of Mexico. Although Lawrence's fascination with forms of power and domination leads him in nonpastoral directions, he depends on the collision of instinct and civilization, of life and death forces, to empower much of his fiction. Thus, continuities between "pastoral" and "nonpastoral" are evident. In the work of all three novelists, the provincial community figures importantly, though often it cannot sustain the hero or heroine; and strategic contrasts of simple and complex control both plot and theme in much of their fiction. The novels I have selected for study are simply those that express, most persuasively and most fully, the pastoral impulse.

Grouped together, then, are the important pastoral novels of three major writers within a workable period in which the pastoral impulse powerfully animated the literary imagination. The evolution from rural order to industrial state called for a response. If rapid industrialization was making the rural world obsolete, yet the process of change—apprehended in ways that illuminate human experience—was transformed into art by the pastoral novelist. By studying these seven novels, we can see how prose fiction uses pastoral to express eternal human values in an age of transition.

Chapter 2

The Development
of the Pastoral Novel

IN THE LITERATURE of the Western world, the pastoral tradition is long and varied. It has been the record of one avenue of man's adaptation to his environment. In examining such a record, this chapter aims not to give a complete history of the pastoral tradition. Although no comprehensive modern study has yet been written, the studies cited in chapter 1, taken together, provide a quite useful background for the student of pastoral. Instead, this chapter aims only to provide the line of development out of which the pastoral novel ultimately struggled into being. Because I see the expert fusion of the pastoral vision with modern realism as forming the *locus* of the pastoral novel, defining its achievement, I lean heavily toward traditional works that reveal a similar fusion of pastoral and realistic elements. I have, in other words, limited my discussion not to works at the center of the genre but to pastoral works that resonate in the pastoral novel.

The roots of pastoral probably lie deep in the myth of primitive peoples. In classical antiquity pastoral was stimulated by Greek and Roman primitivistic thought, especially the discovery and praise of the Golden Age. Theocritus and Vergil, as the earliest practitioners of the pastoral form, came to be the chief influences on the widespread writing of pastoral poetry in the Renaissance and occasionally afterward. But the advent of scientific skepticism in the eighteenth and nineteenth centuries gradually altered the artist's characteristic way of looking at the world. Since traditional pastoral was uncongenial to an empirical bent of mind, its form was appropriately modified. The fundamental pastoral impulse did not, however, die but was successfully adapted to a new set of conditions in which a realistic bias was imposed on traditional pastoral attitudes. The first comparatively modern literary figure to demonstrate the possibilities of the pastoral form adapted to realistic subject matter was, I believe, Wordsworth. And in the last half of the nineteenth century, another change occurred: George Eliot, Thomas Hardy, and, later, D. H. Lawrence showed that the pastoral impulse could be adapted to serious prose fiction.

Although it is often said that pastoral poetry derives from spontaneous shepherd-songs, W. W. Greg has said that the shepherd-songs became distinctly pastoral only after they were divorced from the life of shepherds and were sung nostalgically within the city walls. The contrast between the simplicity of the country and the complexity of the city became a permanent feature of pastoral literature. The earliest recorded pastoral poetry, that of Theocritus, springs directly from the contrast between childhood memories of country life in Sicily and the complex city life of Alexandria.[1] The same kind of tension proves to be a generative force in the pastoral novel. Out of this contrast between pastoral life and a more complex civilization arises the idea, very frequent in pastoral, of the Golden Age. The imaginative ideal of an age of innocence and simplicity sprang from the complexities of Roman civilization, and it was Vergil in his *Eclogues* who first associated the Golden Age with the simplicity of pastoral life. Although later a polite convention, the idea of the Golden Age originally answered some deep inner need in the human psyche to escape the pressures of sophistication. In its beginnings, pastoral was essentially a vehicle of reaction against the world of urban culture and refinement.

The legend of the Golden Age, which is both central and pervasive in the pastoral form, is one of the most significant elements in primitivistic thought, to which pastoral is related. If we define chronological primitivism (with Lovejoy and Boas) as a theory that locates the time when the best condition of human life may be supposed to occur, then the legend of the Golden Age is the earliest manifestation of chronological primitivism.[2] Hesiod, a Greek poet of the eighth century B.C., was the first to tell, in his *Works and Days*, the myth of the Five Ages—the Golden Age (best), the Age of Silver, the Age of Bronze, the Age of Heroes, and the Age of Iron (always the contemporary age). Of the Golden Age he says: "First of all the deathless gods who dwell on Olympus made a golden race of mortal men. . . . And they lived like gods without sorrow of heart, remote and free from toil and grief: miserable age rested not on them; but with legs and arms never failing they made merry with feasting beyond the reach of all evils . . . and they had all good things; for the fruitful earth unforced bore them fruit abundantly and without stint. They dwelt in ease and peace upon their lands with many good things, rich in flocks and loved by the blessed

---

[1] Walter W. Greg, *Pastoral Poetry and Pastoral Drama* (1906; rpt. New York: Russell & Russell, 1959), pp. 4–5. This chapter is indebted to Greg's pioneering book. On the origin of pastoral, see now Thomas G. Rosenmeyer, *The Green Cabinet* (Berkeley and Los Angeles: Univ. of California Press, 1969), ch. 2.

[2] Arthur O. Lovejoy and George Boas, *Primitivism and Related Ideas in Antiquity* (Baltimore: Johns Hopkins Press, 1935), pp. 1, 24. On the Golden Age see also Rosenmeyer, *Green Cabinet*, pp. 74f. and 214–23.

gods."[3] Notable are the freedom from toil and sorrow, the spontaneous production of the earth, and the absence of war in the "golden race"— a state of perfect luxury whose connections with later pastoral works are its peace, its harmony with the natural world, and its formulation of an ideal in the past. In the *Metamorphoses* Ovid simplifies the Ages to two—the age of fortunate primitive man who lived when the age was golden under the god Saturn, and that of unfortunate modern man who lived under the rule of Zeus. It is this version of the Golden-Age story that has influenced later literature.[4]

The Greek poet Theocritus founded the pastoral tradition in the third century B.C. when he wrote a collection of thirty *Idylls*, poems that focused not on the intrigue and sophistication of the court at Alexandria but on the countryside of Sicily. The strong feeling for the contrast between town and country came to life when urban culture had become far enough removed from the conditions of real rural life for its hardships to be nearly forgotten; and as a result pastoral evoked the charms of rustic life in allusive, polished verse written for a sophisticated urban audience.[5] In his poetry Theocritus offered a stylized version of rustic activities such as song contests, laments of unrequited affection, and songs of love which he had heard and observed in Sicily and on the island of Cos. He recorded his memories fondly, with faithfulness of detail, and was usually satisfied to offer in his idylls a straightforward, nonallegorical account of the simplicity and naïveté of rustic culture. His bucolic idylls take us to a pastoral world that depicts an imagined life of leisure, enhanced by nature's beneficence, in which rustic figures sing and pipe of love. But if Theocritus transformed the pastoral life of Sicily into poetry, he took care not to dissociate his subject from reality or to create an illusion of total innocence. His art has frequently the vigor and earthiness of realism because it has as its inspiration actual human nature, not a philosophical or theoretical ideal. The art of

[3] Hesiod, *Works and Days*, Loeb Classical Library (Cambridge: Harvard Univ. Press, 1936), ll. 109–20.

[4] Lovejoy and Boas, pp. 43, 49. The other area of primitivism closely akin to the development of pastoral is cultural primitivism—the discontent of the civilized with civilization. If from chronological primitivism pastoral adapts the idea of the Golden Age, from cultural primitivism it adapts both the discontent with civilization and the resulting preference for a simpler way of life.

Raymond Williams' *The Country and the City* (New York: Oxford Univ. Press, 1973), which arrived while I was reading proof, traces in admirable detail the way every age has yearned for a rural Golden Age. But whereas Williams is concerned with the historical legitimacy of pastoral feelings, I am concerned with pastoral as a mode of traditional literary expression available to George Eliot, Hardy, and Lawrence.

[5] See Barriss Mills, trans., *The Idylls of Theokritos* (West Lafayette, Ind.: Purdue Univ. Studies, 1963), p. vii, and Greg, p. 7.

George Eliot, Hardy, and Lawrence is in this respect the same: its sympathy with actual humankind assures its nostalgia for the past of a solid foundation in reality.

The characteristic quality of traditional pastoral is captured in the seventh idyll of Theocritus. Here the reader finds a highly lyrical description of a paradise in nature, viewed by three men escaping from the city to attend a harvest festival. After a singing match with a goatherd, the three friends join the harvest party and

laid ourselves down rejoicing on deep couches of sweet rush and in the fresh-stripped vine-leaves. Many a poplar and elm murmured above our heads, and near at hand the sacred water from the cave of the Nymphs fell splashing. On the shady boughs the dusky cicadas were busy with their chatter, and the tree-frog far off cried in the dense thorn-brake. Larks and finches sang, the dove made moan, and bees flitted humming about the springs. All things were fragrant of rich harvest and of fruit-time. Pears at our feet and apples at our side were rolling plentifully, and the branches hung down to the ground with their burden of sloes.[6]

As a *locus amoenus*, this fertile paradise boasts shade, water, music, and fruit—ingredients of the *locus amoenus* that will recur later in *Adam Bede* and *Lady Chatterley's Lover* and (in inverted form) *The Woodlanders*. Similarly, *Idyll* 8, much imitated by Vergil, dramatizes a singing contest between Daphnis and Menalcas and features many concrete suggestions of real rural life. Variations of the song contest appear in *Adam Bede*, *Far from the Madding Crowd*, and *The White Peacock* as clear parallels to classical pastoral.

If *Idylls* 7 and 8 characterize the tradition, *Idyll* 10, "The Reapers," illustrates unusually well the tension between pastoral and realism that later vitalizes the pastoral novel. A dialogue between Milon and Bucaeus, *Idyll* 10 dramatizes the conflict of work with love. Milon playfully admonishes his youthful companion: "Bucaeus my man, what's the matter with you, my poor fellow? You can't drive your swathe straight as you used, nor do you keep up with your neighbour in the reaping." Bucaeus, lovesick and unable to sleep, confesses his negligence: "the land before my door is all unhoed since the sowing." Theocritus, having staged this amusing battle between toil and romance, resolves the conflict with a pair of songs. Milon himself declares the appropriate balance between work, music, and love when he says to Bucaeus: "just lay the crop on the ground, and strike up some love-song for the girl. You'll work happier." If Bucaeus proceeds to deliver a rhapsody to his "honey-hued" love, Milon in his song seeks Demeter's

[6] A. S. F. Gow, *Theocritus*, 2d ed. (Cambridge: Univ. Press, 1952), pp. 65–67. All quotations from Theocritus are from this edition.

blessing on the fields ("grant this crop be easy harvested and fruitful exceedingly") and sets in motion therefore a pleasing tension between labor and beauty. Milon, given the last word, concludes the poem by noting the fusion he has created between georgic and pastoral: "That's the stuff for men that work in the sun to sing."

Using Theocritus as their model, poets began to imitate their master in theme, meter, and dialect, largely reproducing the possibilities of the form Theocritus had created. Vergil, however, who was the first great successor of Theocritus and whose *Eclogues* are alluded to in the pastoral novels of George Eliot and Hardy and Lawrence, considerably altered the pastoral form. Vergil turned the bucolic eclogue into a form based upon polished artifice. Not content with the simplicity and the direct rural inspiration evident in Theocritus, Vergil began to separate pastoral from actual rural life: his shepherds are complex, and his landscape becomes distant and imaginary, as in *Eclogues* 7 and 10 whose setting is the idealized land of country life, sensitive to feeling and poetry, which Vergil calls Arcadia.[7] His eclogues, removed from real rural society, also serve to convey allegory or panegyric.

Vergil's ten *Eclogues*, written between 42 and 39 B.C., show profoundly the influence of Theocritus. Yet Vergil's pastoral is more polished and decorous and serene. Frank Kermode remarks that Vergil's pastoral poetry for the first time cultivates simplicity in stylized language and "uses the country scene and rustic episode for allegorical purposes." *Eclogue* 5, to cite an example, imitates the first idyll of Theocritus with a lament for the dead Daphnis. But the poem is almost certainly about Julius Caesar too.[8] If the objectivity of the Theocritian idyll disappears, still the *Eclogues* extend the earlier limits of the genre. The somber chords of *Eclogues* 1 and 9 blend problematic strains of actual life into the idealized pastoral world. Vergil's shepherds will not serve as vehicles of comedy or pathos alone, says Brooks Otis; "they are serious lovers or sufferers whom we can take seriously because we empathetically follow their feelings and participate in their tragedy."[9] This melancholy represents an important new note in pastoral poetry.

---

[7] For a discussion of Arcadia, see Gilbert Highet, *The Classical Tradition* (1949; rpt. London: Oxford Univ. Press, 1967), p. 163, and Rosenmeyer, ch. 11.

[8] Frank Kermode, *English Pastoral Poetry* (London: Harrap, 1952), pp. 25–26. The latest commentator on the *Eclogues*, Michael C. J. Putnam, says however: "Questions of fact . . . stand in the way of a direct equation between Daphnis and Julius Caesar. Nevertheless one cannot but presume that a contemporary of Virgil would have tended at first to form such an opinion, after reading Menalcas' lines. It is perhaps the poet's greatest achievement in *Eclogue* 5 to turn the idea of a literal apotheosis to specifically intellectual purposes" (*Virgil's Pastoral Art* [Princeton: Princeton Univ. Press, 1970], pp. 189–90).

[9] Brooks Otis, *Virgil* (Oxford: Clarendon Press, 1963), pp. 127–28.

In establishing the pervasive fiction of the Golden Age, Vergil's fourth eclogue, written in 40 B.C., proved the most influential on the pastoral tradition. While all of antiquity placed the dream of mankind's happy state at the beginning of time, Vergil projected that dream into the future.[10] At the opening of the poem we meet a newborn child and a prophecy of a change: "a great order of ages arises anew." As the child develops, natural evil disappears and the earth recovers its original spontaneity. When the boy matures into a man, natural spontaneity has eliminated the need for commerce or agriculture. An era of peace begins. George Eliot, Hardy, and Lawrence create in their pastoral novels a version of the Golden Age not only possible, but within the actual memory of the writer.

Two of Vergil's *Eclogues*, 1 and 9, nicely illustrate the fusion of realistic and pastoral material that characterizes the pastoral novel. Both show, if briefly, the collision of the historical process with the timeless pastoral world of beauty, leisure, and song. In *Eclogue* 1, Meliboeus and his goats are driven from the land, which the state has awarded to a soldier, while Tityrus remains to enjoy the bucolic life:

> Tityrus, here you loll, your slim reed-pipe serenading
> The woodland spirit beneath a spread of sheltering beech,
> While I must leave my home place, the fields so dear to me.
> [ll. 1–3] [11]

In *Eclogue* 9, Moeris against his will must drive a flock of goats to Rome for another man's profit:

> Oh, Lycidas, that I should have lived to see an outsider
> Take over my little farm—a thing I have never feared—
> And tell me, 'You're dispossessed, you old tenants, you've got to go.'
> [ll. 2–4]

The singing of songs only temporarily erases the painful recognition of change. "Time bears all away," Moeris laments. The theme of dispossession, which enters pastoral with Vergil's *Eclogues*, recurs frequently in the pastoral novel, a cruel reminder that historical process alters the landscape and destroys the pastoral world. Threatened by dispossession (or actually dispossessed) are the Poysers, Gabriel Oak, Giles Winterborne, Marty South, the Saxtons, and Connie and Mellors. One reason why pastoral as a form prefers to fix the historical moment in the past

[10] Renato Poggioli, "The Oaten Flute," *Harvard Library Bulletin*, 11 (1957), 163.

[11] *The Eclogues and Georgics of Virgil*, tr. C. Day Lewis, Anchor Books (Garden City, N.Y.: Doubleday, 1964). All translations of the *Eclogues* and the *Georgics* are by Lewis.

is that it so clearly recognizes time as the enemy of stability and peace. What is past has released itself from the power of time.

If not usually regarded as pastoral, Vergil's didactic poem on agriculture, the *Georgics*, is of special significance because it prefigures, early, some salient tensions in the pastoral novels of George Eliot, Hardy, and Lawrence: glorified work, contrasts of city and country, idealized farm life yet also realistic details of the agricultural process (found especially in Hardy), and finally man's intimate relationship to nature. Composed between 37 and 29 B.C., upon Augustus' message of peace for rural Italy after the civil wars, the poem was written to promote a "back-to-the-farm" movement in Italy by offering both practical advice on the methods of successful agriculture and rhapsodic praise of the rural world. In Book I man's struggle with inanimate nature is a harsh one; he must *work* (a central idea in the pastoral novel later) if he is to discover the basic arts of civilization.[12] The gospel of work that Vergil sets forth reverses the original valuation of the Age of Saturn and the Age of Jupiter:

> For the Father of agriculture
> Gave us a hard calling: he first decreed it an art
> To work the fields, sent worries to sharpen our mortal wits
> And would not allow his realm to grow listless from lethargy.
> Before Jove's time no settlers brought the land under subjection;
>
> . . . . .
>
> All produce went to a common pool, and earth unprompted
> Was free with all her fruits.
>
> [I.121–28]

But the imposition of arduous labor is a gain rather than a loss. It was for man's benefit that Jove introduced toil: man could earn his own subsistence and thus would not grow "listless from lethargy." As Vergil remarks in a celebrated sentence, "Labor omnia vicit / improbus" (Unremitting labor overcomes all difficulties).

Book II in contrast describes the happy cooperation between man and nature, and identifies Italy as a region befitting the Age of Gold. The equation of a specific geographical area with the ideal of a Golden Age anticipates the pastoral novel: Hayslope, Raveloe, Mellstock, Weatherbury, Little Hintock, the Nethermere Valley, Wragby Wood all represent an ideal united with a specific *locus*. For Vergil, Italy corresponds to the prelapsarian paradise. In Italy, the "land of Saturn," we find the lush fertility and the continual spring of other portraits of the Golden Age. Italy is

[12] Otis, pp. 148–52; see also pp. 136, 139.

> a country fulfilled with heavy corn and
> Campanian wine, possessed by olives and prosperous herds.
>
> .   .   .   .   .   .
>
> Here is continual spring and a summer beyond her season;
> Cattle bear twice yearly, apples a second crop.
>
> [II.143–50]

This description contrasts sharply with the severe picture of the Iron Age in Book I. Through diligent labor, man can create harmony with nature.

Besides a new conception of the Golden Age, Vergil's *Georgics* manifests other important parallels to the pastoral novel—the lavish praise of rural life and its intimate relationship to nature, the sharply etched contrast between city and country life, and the renunciation of ambition and courtly splendor. These underlying attitudes emerge in Book II:

> Oh, too lucky for words, if only he knew his luck,
> Is the countryman who far from the clash of armaments
> Lives, and rewarding earth is lavish of all he needs!
> True, no mansion tall with a swanky gate throws up
> In the morning a mob of callers to crowd him out. . . .
>
> .   .   .   .   .   .
>
> But calm security and a life that will not cheat you,
> Rich in its own rewards are here: the broad ease of the farmlands,
> Caves, living lakes, and combes that are cool even at midsummer,
> Mooing of herds, and slumber mild in the trees' shade.
> Here are glades game-hunted,
> Lads hardened to labour, inured to simple ways,
> Reverence for God, respect for the family.
>
> [II.458–73]

The marked similarities between pastoral and the *Georgics* suggest that Vergil's poem is a semipastoral work that bears much the same relation to his own *Eclogues* and to Theocritus' *Idylls* as the pastoral novels of George Eliot, Hardy, and Lawrence bear to the works that cumulatively became traditional pastoral. In both the *Georgics* and the pastoral novel, the necessity of work is not only recognized but glorified as a condition which ensures order, preserves man's kinship to the natural world (which unconsciously labors to maintain its own form of order), and provides interest and variety in life. Fundamentally, like the pastoral novel later, the *Georgics* is realistic in intent. Both evoke real life warmly and charmingly in order to commemorate the rural values of harmony with nature, humility, and contentment. In these ways the *Georgics*, especially Book II, anticipates the pastoral novel. If its in-

fluence is not direct, that is because its aim throughout is to teach and
promote, rather than to re-create imaginatively the rural past.

Compared to the importance of Vergil's work, the Middle Ages con-
tributed nothing significant to the development of the pastoral novel.
We turn instead to some Renaissance works of pastoral.

Frank Kermode has written that "the Renaissance, which saw the beginning of the change to something like modern town-life, had its own
nostalgia for simplicity, its own deep though ambiguous feelings about
the countryside and its inhabitants, its own myth of the natural man,
and his special sympathy with created Nature."[13] As we have seen,
pastoral develops from the tension between town and country, a tension
subordinate to the more universal antithesis between art and nature.
The tension between rural and urban modes of life was perhaps felt
more poignantly during the Renaissance than in any century that has
followed. London was gradually emerging (like Alexandria or Rome
earlier, or New York later) as a modern metropolis with its own dis-
tinctively urban values, while its inhabitants were still essentially rural
in their training and traditions. If there was the traditional laughter at
the rude manners of country people, there was also a tendency to idealize
them as a nostalgic reminder of the traditional order.

In the Renaissance, the pastoral tradition witnessed (in Petrarch and
Mantuan, e.g.) the full flowering of the allegorical pastoral initiated
by Vergil. Because changes in religious outlook brought about a weakening of allegorical modes of thinking, however, the pastoral novel shows
scarcely any reflection of allegorical pastoral, and so I consider instead
the spontaneous pastoral impulse in England. In English pastoral, Greg
has isolated two distinct and recurring tendencies: the spontaneous and
popular pastoral impulse, and the foreign and literary pastoral influence.[14] The spontaneous impulse was stronger and more important, and
attracted the attention of Spenser, who stands as the first of several English writers to combine successfully the native pastoral impulse and the
foreign literary tradition. Spenser's *The Shepheardes Calender* (1579)
experiments boldly with meter and diction by using archaic and dialectal
words effectively and by adopting a rough, antilyrical meter where appropriate. Spenser's eclogues, although they probably did not influence
the pastoral novel, provided a model for experimentation and the use

[13] *English Pastoral Poetry*, p. 36; Kermode's introduction contains a valuable
discussion of Renaissance pastoral.

[14] Cf. Edmund K. Chambers' earlier distinction between "transparent, sensuous,
melodious" pastoral poetry and pastoral poetry that perfers "the sombre, the obscure, the intricate" (*English Pastorals* [London: Blackie, 1895], p. xviii).

of dialect. If his shepherds are remote from the reader, placed as they are in an ideal landscape, the pastoral philosophy they express encapsulates the tradition. "June," for example, illustrates the shepherd's denial of ambition, which is echoed later by Hardy's Gabriel Oak and Giles Winterborne. A shepherd should neither "strive to win renown, or passe the rest," nor "follow flying fame / But feed his flock in fields, where falls hem best." In its concern with man's relationship to the cycle of nature and with matters of universal significance—love, death, or art— *The Shepheardes Calender* like the pastoral novel ranks as serious literature.

If much Renaissance pastoral verse lacks originality, the fault lies in the requirements of an age that demanded the familiarities of convention. The same perhaps can be said for the pastoral romance in the Renaissance. It should be noted, at the outset, that despite similarities, the pastoral romance and the pastoral novels of George Eliot, Hardy, and Lawrence differ considerably. It is true that both deal ostensibly with rural life and are written in prose. Both too share the pastoral ideal and have techniques in common (contrasts and structural devices, e.g.). But in the pastoral romance rural life is still a convention; it is generally a background for fantastic adventure, for allegory, and for an escape from actuality. In the pastoral novel rural life is utilized differently, to reveal an integrated culture whose values are more essential and significant than those of urban life. Unlike most pastoral romances, the pastoral novel successfully interweaves pastoral and realism.

In the English pastoral romance, the main elements are the separation of lovers, their exceptional loyalty, an elaborate plot, unusual chance adventures often among shepherds, mistaken or disguised identities, and an elegant and formal style. The rearrangement of romantic relationships during the course of the romance—in *Rosalynde*, e.g.— anticipates *Adam Bede*, *The Woodlanders*, and *The White Peacock*. Although many prose pastoral romances appeared in the Renaissance, those outstanding are Robert Greene's *Menaphon*, Thomas Lodge's *Rosalynde*, and Sir Philip Sidney's *Arcadia*. Greene's *Menaphon* (1589) demonstrates the requirements of the type, with its secret marriage of the daughter of the king of Arcadia, its subsequent banishments and shipwreck, its pastoral disguising and amorous confusion, its revealed identities and happy ending, and its euphuistic style. Opening, like the *Arcadia*, with a shipwreck, *Menaphon* focuses on the princess Sephistia, who disguises herself as a shepherdess and who, like Rosalynde and Alinda, enters the bucolic life. Around Sephistia swarm many suitors, including both shepherds and disguised members of her own family. When identities are revealed, the number of marriages that follow sparks our recollection of the felicitous endings of both *As You Like It* and *Under the Greenwood Tree.* The realignment of romantic ties is achieved in the pastoral romance by stripping away costumed disguises; in the pastoral novel, it is the process of peeling a false identity that achieves the realignment (e.g., Hetty Sorrel, Fancy Day, Bathsheba Everdene, Connie Chatterley, and Oliver Mellors).

By far the most influential of the pastoral romances (and the most important for our purposes) is Sidney's *Arcadia* (1593). Like other pastoral romances, its plot is intricate, digressive, and episodic; it combines prose and verse; and it offers a wide variety of tales.[15] By adding numerous nonpastoral episodes and saturating the narrative with argumentation, the romance experiments with the *fusion*, in a complicated plot, of pastoral landscape and chivalric adventure. The *Arcadia*, with its contrasting locales and contrasting kinds of action, features a center (two lodges, an arbor, and a cave), an inner circle (Basilius' pastoral retreat), a middle circle (Arcadia proper, the mean between outer and inner circles), and finally the outer circle (urban, complex, sophisticated).[16] "The action of the pastoral romance," says Walter R. Davis, "is simply the progress of the hero through the various areas of the setting: from the outer circle into the inner circle, hence to the center, and out again." The standard pastoral romance has therefore a three-part pattern: "disintegration in the turbulent outer circle, education in the pastoral circle, and rebirth at the sacred center." In Sidney's *Arcadia*, Pyrocles and Musidorus, shipwrecked, fall in love with the princesses Pamela and Philoclea, assume pastoral disguises, win the love of their mistresses, achieve harmony of soul, and at last return to the world from which they came.

Despite analogical differences and differences in language levels, the pastoral novel is like Sidney's *Arcadia* in a number of ways. Both feature incursions from outside the pastoral world and thus city-country contrasts. At the plot center of both we find sensual and nonsensual love, located in a pastoral setting and culminating usually in marriage. And in *Adam Bede* and especially in *Lady Chatterley's Lover*, the *Arcadia's* pastoral pattern of escape-reorientation-return is beautifully embodied. But of special interest in both Sidney's romance and the pastoral novel is the full interaction of pastoral and realistic elements, of stasis and

[15] See Walter R. Davis, *A Map of Arcadia: Sidney's Romance in Its Tradition* (New Haven: Yale Univ. Press, 1965), p. 192, and Margaret Schlauch, *Antecedents of the English Novel: 1400–1600* (Warszawa, Poland: PWN—Polish Scientific Publishers, 1963), p. 192. Sidney's *Arcadia* exists in three forms—the *Old Arcadia*, written between 1577 and 1580, the *New Arcadia*, a partial revision of the old, published in 1590, and the revised and unrevised versions published together in 1593 as the *Arcadia* by Sidney's sister, the Countess of Pembroke.

[16] Davis, pp. 26, 35–37, 51–52. The quotations that follow are from p. 38.

flux, an interaction that forms a hallmark of the pastoral novel. In her study of the *Old Arcadia*, Elizabeth Dipple argues that since literary heroes mix with comic shepherds and since therefore "literary idealism co-exists with unadorned, quasi-historical realism," the *Old Arcadia* is not generically in the mainstream of pastoral.[17] "The work," she says, "moves instantaneously from literary stasis to the dynamic flux of realistic examination, from the timeless world of pastoral to the world of hopelessly flawed character and action" (p. 320). Particularly in this way does the *Arcadia* anticipate the pastoral novel.

In the Renaissance, English pastoral drama was a more significant and influential form than the pastoral romance. The English pastoral drama was born of the Italian parents *Il pastor fido* (1590) of Guarini and the *Aminta* (1590) of Tasso, Arcadian pastoral dramas that produce echoes, as we will see, in *The Woodlanders* and *Lady Chatterley's Lover*. One highly significant play reverberating in the pastoral novel is *As You Like It* (1600), which borrows its plot from Lodge's *Rosalynde*. In *As You Like It* Shakespeare passes judgment on the pastoral ideal by satirizing it. He offers three degrees of idealization which interact with one another: Phebe and Silvius as refined Arcadians of pastoral convention, Celia and Rosalind and Orlando as courtly characters, and Audrey and William as farcical rustics. Corin, anticipating the pastoral figures of George Eliot, Hardy, and Lawrence, is an exception. He is a real shepherd. "Sir," he says to Touchstone, "I am a true laborer; I earn that I eat, get that I wear, owe no man hate, envy no man's happiness, glad of other men's good, content with my harm; and the greatest of my pride is to see my ewes graze and my lambs suck" (III.ii.73–77). But while Shakespeare presents the conventional pastoral world, he mocks it by introducing characters who scorn the idealists. Touchstone, for example, prefers the court even while he is in Arden: "When I was at home, I was in a better place" (II.iv.16–17). When Rosalind finds Orlando's verses hanging from a tree, Touchstone says: "Truly the tree yields bad fruit" (III.ii.115–16). Reality is brought up sharply against the dream. Yet Shakespeare allows this criticism of his ideal world. In the words of Harold Jenkins, "Shakespeare . . . builds up his ideal world and lets his idealists scorn the real one. But into their midst he introduces people who mock their ideals and others who mock *them*. One must not say that Shakespeare never judges, but one judgement is always being modified by another."[18] By undercutting pastoral conventions, Shakespeare suggests that the pastoral ideal is not an attainable ideal but an *informative* ideal, one that stirs the audience

[17] "Harmony and Pastoral in the *Old Arcadia*," *ELH*, 35 (1968), 318.
[18] "As You Like It," *Shakespeare: Modern Essays in Criticism*, ed. Leonard F. Dean (New York: Oxford Univ. Press, 1961), p. 117.

to consider life's potential as well as its actualities.[19] Thus pastoral attracts Shakespeare's imagination, yet he fails finally to give it his full support. Seldom afterward will the pastoral ideal be purely represented or fully applauded by writers of the first rank.

The seventeenth century shows a notable lack of interest in pastoral. Although one can point to Milton's mixture of pastoral and epic genres in *Paradise Lost* and its importance to George Eliot and Lawrence, works that illustrate the century's interest in pastoral are *Lycidas* (1637) and Andrew Marvell's pastoral poetry (published 1681).[20] Even *Lycidas*, the best and most famous of the pastoral elegies, illustrates the dialectic between pastoral and realism that, I argue, lies implicit in the genre and reaches its height in the pastoral novel. In Milton's poem, passages that follow the conventions of the elegy alternate with passages in which realism threatens to disrupt the poem's cool impersonality. Juxtaposed to the usual procession of mourners, for example, is St. Peter's jarring denunciation of the corrupt Anglican clergy, who

> Creep and intrude and climb into the fold!
> Of other care they little reck'ning make
> Than how to scramble at the shearers' feast,
> And shove away the worthy bidden guest.
>
> [ll. 115–18]

Then the poet bids the Sicilian Muse return to inspire the magnificent catalogue of flowers that follow. The poem as a whole progresses in this way. In the best discussion of the elegy's blend of pastoral and realism, R. L. Brett remarks that "the movement backwards and forwards from pastoralism to a rejection of pastoralism is seen as one of the chief means by which Milton expresses his meaning."[21]

Marvell critically examines and complicates pastoral, notably in the four Mower poems, "The Garden," and "Upon Appleton House." Rosalie Colie argues that what connects the Mower poems is that each of the four raises a different question about the pastoral convention.[22] Like

[19] See Albert R. Cirillo's helpful essay, "*As You Like It*: Pastoralism Gone Awry," *ELH*, 38 (1971), 19–39.

[20] On Milton's use of pastoral in *Paradise Lost*, see John R. Knott, Jr., *Milton's Pastoral Vision* (Chicago: Univ. of Chicago Press, 1971).

[21] *Reason and Imagination* (London: Oxford Univ. Press, 1960), p. 46. See also Jon S. Lawry, " 'Eager Thought': Dialectic in *Lycidas*," *PMLA*, 77 (1962), 27–32, and Harold E. Toliver, *Pastoral Forms and Attitudes* (Berkeley and Los Angeles: Univ. of California Press, 1971), pp. 167–76.

[22] "*My Ecchoing Song*": *Andrew Marvell's Poetry of Criticism* (Princeton: Princeton Univ. Press, 1970), p. 30. Cf. Donald M. Friedman, *Marvell's Pastoral Art*

Shakespeare in *As You Like It*, Marvell takes no final stand on the pastoral mode; instead, he exalts pastoral values even as he questions and intellectualizes them (Colie, p. 40). "The Garden," like the pastoral novel later, mixes thematic genres, combining pastoral themes "with the modes of religious meditation, satire, and the philosophical lyric."[23] Longer, more complex, and more enigmatic, "Upon Appleton House" does the same, combining the pastoral device of the *locus amoenus* with topographical panegyric, epic features, and a richly developed allegory.[24] In Marvell's pastoral poems, as in *Adam Bede* or *The Woodlanders* or *Lady Chatterley's Lover*, ideas are with ease expressed in various but conjoined literary modes, which in turn express varying attitudes toward life. "Pure" pastoral has been abandoned.

After the Restoration and into the eighteenth century, pastoral flourished for a time, but the traditional form grew increasingly artificial and sterile. The neoclassical age, placing a premium on imitation, created frigidity rather than vitality in pastoral. Largely cut off from its country roots, traditional pastoral exhausted itself in the pastorals of Pope, Gay, Ambrose Philips, Allan Ramsey, and William Shenstone. Instead, much energy was spent by French and English critics of the late seventeenth and early eighteenth centuries developing definitions and rules to govern the composition of pastoral. J. E. Congleton shows that the eighteenth century harbored three divergent groups of writers expressing themselves on pastoral: the neoclassicists (Pope and Gay), followers of the French critic Rapin (whose "Treatise" of 1684 is central to neoclassical pastoral theory); the rationalists (Addison and Johnson) who followed the ideas of the French critic Fontenelle; and the pre-Romantics (Joseph Warton and Blair) who modified the rationalist critics before them.[25]

Contending that Nature and the Ancients were the same and that the pastoral poet should imitate the ancient masters of bucolic poetry to create art of the highest order, the English followers of Rapin in the late seventeenth and early eighteenth centuries frowned upon the fusion of pastoral and realism implicit in the genre. As Pope remarks in his

---

(Berkeley and Los Angeles: Univ. of California Press, 1970), p. 101: "The 'Mower' poems in particular are immensely complicated examples of his incessant modifying and re-examination of literary forms."

[23] Harold E. Toliver, *Marvell's Ironic Vision* (New Haven: Yale Univ. Press, 1965), p. 138. Cf. Colie, p. 20.

[24] See David Evett, " 'Paradice's Only Map': The *Topos* of the *Locus Amoenus* and the Structure of *Upon Appleton House*," *PMLA*, 85 (1970), 504f. But cf. Rosenmeyer (p. 207), who believes that the poem is not primarily a pastoral since it synthesizes "privileged culture and rustic strength."

[25] *Theories of Pastoral Poetry in England: 1684–1798* (Gainesville: Univ. of Florida Press, 1952), p. 301.

"Discourse on Pastoral Poetry" (1717), writers of pastoral "are not to describe our shepherds as shepherds at this day really are, but as they may be conceived then to have been; when the best of men followed the employment." The poet should expose the best side only of a shepherd's life, and conceal its miseries. Although a few later writers practiced the form, Pope's *Pastorals* represents probably the last significant illustration of traditional pastoral. Geoffrey Tillotson remarks that "an age which valued satire could only amuse itself in pastoral. Man is the theme still, but it is man as a pretty creature, provided with set and toy emotions which last only to the end of the poem."[26] The pastoral form needed new vitality, needed to rediscover its roots in actual rural life. It is a thesis of this study that the fundamental pastoral impulse—the impulse to discover an ideal or Golden-Age world in a small, integrated rural culture in the past—assumes new literary forms in the late eighteenth and early nineteenth centuries and adapts itself to a set of new assumptions about human nature which, since about 1800, have tended to prevail.

When we turn to the viewpoint of the rationalist critics, we note the beginnings of a marked change in attitude toward pastoral poetry, a change that anticipates the realistic attitudes of later centuries. Best illustrating this altered viewpoint are Dr. Johnson's essays No. 36 and particularly No. 37 in *The Rambler* (1750). These essays attach little value to neoclassical rules for composing pastoral poetry. Instead, Dr. Johnson's definition of pastoral is simple and inclusive: "Pastoral being the *representation of an action or passion, by its effects upon a country life,* has nothing peculiar but its confinement to rural imagery." Pastoral is "a representation of rural nature"; whatever may commonly happen in the country "may afford a subject for a pastoral poet."[27] A rationalist, Johnson rejects the convention of the Golden Age. He insists that pastoral poetry should concern itself with subjects drawn from other kinds of rural life than "of men actually tending sheep," and decries both the allegorical pastoral and the incongruity (in *The Shepheardes Calender,* e.g.) "of joining elegance of thought with coarseness of diction." Wishing to bring pastoral poetry closer to real rural life, Dr. Johnson recommends the abandonment of conventional pastoral and in this way helps prepare for the development of the pastoral novel.

The pre-Romantic critics, like the rationalists before them, preferred realistic characters and situations. For them, the primary purpose of pastoral was to describe the beauties of rural scenery and to portray the simple lives of those who lived close to the soil. Joseph Warton in "An

[26] *On the Poetry of Pope* (Oxford: Clarendon Press, 1938), p. 80.

[27] *Rambler* no. 37, in *The Critical Opinions of Samuel Johnson,* ed. Joseph E. Brown (1926; rpt. New York: Russell & Russell, 1961), pp. 183–85.

Essay on the Genius and Writings of Pope" (1756) reinterprets the development of pastoral. Warton suggests that the poets who followed Theocritus mistakenly believed that the beauties he described were too magnificent to be real and therefore ascribed them to a fictitious Golden Age. Warton thus equates the convention of the Golden Age with real nature and actual rural life. Congleton (p. 116) observes that Warton replaces chronological primitivism (the earliest age as best) with cultural primitivism (the desire for simplicity) and so lays a fresh foundation for the writing of pastoral poetry, since the Golden Age can now occur even in the present. Hugh Blair in his essay "Pastoral Poetry" (1783) wants, like Johnson, to bring pastoral closer to actual rural life and real external nature, and thus to widen its range: "If it be not exactly real life which [the pastoral poet] presents to us, it must, however, be somewhat that resembles it."[28] Such remarks push us in the direction of Wordsworth and the pastoral novel.

Congleton concludes that "*Michael* aside, no notable pastorals were written in England after the eighteenth century. . . . When the Romantic critics pushed pastoral theory into the realm of realism, they exceeded the bounds of the genre" (p. 315). We must disagree, although Congleton presumably speaks of traditional pastoral whereas this study treats the pastoral impulse, which may clothe itself in varying forms. The increasing emphasis on realism forced the genre to enlarge its scope. Thus a version of traditional pastoral gradually replaced traditional pastoral itself. The pastoral impulse shed its outward and conventional form, became semirealistic, and later—in the nineteenth century—took fiction as well as poetry for its linguistic embodiment.

If we examine the pre-Romantic literature of the eighteenth century, we find several poems which—though not of the traditional pastoral canon—reflect the tendency to treat rural life with greater realism while simultaneously maintaining a nostalgic tone. Such a tendency directly anticipates Wordsworth and the pastoral novels of George Eliot, Hardy, and Lawrence because it directs attention away from the artificial world of traditional pastoral.

To understand the later eighteenth-century response to rural life, we should acknowledge the peculiar social and economic conditions out of which that response developed. By ancient tradition, laborers in English villages maintained unwritten property rights to land called "the commons," where they could keep cattle or hogs, gather firewood, and plant gardens. During the late eighteenth century the process of "enclosure" gathered momentum, and by 1850 it was completed. Village landlords, learning profitable farming methods and wanting vast private parks,

[28] *Lectures on Rhetoric and Belles Lettres* (London, 1787), III, 118.

wished to extend their property. During enclosure the village commons were bought, traditional property rights went unrecognized, country laborers and small farmers were forced off the land, and rural life for much of the population came to a close. Hardship was the rule for these laborers, who largely migrated to the new industrial towns. Those who remained scarcely subsisted.[29] In his later novels, Hardy dramatizes the last manifestations of their plight.

During this agricultural revolution a body of literature developed which lamented the death of the old order of peasant life. Wherever the peasant was idealized in literature, there was an implied negative reaction to the agricultural revolution, for idealization of the past is generally a means of protest against the loss of the values it represents. One of the first hints of change appears in Gray's "Elegy Written in a Country Churchyard" (1751). Although the "Elegy" preceded full-scale enclosure, it sets the tone for the later eighteenth-century period, which T. S. Eliot calls a "rural, pastoral, meditative age."[30] The obscure graveyard stirs the poet to ruminate on the death of those who might have been as celebrated as Milton. Yet, undisturbed by ambition, they achieved a steady calm in their lives:

> Far from the madding crowd's ignoble strife,
>   Their sober wishes never learn'd to stray;
> Along the cool sequester'd vale of life
>   They kept the noiseless tenour of their way.
>
> [ll. 73–76][31]

As in traditional pastoral the isolation from struggle and conflict, and the contentment and peace of rural life are praised, for "paths of glory lead but to the grave."

We see the influence of the "Elegy" in Goldsmith's "The Deserted Village" (1770), another in a series of alloyed pastorals that pit idyll against troubled reality. The poem descries the agricultural revolution that was evicting the peasantry from their homes. The same kind of social concern is expressed by Hardy and Lawrence, a concern with the change and attenuation which in varying degrees characterized rural life from "enclosure" to the twentieth century. Goldsmith, in lyrical elegiac couplets, writes of sweet Auburn, "loveliest village of the plain," whose bowers held "innocence and ease":

[29] See Kenneth MacLean, *Agrarian Age: A Background for Wordsworth* (New Haven: Yale Univ. Press, 1950), pp. 12–21.

[30] "Poetry in the Eighteenth Century," in *From Dryden to Johnson*, ed. Boris Ford (London: Penguin, 1957), p. 275.

[31] Quotations from the poetry of Gray, Goldsmith, and Crabbe are from *Enlightened England*, ed. Wylie Sypher (New York: Norton, 1962).

> These were thy charms, sweet village! Sports like these,
> With sweet succession, taught ev'n toil to please;
> These round thy bowers their chearful influence shed,
> These were thy charms—But all these charms are fled.
>
> [ll. 31–34]

The cause of the loss of rural charm? "Vain transitory splendor!"—the same splendor condemned by Vergil in the *Georgics.* The English peasantry is "by luxury betrayed." Goldsmith compares "luxury"—the growth of wealth and extravagant country estates—to "rural virtue"—the ancient agricultural economy of vigorous and independent peasants. It is the same city-country contrast found in traditional pastoral. But Goldsmith discards the stylized artifice of the traditional genre while retaining the political overtones and the theme of dispossession found in Vergil's *Eclogues.* The poem thus nostalgically laments an immemorial way of life and attacks the forces that were corrupting rural life:

> Teach erring man to spurn the rage of gain;
> Teach him, that states of native strength possesst
> Though very poor, may still be very blest.
>
> [ll. 424–26]

Though the poem omits the *otium* and the spiritual landscape of the traditional pastoral lyric, Goldsmith's pastoral sentiment is obvious.[32] The poet glorifies poverty because it contributes to innocence and contentment. The peasant world is here an idealized world nostalgically recaptured, with regret at its passing, yet without sentimentality. "The Deserted Village," unlike the *Pastorals* of Pope, idealizes real peasants and an actual geographical location. In this respect it anticipates both the poetry of Wordsworth and the pastoral novel.

Foreshadowing the pastoral novel differently, Fielding, Smollett, Sterne, and Goldsmith are all attracted to the rural ideal in their fiction.[33] The first half of Goldsmith's *The Vicar of Wakefield* (1766) perhaps best typifies the spirit of pastoral in eighteenth-century fiction,

---

[32] John F. Lynen, however, remarks of "The Deserted Village" that "while it manifests the nostalgia and admiration for rural simplicity so important in pastoralism, the poem is one of social protest and focuses attention upon the actual state of the country in a way quite foreign to pastoral. . . . Goldsmith's humanitarianism and his failure to use the traditional imagery of pastoral are both indicative of a quite different approach to rural life" (*The Pastoral Art of Robert Frost* [New Haven: Yale Univ. Press, 1960], pp. 16*n*–17*n*). I would counter that the poem shows the *direction* in which pastoral is moving, and that, more important, Vergil's first and ninth eclogues focus explicitly on the actual conditions of Italy.

[33] See, e.g., Jeffrey L. Duncan, "The Rural Ideal in Eighteenth-Century Fiction," *Studies in English Literature,* 8 (1968), 517–35.

although it uses pastoral primarily as a means of creating sentiment or as a method of easy contrast, rather than as a vehicle that interprets the novelist's perception of the conflict between rural and urban. Moving in a reverse direction from *Silas Marner*, the novel begins on a note of sweet and mellow charm. Having lost their fortune, the Primrose family retire to a distant neighborhood, "consisting of farmers, who tilled their own grounds, and were equal strangers to opulence and poverty. As they had almost all the conveniences of life within themselves, they seldom visited towns or cities in search of superfluity. Remote from the polite, they still retained a primaeval simplicity of manners, and frugal by long habit, they scarce knew that temperance was a virtue. They wrought with chearfulness on days of labour; but observed festivals as intervals of idleness and pleasure."[34] Innocent and beautiful, both landscape and neighbors are idealized in the tradition of Sidney's description of Arcadia. In telling the story Dr. Primrose concentrates on the "intervals of idleness and pleasure," on neighbors and holidays and simple domestic joys. This concentration adds much to the idyllic atmosphere, although the mention of labor, not part of traditional pastoral, looks ahead to the pastoral novel. But before half the story has passed, misfortune invades the Vicar's rural retreat, leaving in its wake destruction and sustained adversity of a proportion that is foreign to pastoral. The nearest precedent is perhaps Sidney's *Arcadia* or *Daphnis and Chloe*, in their blending of pastoral and nonpastoral elements; later the pastoral novel also alternates pastoral and realism, though more subtly and without the jarring shift from one mode to another. The two weddings that close Goldsmith's novel are the only reminders of the opening half.

In contrast, Crabbe's treatment of rural life, harshly literal, reflects a strong antipastoral bias that leads us still closer to a realistic conception of pastoral and thus to the fiction of George Eliot, Hardy, and Lawrence. As Wylie Sypher observes, "Crabbe offsets the idyllic 'Deserted Village' of Goldsmith as well as the more monumental and contemplative pastoral of Wordsworth."[35] Depending on a contrast rather than a fusion of pastoral and realism, *The Village* (1783) reveals the gathering dissatisfaction with the sentimental portrayal of an idealized rural life dissociated from actual conditions and, in doing so, anticipates Book VIII of *The Prelude*. Crabbe writes:

> Fled are those times when, in harmonious strains,
> The rustic poet praised his native plains.
> No shepherd now, in smooth alternate verse,

[34] *The Vicar of Wakefield*, in vol. IV of *Collected Works of Oliver Goldsmith*, ed. Arthur Friedman (Oxford: Clarendon Press, 1966), pp. 31–32.
[35] *Enlightened England*, pp. 1331–32.

> Their country's beauty or their nymphs' rehearse;
> Yet still for these we frame the tender strain,
> Still in our lays fond Corydons complain,
>
>   .   .   .   .   .
>
> From truth and Nature shall we widely stray,
> Where Virgil, not where Fancy, leads the way?
>   Yet, thus the Muses sing of happy swains,
> Because the Muses never knew their pains.
> They boast their peasants' pipes; but peasants now
> Resign their pipes and plod behind the plow.
>
>   [I.7–12, 19–24]

Crabbe sees in pastoral only leisure and dishonesty; he has no praise, either, for the rural world but concentrates on its wretchedness and harsh penury. He intends to picture existing conditions and to dispel the literary view of village life. Like Gay, who burlesqued pastoral in his *Shepherd's Week* (1714), Crabbe provides one link in the chain of alterations and additions to the pastoral form.[36] But if Crabbe describes factually the conditions of humble rural life, Wordsworth wishes instead to evoke imaginatively these same conditions.

It is usually agreed that *Lyrical Ballads* (1798) marks a change in the nature and direction of English literature. But *Lyrical Ballads* also inaugurates a change in attitude toward peasants and rural life. Wordsworth proves highly significant to our study not only because of this change but because his ideas and attitudes strongly influenced George Eliot, who in turn provided fictional direction for Thomas Hardy and the early D. H. Lawrence. The critical document that illustrates this change is Wordsworth's "Preface" to the 1800 edition of *Lyrical Ballads* in which he proposes to treat incidents and situations from humble, rustic life and to relate them "in a selection of language really used by men." Here Wordsworth, aided by Dr. Johnson half a century earlier, deals the blow that destroys traditional pastoral as a vital source of inspiration to men of letters. The result: conventional pastoral completes its metamorphosis into a form of pastoral heavily mixed with real rural life. If simplicity and a love of nature were already part of traditional pastoral, mimetic representation was not. Wordsworth in the "Preface" invites us to reconsider rural life sincerely and directly, to rediscover its permanent value. M. H. Abrams has written that Wordsworth's criticism

---

[36] See Varley Lang, "Crabbe and the Eighteenth Century," *ELH*, 5 (1938), 305, and Oliver F. Sigworth, *Nature's Sternest Painter: Five Essays on the Poetry of George Crabbe* (Tucson: Univ. of Arizona Press, 1965), pp. 16–17, 61–62.

reflects the discovery of literary subject matter in the habits and speech of those living close to the soil, comparatively insulated from urban contact. "Wordsworth, by doctrine and example, brought into the literary province the store of materials which has been richly exploited by writers from Thomas Hardy to William Faulkner."[37] The essential character of the pastoral novel develops from the subtle and artistic blending of the newly realistic Wordsworthian materials with some techniques and patterns of traditional pastoral.

Yet how is Wordsworth a pastoral poet when many of his characteristic figures—Michael, the old leech-gatherer, the old Cumberland beggar—appear to be realistic? After traditional pastoral undergoes a metamorphosis, it gradually emerges as modern or realistic pastoral, a variation of the conventional genre. Pastoral, as it represents rural life, is brought from a remote and artificial world into a real world. Although Wordsworth adopts in his poetry several characteristics of traditional pastoral—rustic life as poetic setting, sharp contrast between rural and urban, idealization, simplification, harmony of man and nature—his typical figures are more realistic than typical figures of traditional pastoral. Wordsworth maintains loyalties to both camps, as does the pastoral novel later. His figures and landscape are partly idealized, yet partly realistic. David Ferry has said that Wordsworth's poetry, though inimical to prettification or falsification, is "in a serious . . . sense a version of pastoral."[38]

Several of Wordsworth's finest poems show elements of pastoral and so help to define his relationship to the pastoral tradition. "Michael" (1800), subtitled "A Pastoral Poem," shows most clearly the change in attitude toward traditional pastoral. By his subtitle Wordsworth intends to suggest a poem not about refined shepherds remote from actuality but about real contemporary shepherds. Following the lead of eighteenth-century rationalist and pre-Romantic critics, Wordsworth in this poem puts into literary practice the change in attitude toward traditional pastoral and dramatizes the suffering of a humble rustic family when their only son Luke is corrupted by the "dissolute city." By interlacing work and sorrow with pastoral occupations, harmony, and simplicity, Wordsworth in "Michael" makes pastoral realistic. Michael and his wife Isabel are "a proverb in the vale / For endless industry" (ll. 94–

[37] *The Mirror and the Lamp* (New York: Oxford Univ. Press, 1953), pp. 112–13.
[38] *The Limits of Mortality* (Middletown, Conn.: Wesleyan Univ. Press, 1959), p. 91. Cf. Basil Willey: "perhaps the healing power of nature is only felt to the full . . . by those who return to it at intervals after being long 'in populous cities pent'. Even to Wordsworth Nature meant most as long as he could retain a sense of *escape* into it; when he had long been domiciled there it lost its glory and freshness" (*The Eighteenth Century Background* [London: Chatto & Windus, 1940], p. 292).

95).[39] Wordsworth's insistence that "The Shepherd went about his daily work / With confident and cheerful thoughts" offers an obvious literary antecedent for the preoccupation with work in George Eliot's early novels, especially *Adam Bede*, and in the pastoral novels of Hardy and Lawrence as well. *Adam Bede* and *Silas Marner* are, in fact, adaptations of "Michael."

In Wordsworth's poem, Michael and his family not only toil diligently but, like their neighbors, lack material wealth. Yet though they toil and are poor, Wordsworth praises the life they live. He says of Michael:

> Those fields, those hills—what could they less? had laid
> Strong hold on his affections, were to him
> A pleasurable feeling of blind love,
> The pleasure which there is in life itself.
>
> [ll. 74–77]

The shepherd's calling, stripped of ease and luxury, is nonetheless glorified, as in traditional pastoral. Nature, a benign and cheerful influence, accompanies Michael in his daily work. Toward the close of the poem, Wordsworth expresses the rural-urban dialectic essential to pastoral. When Michael recognizes at last the necessity of Luke's departure for the city to redeem their patrimonial fields, Michael intuitively fears that evil men will "Be thy companions." Once in the city, Luke succumbs to urban temptations and, forgetting duty,

> He in the dissolute city gave himself
> To evil courses: ignominy and shame
> Fell on him, so that he was driven at last
> To seek a hiding-place beyond the seas.
>
> [ll. 444–47]

The poem explicitly criticizes urban life. In contrast, rural life functions as a version of the Golden-Age criterion by which poet and reader judge the corrupting atmosphere of the city. Like Hetty Sorrel in *Adam Bede* or Godfrey Cass in *Silas Marner*, Luke fails in his duty when exposed to materialism and the lures of the city. But the invasion of urban values on Luke also affects the rural world and its simple round of duty; when news of his son reaches Michael, he stops work on the sheepfold: "many a day he thither went, / And never lifted up a single stone" (ll. 465–66). The rural world is disrupted by outside forces. After the death of the old couple, the immemorial family farm, like the farms in

[39] *The Poetical Works of William Wordsworth*, vol. II, 2d ed., ed. E. de Selincourt, rev. Helen Darbishire (Oxford: Clarendon Press, 1952). Quotations from "Michael" and "Resolution and Independence" are from this edition.

Vergil's first and ninth eclogues or like the Saxtons' farm in *The White Peacock*, "went into a stranger's hand."

Although a number of Wordsworth's poems manifest elements of pastoral[40] (and still others, such as "Simon Lee," tend to be antipastoral), the poem that most clearly reveals Wordsworth's attitudes toward pastoral is *The Prelude*—particularly Book VIII, the pastoral book. In Book VIII Wordsworth reconsiders his first twenty-one years in order to detect the transfer of his early love of nature to shepherds and other humble people, like Michael or the leech-gatherer or the Highland reaper, who perform their solitary duty as though they were mobilized objects in the landscape. Wordsworth, in showing his early appreciation of the dignity and sacred value of man, comments significantly and in detail on traditional pastoral, distinguishing his own version of pastoral from that of convention in much the same way that George Eliot contrasts Vergil's shepherds to those she describes in *Adam Bede* (p. 82 below) or the way Lawrence treats the pastoral picnic in *The White Peacock* (pp. 187–89 below).

The opening portion of Book VIII hails the joyful marriage of man and nature in Wordsworth's native countryside. The landscape and the shepherds who live among the mountains, in creating his most vivid impressions of the Lake District, shaped in his boyhood mind a version of the Golden Age. Throughout his early manhood, this version offered recurrent inspiration, and his first human love inclined toward shepherds in particular. With its majestic sights, his native region appeared more exquisite "Than is that Paradise of ten thousand Trees, / Or Gehol's famous Gardens . . ." (VIII.122–23).[41] Lovelier by far was his

---

[40] A survey of Wordsworth's collected poems shows that, aside from "Michael" (1800), Wordsworth employed the term *pastoral* to subtitle four other poems, three of them also composed and published in 1800: "The Pet-Lamb: A Pastoral" (1800), "The Oak and the Broom: A Pastoral" (1800), "The Idle Shepherd-Boys; or, Dungeon-Ghyll Force: A Pastoral" (1800), and "Repentence: A Pastoral Ballad" (1804?, 1820). In each poem the term *pastoral* is used loosely to suggest a scene of real rural life.

"Resolution and Independence" (1802) is, William Empson has said, "a genuine pastoral poem if ever there was one" (*Some Versions of Pastoral* [1935; rpt. Norfolk, Conn.: New Directions, 1960], p. 251). Like "Michael," "Resolution and Independence" demonstrates the way in which realism enlarges the concept of traditional pastoral. The leech-gatherer, though feeble and burdened with hardships, becomes for the traveler upon the moor, "like a man from some far region sent, / To give me human strength, by apt admonishment" (ll. 111–12). The endurance of the leech-gatherer gives the traveler the necessary courage to immerse himself again in urban life.

[41] William Wordsworth, *The Prelude*, 2d ed., ed. Ernest de Selincourt, rev. Helen Darbishire (Oxford: Clarendon Press, 1959). Because it reveals more clearly

native countryside than the paradises typically featured in romances: his native region was tangible, inhabited by real shepherds. Though sheepherding and agriculture rank as ancient occupations, the shepherds and other humble people of Wordsworth's native region differ from shepherds of traditional pastoral:

> Smooth life had Flock and Shepherd in old time,
> Long Springs and tepid Winters
>
> . . . . .
>
> where the Pipe was heard
> Of Pan, the invisible God, thrilling the rocks
> With tutelary music, from all harm
> The Fold protecting.
>
> [VIII.312–13, 321–24]

But Wordsworth's shepherds inhabit, he says, another world. They are

> Not such as in Arcadian Fastnesses
> Sequester'd, handed down among themselves,
> So ancient Poets sing, the golden Age;
> Nor such, a second Race, allied to these,
> As Shakespeare in the Wood of Arden plac'd
> Where Phoebe sigh'd for the false Ganymede, . . .
> Nor such as Spenser fabled.
>
> [VIII.183–91]

The Arcadian shepherds of Sidney, Shakespeare, or Spenser, inhabiting literary pastoral, had only love and pleasure to occupy their days.

Wordsworth distinguishes his shepherds equally from rustics who inhabited the alleged golden age of rural England. Although Spenser and others may have observed such quaint rural customs as the Maypole Dance, these festivities represent for Wordsworth only imaginative fragments of yet another ideal world which can have no validity because it has no reality. However beautiful as a memory, this idealized folk world alas

> Was but a dream; the times had scatter'd all
> These lighter graces, and the rural custom
> And manners which it was my chance to see
> In childhood were severe and unadorn'd, . . .
> Yet beautiful, and beauty that was felt.
>
> [VIII.204–10]

---

and more fully Wordsworth's relationship to traditional pastoral, the 1805 text is quoted and is cited by book and line number in my text.

This passage is critical because it illustrates the double nature of Wordsworth's version of pastoral. The rural life which Wordsworth had observed all his life is simple yet substantial, unadorned yet attractive, and
above all severe yet beautiful. Wordsworth's version of pastoral inclines
toward both realism and idealism, directly anticipating the pastoral
novel.

In distinguishing his pastoral region from all ideal worlds, Wordsworth also considers a contemporary form of the Golden Age of classical pastoral—Goslar, Germany—a region offering a "Smooth life" of
"Long Springs and tepid Winters," and a pastoral "Pleasure-ground"
where the shepherd strays, having "no task / More toilsome than to
carve a beechen bowl / For Spring or Fountain" (VIII.343–45). But
Wordsworth's pastoral region is harsher, a more realistic form of pastoral where a sweet life is challenged by suffering and real obstacles,
where " 'tis the Shepherd's task the winter long / To wait upon the
storms" (VIII.359–60).

The shepherd of Wordsworth's pastoral earns praise because, being
free, he "feels himself" in those vast regions where he works. He lives
a "life of hope *and* hazard" and of "hard labour *interchanged* / With
that majestic indolence so dear to native Man" (VIII.387–90; my
italics). Both sides of the coin matter, yet as a child Wordsworth saw
only the idealized form of the shepherd, glorified and ennobled. The
reader suspects that it is this form of pastoral man that dominated
Wordsworth's imagination throughout 1797–1806, the period of his
finest poetry. Of his representative shepherd Wordsworth recalls feeling his presence "As of a Lord or Master; or a Power / Or genius, under
Nature, under God." Then come the critical lines:

> His Form hath flash'd upon me, glorified
> By the deep radiance of the setting sun:
>   . . . Thus was Man
> Ennobled outwardly before mine eyes.
>
>   [VIII.404–11]

The idealized figure of the solitary shepherd yet "Was not a Corin of
the groves," but a man who "suffer'd with the rest / From vice and folly,
wretchedness and fear." Yet throughout *The Prelude* the form glorified
and ennobled is the form we grasp imaginatively, seldom the form that
suffers with the rest of mankind. Thus two conceptions intermingle:
the idealized shepherd of Wordsworth's boyhood; and the partly real,
partly ideal shepherd of his early adulthood, which derives from his
childhood impression. David Ferry argues that Wordsworth confuses
"his vision of man as ideal and his insistence that this ideal *in fact* exists
in such persons as the shepherds of his country" (p. 95). Interestingly,

the revisions for the 1850 text of *The Prelude* show that, with the passing of time, Wordsworth's conception of the Lake District shepherd gradually became more realistic, thus anticipating the fictional development of George Eliot and Thomas Hardy.

Book VIII of *The Prelude*, then, stands as one of many versions of traditional pastoral. Idealized shepherds, with enviable occupations and lives, inhabit a real Golden Age in the near past. Wordsworth intensifies this pastoral feeling when he says that he discovered the "great City" to be almost like "A heart-depressing wilderness indeed," almost like "a wearisome abode":

> ... therefore did I turn
> To you, ye Pathways, and ye lonely Roads
> Sought you enrich'd with everything I prized,
> With human kindness and with Nature's joy.
> [XIII.123–26]

As in the pastoral of tradition, the creation of a beautiful and harmonious Golden Age invites a criticism of the complex urban life opposed to it. Wordsworth values highly his retreat into the rural world because he found there

> Hope to my hope, and to my pleasure peace
> And steadiness, and healing and repose
> To every angry passion. There I heard,
> From mouths of men obscure and lowly, truths
> Replete with honour; sounds in unison
> With loftiest promises of good and fair.
> [XIII.180–85; 1850 text]

Wordsworth is not writing as a traditional pastoralist. Nor is he literal, like Crabbe, in interpreting humble and rustic life. Put simply, he alternates between realism and idealization in his treatment of rural life. Wordsworth's affinities with traditional pastoral are several. He mistrusts the city, and prefers Nature to Art. Harmony and beauty provide central themes; shepherd and setting conjoin. As Herbert Lindenberger comments, "Wordsworth idealizes not only his individual shepherds, but the whole society of dalesmen who, in their ordered, traditional way of living, are contrasted with the brute masses of the city."[42] He renounces worldly ambition for peace and rural solitude. And though it is different in character from traditional pastoral in its preference for realistic details, he creates of his native countryside a Golden Age, a metaphor for the creative potential of the imagination, a landscape of the mind as much as of observed reality. Wordsworth, insisting

[42] *On Wordsworth's "Prelude"* (Princeton: Princeton Univ. Press, 1963), p. 249.

that his shepherds are not of the golden age, is yet nostalgic for that age and eagerly celebrates it.[43] The antipastoral passages in Wordsworth's poetry show, along with his "Preface," how sharply he intended to break from the artificiality of conventional pastoral. But, as his critics have pointed out, Wordsworth simply replaced one kind of pastoralism with another.[44] By creating a realistic pastoral, Wordsworth succeeded however in modifying traditional pastoral. Acknowledging the real, Wordsworth still considers rural life of the Lake District to be the best life attainable, thereby shifting the Golden Age from the long ago of older forms of pastoral to the recent past of Wordsworth's childhood memories.

Two things bring about this change in the conception of pastoral: Wordsworth's frequent mention of toil and hardship, and his desire to take his settings literally. Instead of functioning to disguise the poet's cultured stance, Wordsworth's shepherd comes out of his setting literally.[45] The fundamental pastoral impulse, hardened into the convention of traditional pastoral, needed to be revitalized and brought once again near its roots in country life. After Wordsworth, pastoralism becomes increasingly oriented toward realism and becomes, as it travels through the nineteenth century, increasingly broadened in scope. Renato Poggioli argues that "while creating quasi-pastoral utopias, the modern world destroyed the conventional and traditional pastoral through four cultural trends that arose together and partly coincided. There were the humanitarian outlook, the idea of material progress, the scientific spirit, and artistic realism."[46] In its many modern transformations, the pastoral artist's eye rests more closely on his subject matter than before; he respects fact. Science and empiricism have deeply impressed the literary imagination. Moreover, although the modern pastoralist is nostalgic for the past, he is less inclined to treat the past as allegory or as a landscape of the mind. The modern pastoralist, although he is committed to a portrayal of the positive relationship between man and nature, is less interested in the *otium* of the pleasance than in representing faithfully the spirit of the rural life he either sees or recalls.

Whereas conventional pastoral had demanded that the pastoral world be free from toil and that leisure to sing and pipe be unbroken, the most significant change in the nineteenth-century transformation of the pastoral impulse is the recognition, even glorification, of work. One writer has said that "the bucolic, unlike the georgic, exalts the innocent leisure

[43] For a somewhat different view, see Lindenberger, ibid., p. 245.

[44] See Lindenberger, p. 249, and Ferry, p. 138.

[45] See John Stevenson, "Arcadia Re-Settled: Pastoral Poetry and Romantic Theory," *Studies in English Literature*, 7 (1967), 636.

[46] "The Oaten Flute," p. 175.

of the shepherd over the peasant's hard task."[47] After Wordsworth the pastoral form verges toward the georgic, the literary work which glorifies the toil of the agricultural sphere and which finds supreme expression in Vergil's *Georgics*. A second significant change in pastoral is the shift—anticipated by Wordsworth in the prose-poetry of "Michael" and much of *The Prelude*—to the use of prose rather than poetry in works inspired by the pastoral impulse. A final change occurs in the virtual abandonment of allegorical uses of landscape and character— an interest less in a perfect and pure world of the imagination, and more in a world of imagined reality that depends upon verifiable local details.

It is Wordsworth especially who influences the attitudes and subject matter of George Eliot's early fiction; her early novels have even been called lyrical ballads in prose. A lifelong admirer of Wordsworth and Scott, George Eliot regarded herself as heir to the English Romantics.[48] After a complete reading of Wordsworth, George Eliot said in a letter of 22 November 1839: "I never before met with so many of my own feelings, expressed just as I could like them."[49] Like Wordsworth or Theocritus, George Eliot places strong faith in the value of childhood memories. The remembered past is an essential aspect of her early novels. She describes its value in a vivid passage early in *The Mill on the Floss*: "We could never have loved the earth so well if we had had no childhood in it. . . . What novelty is worth that sweet monotony where everything is known, and *loved* because it is known? . . . These familiar flowers, these well-remembered bird-notes, this sky . . . these are the mother tongue of our imagination, the language that is laden with all the subtle inextricable associations the fleeting hours of our childhood left behind them."[50] Her conservative attitude toward the home scene and its rooted memory parallels Wordsworth's toward his native countryside, and the idea that images of childhood delight are the essential preparation for adulthood parallels Wordsworth's philosophy in "My Heart Leaps Up," "Tintern Abbey," the great "Ode," and Book VIII of *The Prelude*. George Eliot is therefore intimately connected to what Mario Praz calls "this Wordsworthian cult of the mem-

[47] Poggioli, "The Oaten Flute," p. 161.

[48] See, e.g., U. C. Knoepflmacher, *George Eliot's Early Novels* (Berkeley and Los Angeles: Univ. of California Press, 1968), p. 16.

[49] *The George Eliot Letters*, ed. Gordon S. Haight (New Haven: Yale Univ. Press, 1954), I, 34.

[50] George Eliot, *The Mill on the Floss*, ed. Gordon S. Haight, Riverside Edition (Boston: Houghton Mifflin, 1961), pp. 37–38. See also Thomas Pinney, "The Authority of the Past in George Eliot's Novels," *Nineteenth-Century Fiction*, 21 (1966), 131–47.

ories of a childhood spent in the country."[51] In *The Prelude* Wordsworth had made the emotions of humble people attractive by using the
power of language to transfigure the ordinary situations and events of
their lives: "And thus George Eliot takes up, in prose, the programme
announced in Wordsworth's part of the manifesto of *Lyrical Ballads.*"
If, to apply this idea, we limit ourselves to works that are pastoral, we
can discover marked parallels between "Michael" and *Adam Bede*, and
again between "Michael" and *Silas Marner.* In all three, work and duty,
located in a rural landscape, are major thematic elements.

In a number of ways *Adam Bede* adapts Wordsworth's poem, becoming an elaborate prose variation of it. Adam toils daily, like Michael, and both are betrayed in their trust by the fascination of urban
values on those they love: Luke's innocence is betrayed by the dissolute
city, Hetty is betrayed by her materialism and love of finery. Both Adam
and Michael are accorded immense sympathy from their creators. And
just as Luke "began / To slacken in his duty," Hetty neglects her house-
hold duties and detests her responsibility for the Poysers' children. Both
bring suffering and shame to their families and rural communities.
Both are at the end forced to leave their homeland.

As critics have shown, echoes and expressions of Wordsworth's poetry
occur throughout *Silas Marner.*[52] Significantly, George Eliot uses some
lines from "Michael" as an epigraph to *Silas Marner*:

> . . . a child, more than all other gifts
> That earth can offer to declining man,
> Brings hope with it, and forward-looking thoughts.
>
> [ll. 146–48]

Silas Marner also varies Wordsworth's story of Michael, except that the
opening and closing of the novel create a reversed variation of the poem.
Luke's flight to the "dissolute city" is mirrored in Silas' escape to the
rural world. Flight to the urban world creates tragedy; flight to the
rural world brings peace and fulfillment. In "Michael" the story progresses from the happiness of the old couple with their child, to their
grief without him; but Silas Marner's unhappiness is transformed into
joy when he discovers Eppie. A value system is thereby created: the
rural world offers the possibility of a tranquil and rewarded life.

From Wordsworth, George Eliot took many of the ideas and situations that she used in creating her prose version of pastoral: the posi-

---

[51] *The Hero in Eclipse in Victorian Fiction*, tr. Angus Davidson (New York:
Oxford Univ. Press, 1956), p. 373. The quotation that follows is from pp. 322–23.

[52] See, e.g., Praz, *Hero in Eclipse*, p. 404, and Lilian Haddakin, "Silas Marner,"
in *Critical Essays on George Eliot*, ed. Barbara Hardy (New York: Barnes & Noble,
1970), pp. 59–77.

tive conception of the value of rural life, the remembered past re-created as a kind of Golden Age, the rural-urban dichotomy, and an insistence on work and duty. From Wordsworth and earlier pastoralists George Eliot (and Hardy and Lawrence after her) learned above all to fuse pastoral and realistic elements into a satisfying whole.

Since we will be turning to George Eliot in a moment, we should mention one more figure, Sir Walter Scott, who influenced George Eliot and therefore the direction of the pastoral novel, even though Scott, attracted as he was primarily to the arena of political conflicts, cultural clashes, and rebellion, cannot be called a pastoral novelist. In his novels of Scotland's past, with their delineation of the habits and customs of the peasants and with their recognition of the dignity of humble rural life, Scott looks forward to George Eliot. The plot of *Adam Bede*, for example, owes much to *The Heart of Midlothian* (1818). Scott, like George Eliot or Wordsworth, loved the rooted past of a definite locality. And in his kindly pictures of the poor, Scott connects Wordsworth and George Eliot. But where Scott reveled in a romantic past of excitement and picturesque scenery, George Eliot looked to a past more real and more commonplace, where the imagination could transfigure everyday reality into idyllic or elegiac beauty. From Scott as well as other pastoralists, George Eliot learned the re-creation of the regional past, the expressive use of dialect, and the realistic treatment of characters from humble life. Dr. Leavis writes that Scott's "treatment of the remembered past, the strong imaginative piety that gives life and depth to his evocations, was wholly congenial to her."[53] Although Scott recognized the inevitability of progress, he delighted in regional customs and speech. His perception of the dignity and strength of humble rural life proved to be enormously influential on later novelists. In George Eliot's early novels the use of dialect cements the concrete feeling of a definite locale and tends to create the sense of an isolated, circumscribed pastoral world, like that of traditional pastoral. But where Scott sets forth in his best novels an entire culture, a myriad display of all classes,

[53] F. R. Leavis, "Foreword" to *Adam Bede*, Signet Classic Edition (New York: New American Library, 1961), p. viii. See also Kathleen Tillotson, *Novels of the Eighteen-Forties* (1954; rpt. Oxford: Oxford Univ. Press, 1961), p. 142. Maria Edgeworth had already, in her novels of Irish provincial life, discovered the territory which Scott was to explore. Scott, remarks G. M. Young, "set out to do for Scotland what Maria Edgeworth had done for Ireland. . . . She had painted a picture, not of contemporary Ireland, but of an Ireland just fading on the view." Yet she gave him also "the example of an idiom . . . that gives her stories their amazing verisimilitude" (G. M. Young, "Scott and the Historians," in *Sir Walter Scott Lectures: 1940–1948*, by Herbert Grierson et al., [Edinburgh: Univ. Press, 1950], p. 95). She showed Scott, and thus George Eliot, the fertile and varied uses of dialect; and she showed as well the rich possibilities of dealing with a specific region.

George Eliot in her early novels chooses only a piece of Scott's canvas; she portrays largely one level of her culture, the humble rural world of the recent past, or as Scott himself once said, "a period too recent to be romantic, and too far gone by to be familiar." It is a world, tranquil and unhurried, in which life seems simpler and in which man and nature cohere into a fully integrated pastoral community. It is to this kind of world that we turn in George Eliot's first novel, *Adam Bede*.

Chapter 3

Adam Bede

"A Great Temple and A Sacred Song"

GEORGE ELIOT was a pastoral novelist because particular historical and biographical forces made her so. It may be useful to broaden our understanding of the pastoral novel by looking briefly at the pressures that guided George Eliot, and later Hardy and Lawrence, toward the pastoral genre. Grounded in Rousseau's primitivistic thought,[1] the Romantic revolt against restraint and convention allowed ideas of equality and brotherhood to emerge with great force. The history of nineteenth-century England is in large part a record of political, economic, and social democratization. Nowhere does the democratic force exhibit itself more clearly than in the Reform Bill of 1832, which handed the power of government to the middle classes, or in the Chartist Movement of the 1830s and 40s, which campaigned for universal manhood suffrage, or in the Reform Bill of 1867, which granted suffrage to much of the working class. This shift in political power was, moreover, accompanied by a pronounced shift in the relative weight of rural and urban: by 1851 half of the British population lived in towns and cities, and as factory jobs became available, the movement from country to city continued vigorously through the century. In 1841, having spent twenty-two years in and around the country, having made intimate friends of rural landscape and rural people, George Eliot, a metaphor for the larger migratory process, moved to the city of Coventry; then, eight years later, she went to Geneva for most of a year before migrating to London, in 1851, to fill the position of assistant editor of the *Westminster Review*. Although she remained in the city much of her life, the yearning for hedgerows and spring flowers, for an orchard heavy with ripe fruit, for a farm resting beneath a bright sky haunted her imagination throughout her thirty years of London life. In her essay "Looking Backward," from *Theophrastus Such* (1879), George Eliot writes: "Sometimes when I am in a crowded London drawing-room . . . quick flights of memory take me back among my father's parishioners. . . .

---

[1] In a letter to Sara Hennell (9 February 1849), George Eliot wrote: "Rousseau's genius has sent that electric thrill through my intellectual and moral frame which has awakened me to new perceptions, which has made man and nature a fresh world of thought and feeling to me" (*The George Eliot Letters*, ed. Gordon S. Haight [New Haven: Yale Univ. Press, 1954], I, 277).

But my eyes at least have kept their early affectionate joy in our native landscape, which is one deep root of our national life and language." Her nostalgia for Warwickshire, aroused by her experience of London and continental cities to which she traveled, remained intense and stirred her to recollect the varied rural scenes of her childhood. But her break with conventional morality in "marrying" George Henry Lewes, though it perhaps sustains the Romantic revolt, alienated friends and family, and swept away the sense of community she had felt as a child in Griff. Thus the expanding pressures toward democratization, George Eliot's deracination, and the influence of Wordsworth in suggesting humble rural life as appropriate democratic subject matter—all of these helped to direct her toward the pastoral genre.

In 1859 George Eliot published *Adam Bede*, which is at once both a pastoral novel and the earliest important novel to deal largely and realistically with humble rural life. If no one has discussed it as a pastoral novel, critics have often agreed that, in the words of V. S. Pritchett, "*Adam Bede* looks like our supreme novel of pastoral life."[2] Walter Allen concurs that *Adam Bede* is "the finest pastoral novel in English, *Far from the Madding Crowd* not excepted,"[3] and Ian Gregor views the novel within "the whole convention of serious pastoral."[4] *Adam Bede* is not part of traditional pastoral but a modified version of traditional pastoral in which realism is always evident—from the famous artistic credo in chapter 17 to the introduction of death, imprisonment, and exportation into the plot. Yet in the novel's nostalgic re-creation of a rural order distant in time and space from the great urban world, much of

[2] *The Living Novel* (New York: Reynal & Hitchcock, 1947), p. 91. Pritchett is perhaps the first modern critic to suggest the term *pastoral novel*, but the term was used also in 1947 by Harvey Curtis Webster in *On a Darkling Plain* (Chicago: Univ. of Chicago Press): "*The Trumpet Major* . . . marks a return, although not a very rewarding one, to the pastoral novel" (p. 140). In his book *George Eliot's Early Novels* (Berkeley and Los Angeles: Univ. of California Press, 1968), U. C. Knoepflmacher frequently uses the term *pastoral*.

[3] *George Eliot* (1964; rpt. New York: Collier, 1967), p. 105. Allen revised his judgment after closer study of *Adam Bede*. In *The English Novel* (New York: Dutton, 1954), he had written that *Adam Bede* is, "*Far from the Madding Crowd* apart, the finest pastoral novel in English" (p. 258).

[4] "The Two Worlds of 'Adam Bede,'" in Ian Gregor and Brian Nicholas, *The Moral and the Story* (London: Faber & Faber, 1962), p. 13. Barbara Hardy (employing Empson's specialized use of the term "pastoral") calls the novel "that very rare thing, a good pastoral or proletarian novel" (*The Novels of George Eliot* [London: Athlone Press, 1959], p. 39).

the novel gradually creates a pastoral world of resonance, charm, and beauty. The novel's pastoralism reveals itself throughout: in contrasts of city and country, in characterization, in the use of the *locus amoenus* and of the concentric circles of pastoral romance, in the uses of nature and nature imagery, in the use of spatial and temporal distance, and in George Eliot's skillful choice of detail.

Near the end of *Adam Bede* occurs the following passage, rich in typical contrasts of place and time:

Surely all other leisure is hurry compared with a sunny walk through the fields from "afternoon church,"—as such walks used to be in those old leisurely times, when the boat, gliding sleepily along the canal, was the newest locomotive wonder; when Sunday books had most of them old brown-leather covers, and opened with remarkable precision always in one place. Leisure is gone—gone where the spinning-wheels are gone, and the pack-horses, and the slow waggons, and the pedlars, who brought bargains to the door on sunny afternoons. Ingenious philosophers tell you, perhaps, that the great work of the steam-engine is to create leisure for mankind. Do not believe them: it only creates a vacuum for eager thought to rush in. . . . Old Leisure was quite a different personage: he only read one news-paper, innocent of leaders, and was free from that periodicity of sensations which we call post-time. . . . He lived chiefly in the country, among pleasant seats and homesteads, and was fond of sauntering by the fruit-tree wall, and scenting the apricots when they were warmed by the morning sunshine, or of sheltering himself under the orchard boughs at noon, when the summer pears were falling. [Pp. 428–29][5]

The passage, with its unhurried sentences, nostalgically evokes the Golden-Age rural past. In order to create a pastoral world, a world that originated in the impulse to criticize sophisticated urban civilization, George Eliot openly compares the sunny days of pleasant leisure, seen through the warm glow of reminiscence, to the hurry of "our modern standard." Keenly anticipating Hardy's criticism of Sergeant Troy's "post-time" in *Far from the Madding Crowd*, George Eliot pits the industrial present (the "vacuum" created by the steam engine) against the preindustrial rural past. Because pastoral usually comes to life when a sharp contrast is drawn between rural and urban life, contrast provides George Eliot with a fictional technique that helps reveal, with conviction, the values she finds significant. With *Adam Bede*, she once wrote, "I have arrived at faith in the past, but not at faith in the present."[6] Yet

[5] Page numbers refer to George Eliot, *Adam Bede*, Riverside Edition, ed. John Paterson (Boston: Houghton Mifflin, 1968).

[6] Quoted in Robert Speaight, *George Eliot* (London: Arthur Barker, 1954), p. 49.

George Eliot's pastoral world is not a world of perfection. Unhappiness
—even tragedy—can occur, for she is aware that only in the artificial
and conventional Golden Age were the men "all wise and majestic, and
the women all lovely and loving" (p. 131). Still, she suggests, the pastoral world of her creating is the best *real* world to be found. Such a
world achieves sharper clarity, moreover, when viewed in terms of its
industrial counterpart—Dickens' London, Mrs. Gaskell's Manchester,
or the towns pictured in *Sybil* and *Alton Locke*.

Adam Bede, a modified version of traditional pastoral, deals sympathetically and nostalgically with life in the country. Narrated from an
urban point of view, it creates a Golden Age of the pastoral "world"
that it discovers in the rural past. Yet a tension between inside and outside views of country life often appears—a tension between the reality
and the remembrance, between the close view and the distant view. As
a nineteenth-century pastoral novelist, George Eliot attempts to replace
artificial shepherds with real peasants, a conventional countryside with
direct observation of external nature, and a simplified and unreal way
of life with "the faithful representing of commonplace things" (p. 153).
Since the dominant motive of pastoral is the urge to withdraw from
civilization's complexity and power, pastoral normally contrasts rural
and urban. F. R. Leavis rightly observes that in *Adam Bede* "the rural
drama and its setting are seen from the metropolitan point of view" and
that "idealizing and softening" result.[7] Since she and George Henry
Lewes were living in Dresden, Munich, and London during the novel's
composition, George Eliot tended to write *Adam Bede* from an urban
vantage point, and based the novel appropriately on fond recollections
of what she calls "that golden age of childhood." Thus she chides her
urban readers: "when you are among the fields and hedgerows, it is impossible to maintain a consistent superiority to simple natural pleasures"
(p. 139). A marked urban point of view crops up frequently in the
novel (e.g., pp. 17, 34, 225, 235, 240, 299, 347, 433, 445). As Lynen
argues, "The pastoralist must of necessity be a man of sophistication
writing for a sophisticated audience, for to yearn for the rustic life one
must first know the great world from which it offers an escape."[8]

We have already seen that the modern world can never equal "those
old leisurely times" of the remembered past. George Eliot uses the same
pastoral technique of frequent sharp contrasts to identify and to heighten
both the characteristic landscape of the pastoral microcosm and its tra-

---

[7] "Foreword" to *Adam Bede*, Signet Classic Edition (New York: New American
Library, 1961), p. xv.

[8] John F. Lynen, *The Pastoral Art of Robert Frost* (New Haven: Yale Univ. Press,
1960), pp. 12–13.

ditions and people. Early in the novel, she describes the district of Loam-shire to which the village of Hayslope belongs:

On the side of the Green that led towards the church, the broken line of thatched cottages was continued nearly to the churchyard gate; but on the opposite northwestern side, there was nothing to obstruct the view of gently-swelling meadow, and wooded valley, and dark masses of distant hill. That rich undulating district of Loamshire to which Hayslope belonged, lies close to a grim outskirt of Stonyshire, overlooked by its barren hills as a pretty blooming sister may sometimes be seen linked in the arm of a rugged, tall, swarthy brother; and in two or three hours' ride the traveller might exchange a bleak treeless region, intersected by lines of cold grey stone, for one where his road wound under the shelter of woods, or up swelling hills, muffled with hedgerows and long meadow-grass and thick corn; and where at every turn he came upon some fine old country-seat nestled in the valley or crowning the slope, some homestead with its long length of barn and its cluster of golden ricks, some grey steeple looking out from a pretty confusion of trees and thatch and dark-red tiles. [P. 16]

From the passage we learn that Hayslope, in relation to the world beyond, is a land of fertile plenty, of beauty and apparent happiness. Unlike the barren hills and the grim appearance of Stonyshire (Adam calls it "a hungry land"), the district of Loamshire bursts with produc-tivity: woods and thick corn and golden ricks. The narrator contrasts the sterile to the fertile as, earlier, Sidney contrasts Laconia to Arcadia. An impression of growth dominates the passage because of the diction ("blooming," "masses," "golden," "swelling meadow," "pretty con-fusion") and because of the abundance of adjective modifiers and con-nectives that build a rich sense of detail. The favorable connotations of the names of the region—"Hayslope" in "Loamshire"—suggest, them-selves, the idea of growth that the novel explores. Hayslope is filled with children, and of its major inhabitants, only Seth remains unmarried or childless. On the other hand, Dinah is "sterile" until she has made Hay-slope her permanent home.

The pastoral contrast between rural and urban extends beyond the landscape to the occupations of the families of Hayslope and to their provincial traditions. Chapter 7 describes Hetty's working conditions: "The dairy was certainly worth looking at: it was a scene to sicken for with a sort of calenture in hot and dusty streets—such coolness, such purity, such fresh fragrance of new-pressed cheese, of firm butter, of wooden vessels perpetually bathed in pure water; such soft colouring of red earthenware and creamy surfaces, brown wood and polished tin, grey limestone and rich orange-red rust on the iron weights and hooks and hinges" (p. 72). The description is consciously nostalgic and poetic.

With its use of assonance and its frequent suggestion of rhyme, it creates a resonant lyrical quality that conveys a sense of longing and recollection.[9] Later, the diary becomes a "damp temple of cleanliness" (p. 289). And the milking of the cows "was a sight Mrs. Poyser loved," even though she complains to the Squire that " 'it's more than flesh and blood 'ull bear sometimes, to be toiling and striving, and up early and down late' " (p. 71). Although George Eliot, like Hardy, appears to soften the poverty of nineteenth-century agricultural life,[10] she nonetheless succeeds in striking a balanced view between the ideal and the real. Provincial traditions too are opposed to mobility and disorganization. Hayslope has "an inheritance of affections nurtured by a simple family life of common need and common industry, and an inheritance of faculties trained in skilful courageous labour" (p. 181). The men of Hayslope are not Arcadian shepherds but "painstaking honest men, with the skill and conscience to do well the tasks that lie before them" (p. 182). The quotation reveals the inherited virtues and traditions of the world of Hayslope: simplicity, honesty, unity of family and community life, and a common labor that assures meaning and purpose in daily living. These characteristics, viewed as human staples, are offered in opposition to alienation and moral degeneration, increasingly the trademarks of industrialized factory labor.[11]

Just as the Industrial Revolution began to break down the ancient rural patterns of life, the landed gentry in *Adam Bede*—the class that gradually merged with the wealthy urban class—intrudes upon the Hall Farm and violates its happiness. Though the intrusion is a limited one, the class conflict that is found embryonically in *Adam Bede* recurs later as a constant pattern in Thomas Hardy's novels, where the clash is between two dominant classes of people: the gentry and the peasantry.[12] The plot that results from the intrusion is exceedingly simple, since most of the novel creates a world in which the action may convincingly

[9] Compare, however, the following similar passage in which, with her intense nostalgia, George Eliot loses control: "Ah! I think I taste that whey now—with a flavour so delicate that one can hardly distinguish it from an odour, and with that soft gliding warmth that fills one's imagination with a still, happy dreaminess. And the light music of the dropping whey is in my ears, mingling with the twittering of a bird outside the wire network window—the window overlooking the garden, and shaded by tall Gueldres roses" (p. 185).

[10] Compare Richard Jefferies' *Greene Ferne Farm* (1880) in which women toiling in the fields offer a harsh contrast to the lyrical beauty of the natural world that surrounds them. In terms of historical accuracy, Jefferies perhaps corrects the impression of field work that we have from *Adam Bede*.

[11] See, e.g., Charlotte Elizabeth Tonna's *Helen Fleetwood* (1841), a novel that describes actual conditions in the factories of the time.

[12] For a blistering attack on the squire-tenant system, see Richard Jefferies' novel *The Dewy Morn* (1884).

occur. Adam Bede loves Hetty Sorrel, but Hetty loves Arthur Donnithorne, heir to the Donnithorne estate. After Hetty is seduced by Arthur,
she is unworthy of Adam, so Adam marries Dinah Morris. None of the
original romantic relationships mature. Like the amorous relationships
of pastoral romance, the bonds of love created initially are entirely
rearranged by the end of the novel. As in *Far from the Madding
Crowd*, three relationships metamorphose into one mature bond (see
pp. 128–29).

Growing out of the plot, the fundamental moral concern of the novel
is a testing of strength (or the lack of it), a process that weights the
novel's pastoralism with epic density and, in the manner of certain
earlier pastoralists such as Milton, fuses pastoral with other genres. The
strongest figure in the pastoral world of the novel is Adam Bede—
strong physically, mentally, morally, and emotionally. As the village
carpenter, Adam has also, like the pastoral figures in Hardy's *The
Woodlanders*, a remarkably strong sensitivity to trees: "Adam delighted
in a fine tree of all things. . . . Adam's perceptions were more at home
with trees than with other objects" (p. 250). The flaw in character that
brings him pain, however, is an excess of strength, for Adam is "foolishly
sanguine and confident." His pride encourages extreme independence
and thus "too little fellow-feeling," not enough "patience and charity"
toward others (p. 179). Adam, though sympathetic to industrialism,
remains a pastoral figure: upon his promotion to manager of the woods,
he becomes in the course of the novel not only more human but more
fully rural as well.[13]

Like Adam, Dinah Morris is a character who is also strong. If her
courage lies in her Methodist convictions, her weakness lies in her in-
flexible virtue and her overabsorption in religious piety. Set against
Adam and Dinah are the morally weak characters, Hetty Sorrel and
Arthur Donnithorne. Because they have not the power to resist temptation, theirs becomes a "story of sin and sorrow" that combines pastoralism with realism. Though beautiful and appealing, Hetty is vain,
coquettish, materialistic. Hetty's dreams, writes George Eliot, are all of
"wealth and grandeur immeasurable." Her love of money makes her an
antipastoral figure. Hidden beneath her beauty are moral deficiencies,
for Hetty was "a girl who really had nothing more than her beauty to
recommend her" (p. 297). She uses her beauty to purchase material
possessions and social status rather than to win Arthur's love. Her self-
centeredness results in insensitivity to the problems of others, and her
character flaw is therefore her lack of sympathy: "some fatal influence
seems to have shut up her heart against her fellow-creatures" (p. 353).

[13] Mellors in *Lady Chatterley's Lover* also becomes more fully rural as a manager
of woods, although he manages pheasants rather than trees.

Arthur's weakness is different. Though he "was nothing if not good natured," his weakness lies in his lack of resolution and self-mastery. Because he gives way to the emotions that steal over him, Hetty's charms lure him into an affair that is, too soon, consummated. More important to the central pastoral tension of rural versus urban and simplicity versus sophistication, Arthur—essentially a sophisticated urban figure, refined and educated—is inferior to Adam: "The eyes that shed those glances [toward Hetty] were really not half so fine as Adam's" (p. 87). Beside the rugged peasant virility of Adam, Arthur pales into a "delicate-handed gentleman" whose letters have "a faint scent of roses." Because Arthur and Hetty are reared not by their parents but by others, their roots in the community are shallow and impermanent, and they suffer failures as human beings, failures that must be shared by the pastoral world. The novel reveals that pastoral innocence makes no provision for morality and that the two are in fact unrelated. "Long dark eyelashes, now: what can be more exquisite?" comments the narrator. "One begins to suspect at length that there is no direct correlation between eyelashes and morals" (p. 131). Morality must be acquired independently, through experience and through the community traditions that are themselves the profit of immemorial collective experience. By regulating behavior, Hayslope's moral codes help protect the strong characters from the common errors of experience.

Strength is ultimately rewarded in the novel: Adam for example acquires depth through his suffering over Hetty's betrayal. The novel shows that pain and suffering, initially hard to endure, serve to uncover and develop one's sympathy for the problems of others. Trouble and grief—favorite words in the novel—help to make the characters more fully human, and the novel itself illuminates the process of softening various kinds of hardness. In the face of despair both Arthur and Hetty, along with Adam, are humbled. At the end George Eliot remarks that "the fuller life which a sad experience has brought us is worth our own personal share of pain: surely it is not possible to feel otherwise" (p. 442). Thus the world of traditional pastoral, modified by suffering and by a need for moral codes, is brought close to everyday reality. If the world of traditional pastoral is as a whole modified, some aspects of pastoral are impressively sustained: the novel's *locus amoenus* and its pastoral pattern successfully employ the conventions of pastoral.

A study of a single narrative sequence, one that illustrates both a *locus amoenus* and a pastoral pattern, will help to define the way in which the novel uses but varies the conventions of pastoral. Ian Gregor has demonstrated that in *Adam Bede* George Eliot allows two alternating impulses to guide her imagination and to shape the materials of the novel: the pastoral impulse and the moral impulse.[14] Although both have received critical attention, the pastoral impulse has been explored by critics less fully than the moral impulse, partly because pastoral elements by their nature lend themselves to description rather than analysis, but partly too because a comprehensive examination of modern forms of pastoral has not yet been written, thus compounding the difficulties of the critic who wishes to approach the novel from the generic viewpoint of pastoral.[15] In relating the novel to the pastoral tradition, critics have never noticed George Eliot's use of the *locus amoenus*, or "lovely place," in *Adam Bede*. Yet her use of the *locus amoenus* in chapters 12 and 13 strengthens the novel's relationship to traditional pastoral and valuably illuminates her artistic method by showing how, in syncretic fashion, she fuses pastoral conventions and Christian morality.

Originating in antiquity and becoming a standard feature in landscape description, the *locus amoenus*, or "lovely place," quickly formed part of the landscape of both pastoral and erotic poetry; it became the pagan counterpart of the Garden of Eden.[16] E. R. Curtius (p. 195) defines the *locus amoenus* as a natural site, both shaded and beautiful, whose basic ingredients are trees, a meadow, and a spring or brook. Whether we speak of its physical contours or of its emotional and moral values, *Adam Bede* varies only slightly the traditional representation of the *locus amoenus*. Topographically, the *locus amoenus* in *Adam Bede* is a grove of trees—Arthur calls it "a sacred grove"—which skirts one side of a privately owned but unenclosed game preserve called Donnithorne Chase. The grove is a "delicious labyrinthine wood . . . of beeches and limes" (p. 111), but called Fir-tree Grove because of the firs that form a circle around a little cabin at the center. At the edge of the Grove runs a brook (p. 255). Instead of a meadow, the Grove boasts narrow paths edged with moss and a "thick carpet of fir-needles" (p. 256). At the center of the *locus amoenus*, within the circle of firs, hides the little cabin called the Hermitage, "which stood in the heart of the wood" (p. 114). As its name implies, the Hermitage is "a retreat," a "den"; and in this retreat Arthur Donnithorne and Hetty Sorrel can express themselves sexually because the Grove, as an image of the Garden of Eden, encourages innocence to manifest itself. Pastoral has

[14] Gregor, "The Two Worlds of 'Adam Bede,' " p. 15.

[15] The following essays treat the pastoral impulse in *Adam Bede*: R. A. Foakes, "*Adam Bede* Reconsidered," *English*, 12 (1959), 173–76; Gregor, pp. 13–32; Knoepflmacher, ch. 4 of *George Eliot's Early Novels*; and John Paterson, "Introduction" to *Adam Bede*, Riverside Edition, pp. v–xxxiii.

[16] See E. R. Curtius, *European Literature and the Latin Middle Ages*, tr. Willard R. Trask (Princeton: Princeton Univ. Press, 1953), pp. 192–200.

traditionally defined sexual activity as innocent. Almost from the beginning, says David Evett, the *locus amoenus* and sexuality have enjoyed a close symbiotic relationship.[17]

The *locus amoenus* traditionally has had both sensual and moral
functions. Although its sensual function has been favored in literature
(by Theocritus, Vergil, Longus, and Tasso, e.g.), its moral function has
found vivid expression in the Bower of Bliss and in the Garden of Eden.
If D. H. Lawrence follows one tradition in stressing the sensually regenerative function of a *locus amoenus* in *Lady Chatterley's Lover*,
George Eliot tends to combine both functions in *Adam Bede* by creating a sensual haven and then stressing the moral implications of the
meetings between Hetty and Arthur in Fir-tree Grove. Her model for
these chapters of the novel appears to be *Paradise Lost*, which also combines both functions of the *locus amoenus*.[18] Initially, the sensuality of
these meetings dominates George Eliot's analysis. In the "delicious
labyrinthine wood," Arthur is ready to surrender himself to the "delicious feeling" of loving Hetty (p. 114). "He would like to satisfy his
soul" by looking at Hetty's beautiful eyelashes for a whole day (p. 115).
"He is going to see Hetty again: that is the longing which has been
growing through the last three hours to a feverish thirst" (p. 117).
When he meets Hetty, and embraces and kisses her, the ecstasy suspends
the lovers in a timeless world of myth and pastoral innocence, detached
from morality: "for a long moment time has vanished. He may be a
shepherd in Arcadia for aught he knows, he may be the first youth
kissing the first maiden, he may be Eros himself, sipping the lips of
Psyche—it is all one" (pp. 117–18). As their infatuation wears thin,
George Eliot turns from sensuality to the moral consequences of their
meetings, largely because the philosophy underlying the scene stresses
the consequences of an action over its immediate pleasurable value to
the characters, but also because the author's aim was to study an inter-
related community rather than a private affair. Thus for Arthur, memory—the guardian of morality—masters the timeless world of pastoral
and gives it temporal weight. While in the Grove, Arthur at one point
remembers even to look at his watch. George Eliot, like Marvell in the
"Mower" poems, sees a tyrannous force operating to destroy the pastoral world—the force that stirs the mind to remember duty to community. The memory of a kiss triggers "something bitter . . . to mingle
itself with the fountain of sweets" (p. 118). Guilt follows their viola-

[17] " 'Paradice's Only Map': The *Topos* of the *Locus Amoenus* and the Structure
of Marvell's *Upon Appleton House*," *PMLA*, 85 (1970), 506.

[18] Knoepflmacher (p. 91) has rightly pointed to George Eliot's "highly imaginative appropriation of *Paradise Lost*," although he has not noticed the Grove as a
locus amoenus.

tion of the community's moral law: they must hide their "secret" and must never betray "that there had been the least intimacy between them" (p. 264). Arthur once filled Hetty with a "bewildering delicious surprise"; now the short poisonous delights of their intimacy spoil forever "all the little joys that had once made the sweetness of her life" (pp. 281–82). They have sinned (see pp. 346, 354).[19]

Ian Gregor's remark that the novel employs both pastoral and moral modes has special applicability to the *locus amoenus* I have described, which combines both sensual and moral dimensions, both sweetness and poison. Escaping into the *locus amoenus*, the characters lose not only their sense of time but their sense of perspective; soon, however, the trees in the landscape stimulate moral associations in the characters' minds. The two modes, pastoral and moral, alternate in this way. As memory and perspective collide with the temporary waning of his passion for Hetty, Arthur is "glad to get out of the Grove" and into the Chase (p. 118): his "evil genius," he believes, haunts the Grove. The beeches and limes of the Grove, vaguely enervating, appear languorous and weak, a reflection of Arthur's failing resolution and a mirror of his nature. On the other hand, sturdy oaks fill the Chase beyond Fir-tree Grove. Like the ancient oak trees in Lawrence's Wragby Wood, "the strong knotted old oaks had no bending languor in them—the sight of them would give a man some energy" (p. 118). Then Arthur "lost himself" in the Chase until light fades into darkness, George Eliot successfully imaging his moral plight in terms of natural phenomena. The natural world accommodates therefore both pastoral and moral modes. If it provides a place of retreat for the lovers, it also defines Arthur's unsuccessful struggle against his impulses. " 'And I *did* struggle,' " he tells Adam (p. 393). Because morality invades the *locus amoenus*, the pastoral retreat into the Grove is ambiguous: sexual freedom is compromised by conscience, even within the Grove that encourages, by its location and atmosphere, the possibility of freedom. Like Milton, George Eliot attempts in such a scene as "Evening in the Wood" (chapter 13) to Christianize the pastoral, to draw the *locus amoenus* of traditional pastoral within the moral framework of Christianity. Just as Adam and Eve must learn to temper pleasure with God's law, so must Hetty and Arthur learn to balance the moral demands of their community (which are specifically Christian) with their desire for personal satisfaction.

While the Grove as a *locus amoenus* connects the novel to pastoral, the circular configuration around a quasi-supernatural center connects

19 R. A. Foakes puts the matter this way: "Hetty's discovery that she is pregnant, and Arthur's reactions to his predicament, do not emerge as a consciousness of sin . . . so much as a bitter awareness of having offended against their society" (p. 175).

the novel to pastoral romance, where a change of location signifies a change of personality. Grove and configuration intersect since the *locus amoenus*, as the Grove, forms part of the circular pattern. As Walter R. Davis has shown, heroes of pastoral romance journey from the outer world (Hayslope) to a pastoral circle (the Grove) and on to a sacred center (the Hermitage) where they are reborn.[20] In large part, the attraction between Hetty and Arthur follows this pattern. Journeying from Hayslope through Donnithorne Chase to the Grove, and then through the circle of fir-trees surrounding the Hermitage, Hetty and Arthur reach the cabin "in the heart of the wood." There, at the sacred center apart from the community, they seek behavior worthy of the landscape they have discovered: they consummate their love. Like heroes of pastoral romance, who are altered and even transformed by their experiences at the pastoral center, Hetty and Arthur emerge from their sexual union changed: their experiences have reoriented their sensibilities and have joined them sexually and emotionally. Arthur thinks to himself: "Sweet—sweet little Hetty! The little puss hadn't cared for him half as much as he cared for her; for he was a great fool about her still—was almost afraid of seeing her—indeed, had not cared much to look at any other woman since he parted from her. That little figure coming towards him in the Grove, those dark-fringed childish eyes, the lovely lips put up to kiss him—that picture had got no fainter with the lapse of months" (p. 368). Hetty too falls in love. But at the same time that Arthur recognizes the social impossibility of marrying Hetty, Hetty imagines that such a marriage will permit her to enter a world of luxury: "alone on her little island of dreams," Hetty imagines herself "a lady in silks and satins."

In pastoral romance, reorientation of the heroes prepares them to return from the pastoral retreat to the world of strife. Similarly, Arthur and Hetty do, in fact, go from the pastoral retreat into the outer world— Arthur returns to the army, and Hetty enters a world full of fear and loneliness. Both leave Hayslope as a direct result of their experiences in the Grove. But in *Adam Bede* reorientation of Hetty and Arthur is short-lived because Arthur cannot shed his awareness of the moral codes that prevail outside the *locus amoenus*. Unlike the heroes of pastoral romance, moreover, Hetty and Arthur are not strongly enough motivated to escape and do not journey far enough from home in order for them to complete their reorientation: the Donnithorne estate signifies lavish plenty and the Poysers' farm permits too readily a "life of ease and luxury" (p. 397). The lovers' failure to complete reorientation means that they cannot escape the intense mental pain which their subsequent

[20] *A Map of Arcadia* (New Haven: Yale Univ. Press, 1965), pp. 34–37.

actions bring upon them—a pain whose intensity urges them not to break but to return to the community's traditional code of conduct. Because their reorientation fails, both must later, after their wanderings, be reconverted—Arthur into a responsible man and Hetty into a half-penitent Christian. Their failure at a sensual conversion will demand, as compensation, a successful moral conversion. George Eliot, in stressing moral consequences, complicates the pastoral pattern: the characters retreat, act, and therefore change; then they return and *suffer* for their actions. The pattern of recovery fuses with a pattern of moral education, both patterns functioning to identify the central concerns of the novel. One way we can see that George Eliot attemps to take traditional pastoral seriously and to make it assume tragic overtones is by examining the effects of these patterns. Whereas the pastoral pattern of recovery rewards experience and blesses its fruits, the pattern of education imposes a penalty on those who engage in experience.

The pastoral pattern functions, then, incompletely in *Adam Bede*. The pastoral elements of the novel only partly control the structure and motion of the characters' personalities. Instead the moral consequences of the characters' deeds, especially feelings of guilt, also control the shape of events—in particular, Arthur's journey to Windsor and Hetty's subsequent journey in search of Arthur. Yet since the characters both *want* change (both are bored with Hayslope) and since a transformation was not fully effected within the sacred Grove, other changes occur. Hetty's delights curdle; the sweetness of innocence blossoms into the poison of experience. Instead of joy, "she would carry about for ever a hopeless thirst and longing" (p. 282). Her "dream had vanished" (p. 307). Hetty's experiences in the *locus amoenus* prepare her not to return to the ordinary world but to escape from it—into a world that is more than ordinarily cruel. Hetty's experiences invert the traditional pastoral pattern. Instead of reorientation in order to face reality with courage and strength, Hetty's experiences in the pastoral circle (and their consequences) make her unable to adapt to Hayslope life.

For Arthur the function of the *locus amoenus* is more complex. The sacred Grove, by weakening resolution and conscience, encourages sensuality and directs his love to Hetty. It intensifies emotion. The soft air "did not help his resolutions, as he . . . looked into the leafy distance" (p. 114); and his debate with himself at the Hermitage had "come to nothing" (p. 118). But in addition to sensuality, the Grove also encourages meditation and introspection and thus intensifies mental processes. By using a shaded bower to discourage intrusion or interruption, pastoral has always aimed to create a withdrawal that encourages contemplation. Thus after one of his first meetings with Hetty, Arthur meditates "more than an hour . . . at the Hermitage" (p. 115). When he learns about his part in Hetty's crime, he starts out "for a lonely walk, that he might look fixedly at the new future before him, and confirm himself in a sad resolution. He thought he could do that best in the Grove" (p. 387). The result is that he determines to leave Hayslope. For Arthur, then, the sacred Grove functions paradoxically to intensify emotional and contemplative processes by means of the calm, sweet atmosphere that prevails in the wood.

The *locus amoenus* affects not only Hetty and Arthur, but everyone exposed to it. When Adam beholds the lovers in the Grove, he accuses Arthur of deceit, and the two men "fought with the instinctive fierceness of panthers." Although fighting occurs in the *locus amoenus* and thus contradicts our expectations,[21] the function of the *locus amoenus* in the novel does not really change. The physical contact between enemies is like the sexual contact between lovers: both intensify emotion and express instinctual impulses—impulses of protection or propagation. If for Adam the Grove is a place for discovering the force of instinct, it is also a place for reconciliation. After Arthur and Adam reveal their feelings and heal the breach, "Adam left the Hermitage, feeling that sorrow was more bearable now hatred was gone" (p. 394). His experiences in the Grove, together with his despair over Hetty's suffering, help to transform hardness into sympathy for others. In Adam's case a pattern of moral education—a pattern of act, suffer, and change— emerges from his actions instead of the pastoral pattern of recovery.

The *locus amoenus*, then, by changing the direction of Arthur and Hetty and Adam, closely resembles the *locus amoenus* of traditional works both in its topographical characteristics and in its power to redirect those who come within its boundaries. Its "sacredness" depends on its power to transform the lives of those who enter it. At the center of the Grove, the Hermitage provides experience in an especially intense and heightened form. Whether George Eliot was aware of the *locus amoenus* and its functions in earlier works cannot be known with certainty.[22] But what can be said unequivocally is that the Grove and the Hermitage in *Adam Bede*, fusing as they do both pastoral and Christian materials, show unusual similarities to the *locus amoenus* and its functions in traditional pastoral works, and illustrate as well George Eliot's artistic method. The fact that the Grove reveals so clear a relationship to the *locus amoenus* and thus to pastoral helps, I think, to

[21] It is, however, important to note that the fight in the wood was not in George Eliot's mind as she composed the novel but was added at Lewes's suggestion. See her journal entry for 16 Nov. 1858 in Cross's *Life*.

[22] Thomas Pinney's edition of *Essays of George Eliot* (New York: Columbia Univ. Press, 1963) makes no reference to the *locus amoenus* or to similar literary landscapes.

provide an established and significant literary context into which *Adam Bede* may be placed and at the same time to extend the boundaries of an ancient genre. Simultaneously, *Adam Bede* sustains and modifies the pastoral tradition.

The nature of the novel's modification of pastoral is of special interest. The novel's Christian coloring brings with it an epic density and seriousness. The novel's moral insistence on sin and guilt and redemption, in accord with Christian ideas of salvation, challenges a major assumption of pastoral—that moral innocence will equip country people with the means of discovering sustained happiness. Unlike Hardy, who praises innocence and instinct, George Eliot in *Adam Bede* links innocence with sin and suffering (the expression of Hetty's instinct isolates her from the community). George Eliot suggests that experience alone can teach compassion and thus the means of redemption, although in *Silas Marner*, it should be noted, she connects Eppie with innocence and the tutelage of nature without ever suggesting that moral deficiences inhere in pastoral innocence. At its deepest level, then, *Adam Bede* offers a criticism of pastoral. The novel shows greater admiration for moral experience and its fruits than for the intuitive morality on which innocence must rely for guidance. *Adam Bede* presents the community and the values of Hayslope for our approval but at the same time offers evidence of the potential insufficiency of these values.

We study a novel usefully if, in addition to identifying traditional patterns of landscape and moral structure, we search for the patterns of language and thought that capture the novel's pulsebeat and pierce to its essence. When we examine *Adam Bede*, we discover two aspects that have particular significance in revealing the essential pastoral quality of the novel: the use of nature, long an essential part of the pastoral vision, and the concept of work, which enlarges the scope of pastoral. Because the pastoral novel treats rural life with unusual sympathy, full treatment of the natural world places the characters harmoniously into their surroundings and implicitly comments upon them, illustrating the way in which landscape and character are, in most pastoral novels, reflections of each other.

In *Adam Bede*, the word *nature* has three distinct meanings. In most instances, "nature" stands for the laws of the universe which control men (the neoclassical view); frequently it means the distinct temperament of an individual, the "law" of a unique person that is unshared by his fellow men (a romantic view); but it also denotes the natural world of observable phenomena (a universal view). In discovering how George Eliot creates a pastoral world, this last denotation of nature—

to mean natural world—has most importance. Awareness of the land is pronounced in *Adam Bede*. Evocative invocations to nature are frequent, usually landscape descriptions of brooks, fields, woods, sun, and sky—the visible outlines of the landscape. Because they are generally external descriptions and appear to be written from a distance, we do not see in George Eliot's landscape descriptions the inner view of the natural world, the extraordinary kinship evoked between a community and its natural environment, that we see in Wordsworth or Hardy or Lawrence.[23] Nature for George Eliot seems, rather, to exist largely for moral purposes: for its reassuring psychological-spiritual effect, for its power to teach endurance, and for the opportunity it provides men to work.

It is therefore not primarily in landscape description but in the use of metaphorical language that the depth of George Eliot's feeling for nature can be found and that nature enlarges our understanding of the novel. Since the pastoral vision is a vision of the harmony between man and his environment, one of the favorite techniques of the pastoral novelist is to reveal in depth the interpenetration and mystical correspondence between nature and humanity. In *Adam Bede* the metaphorical language, focusing largely on the natural world, identifies most clearly the relationship between man and nature that exists in George Eliot's mind. When George Eliot creates an imaginative analogy between the human and the natural, she suggests a complex dimension, a connecting bond between man and nature, that lies beneath the narrative surface.

George Eliot conceives of nature only as it relates to human life, thereby properly reinforcing the moral basis of her art. Virtually never does she conceive, metaphorically, of the human in terms of the natural, as do Hardy or Lawrence later: they carry to fuller development what exists in larval stage in *Adam Bede*. George Eliot uses metaphorical language mainly to evoke plant and animal life rather than inanimate nature. Flower imagery refers exclusively to women: George Eliot writes of "blooming daughters," of "blooming youth," or of Hetty in comparison to "a little blossom" or "a bud first opening her heart with wondering rapture to the morning." To image Hetty as a "bud" perfectly reveals her character: she is soon to be fertilized, she is beautiful, but she is undeveloped. The imaginative comparison is George Eliot's method not only of suggesting her character in a single metaphor but also of making an implied moral judgment upon her. Hetty is one of the luxuriant plants in the garden at the Hall Farm, blooming and

---

[23] George Eliot, however, was strongly influenced by Wordsworth. The epigraph of the novel comes from Wordsworth's *The Excursion*, and during the writing of *Adam Bede* she was rereading his poems.

bearing fruit but, in spite of her pastoral environment, having no human attachment or extension of sympathy, no awareness of morality. George Eliot clarifies her character in another metaphor: "There are some plants that have hardly any roots: you may tear them from their native nook of rock or wall, and just lay them over your ornamental flower-pot, and they blossom none the worse. Hetty could have cast all her past life behind her, and never cared to be reminded of it again" (p. 132). In addition to being like a plant, Hetty possesses also the innocence of animals, for her beauty is "like that of kittens, or very small downy ducks making gentle rippling noises with their soft bills" (p. 72). And when, after she has murdered her illegitimate baby, we are told that she watches Dinah "like an animal that gazes, and gazes and keeps aloof," we are convinced that Hetty, more than the other characters, belongs to the premoral world of plants and animals. The metaphors have shown us that she is a delicate and beautiful growth out of the fecundity of the earth, uncaring of moral complexities because she is unaware of them. The pathos in her character is that, unequipped, she must act in a human world. Thus pastoral innocence is tested in the real world.

The flower imagery functions in yet another way. Early, we learn of "the tall red sorrel" that grows along the bushy hedgerows. Shortly we meet Hetty Sorrel in the dairy and make a connection between Hetty's name and the redness of the plant. She wears "rose-coloured ribbons," moreover, and her hat "was trimmed with pink"; at church, she unfurls to a "round pink-and-white figure." During her intimacy with Arthur, she drops her "little pink silk handkerchief," and afterward, George Eliot carefully describes Hetty as holding in her hand a "wonderful pink-and-white hothouse plant." She looked "as if she had been made of roses." A few pages later, an extended passage subtly associating Hetty with bright red bunches of currants confirms for us her warmly sensual nature and implies Arthur's violation of her virginity. If we have been carefully attuned to George Eliot's plant and color imagery, then the sexual intimacy between Hetty and Arthur comes as a smaller surprise later in the novel,[24] for George Eliot's method of defining Hetty's character through plant imagery is surprisingly acute: it is a subtle foreshadowing device that helps to unify the book. In perfect complement, we always see Dinah in terms of lilies and white flowers.

Like many pastoral works, the novel throughout emphasizes natural growth. In the world of nature the emphasis is on sprouting seeds, de-

[24] V. S. Pritchett, however, finds that it is "for reasons of Victorian convention" that George Eliot does not reveal more of the seduction than she does; "the result," he adds, "is that we have no real reason for believing that Hetty has been seduced. Her baby appears inexplicably" (p. 93).

veloping plants, blooming flowers, ripening fruit. In the case of Adam, the stress is on moral growth, an expanded awareness of the common human plight. In the case of Hetty, it is appropriately on physical growth —the development of the baby within her body, followed by death. The fruit rapidly returns to the earth, a characteristic of the natural world alone. The child-murder, in essence, contracts the human cycle of birth and death into a seasonal cycle of nature—further proof of Hetty's elemental and instinctive nature operating below the level of responsibility.

The other clear pattern of metaphorical language, heightening the kinship between man and nature in the pastoral world, concerns the animal kingdom. Here metaphor also defines character. More important, it functions within the pastoral framework of the novel since George Eliot's metaphors emphasize domestic animals—sheep, cattle, fowls, swine, dogs, cats. Adam is "like thy dog Gyp" (p. 10), Dinah gathers the villagers "as a hen gathereth her chickens under her wings" (p. 27), Hetty is a "poor wandering lamb" (p. 30), people are "like sheep a bleatin' i' th' fold" (p. 50), Will is "like a cow i' wet clay" (p. 51), folks are "like poultry a-scratching on a gravel bank" (p. 67), Hetty is a "kitten-like maiden" (p. 73). Again, the human world exists as the tenor of the metaphor, and the animal world the vehicle. With almost no mention of wild animals or insects, George Eliot has thereby made a clear selection, which is suggestive because it implies not a representative animal world but a "civilized," limited, contained order that mirrors the community life lying one step above it. The characters are compared to animals within their immediately surrounding environment. The emphasis on domestic animals has the effect of narrowing the pastoral world to the area of the farmyard. The farmyard is peaceful and harmonious; the great world outside appears hard and violent, in search of prey. As in all pastoral, the "contained" world and the unlimited outer world offer marked contrast.

The emphasis that George Eliot places on work, however, modifies and enlarges the scope of traditional pastoral, where the focus is normally on love without responsibility; her emphasis fortifies pastoral against the charge of escapism. Nailed to the novel's moral signposts, *work*, alone and in combination, is a frequently repeated word, and its frequency suggests George Eliot's preoccupation with the idea. Within the novel itself the attitudes toward work separate clearly. Unlike the stronger characters, the weaker characters do not find their work a source of satisfying expression (a pattern found also in the novels of Hardy). Hetty dislikes the Poyser children and silently wishes not to work; instead, she wishes to become a member of the gentry: "Captain Donnithorne couldn't like her to go on doing work: he would like to see her in nice clothes, and thin shoes and white stockings, perhaps with silk clocks to them" (p. 129). Similarly Arthur presents himself to the reader in terms of pleasures—riding, hunting, or clandestine meetings with Hetty. We never see him at work in Hayslope. " 'It's a desperately dull business,' " he confides to Mr. Irwine, " 'being shut up at the Chase in the summer months, when one can neither hunt nor shoot, so as to make one's self pleasantly sleepy in the evening' " (p. 56); "in this confounded place . . . there was nothing to occupy him imperiously through the livelong day" (p. 119). In contrast the strong and admired characters, such as Adam and Dinah and the Poysers, are fully absorbed in their work and devote their energies to it. For them labor brings pleasure and pride.

Because Adam best represents the author's point of view in the novel, George Eliot makes him the apotheosis of the man who "delights in his work," the kind of man Hardy glorifies in Gabriel Oak or Giles Winterborne. Early in the novel, Adam says to the men in the workshop, " 'Look there, now! I can't abide to see men throw away their tools i' that way, the minute the clock begins to strike, as if they took no pleasure i' their work' " (p. 10). We learn that "to 'make a good job' of anything however small, was always a pleasure to Adam" (p. 248); and he tells Arthur that " 'a foreman, if he's got a conscience, and delights in his work, will do his business as well as if he was a partner' " (p. 141). George Eliot's concept of work, like that advanced by John Ruskin in *The Stones of Venice* (1851–53), has honest enjoyment as its end, but prizes perseverance and accomplishment and the useful employment of a man's time. When Adam is dejected after Hetty's trial, he says to himself: " 'But tomorrow . . . I'll go to work again. I shall learn to like it again some time, maybe; and it's right, whether I like it or not" (p. 388). Work is therefore a part of his personal sense of morality. It is thus fitting that we so often observe the characters at work. We see Adam and Seth in the workshop, Hetty in the dairy, Mrs. Poyser and Lisbeth Bede in their kitchens, or Dinah preaching. As an outlet for emotion and as a pattern imposed upon the free flow of time, work is fulfillment in a pastoral world modified by realism. In *Adam Bede* only those characters who are engrossed in their work lead successful lives. When Thias Bede begins to neglect his trade and lose respect for his profession, he fails, and nature reclaims him when he drowns. The lives of Hetty and Arthur offer similar evidence.

In the nineteenth century, we have seen, a significant change introduced work into the world of traditional pastoral. This change occurred distinctly in Wordsworth, whose influence on George Eliot was profound; but the stress on work should also be explained in terms of the social and economic developments of Victorian society. We see anticipations of the Victorian emphasis on work and duty in Wordsworth's "Ode to Duty" (1807), which, as one of George Eliot's favorite poems, is reflected throughout her work. (Lines 41–48, e.g., form the epigraph to chapter 80 of *Middlemarch*.) Here Wordsworth insists on duty as escape from error, needed by both natural and human worlds:

> Stern Daughter of the Voice of God!
> O Duty! if that name thou love
> Who art a light to guide, a rod
> To check the erring, and reprove;
> Thou, who art victory and law
> When empty terrors overawe;
> From vain temptations dost set free;
> And calm'st the weary strife of frail humanity!
>
> [ll. 1–8]

Such a conception of duty derives from the natural world with its harmonious and regular laws. V. S. Pritchett remarks that the importance of work and duty in George Eliot's novels—what he calls "her peasant sense of law"—was encouraged by her rural childhood. In country surroundings the laws and repeated patterns of nature are most clearly evident, and she found poetic value in the ancient traditions and institutions of the agricultural world because they corresponded to the eternal patterns of nature.[25] But the Victorian gospel of work also grew out of both its religious and economic atmosphere, demanding that an individual develop himself and contribute to society; it was encouraged by the sense of doubt that hid behind rapid change. To labor, says Walter Houghton, became "a practical means of exorcising the mood of ennui and despair which so often accompanied the loss of faith." A religion of work that could resolve intellectual confusion and psychological depression thus became the faith of many Victorians.[26]

In *Adam Bede* the Poyser family perhaps best reveals and embodies the work rhythms shared by man and the soil. Because Hetty dislikes her proper work (her hands are "coarsened by butter-making and other work that ladies never did"), she violates the moral order of the pastoral world. She interrupts the work rhythms that would bind her to her butter-making and, indirectly, to the soil. As life at the Hall Farm shows, work as a center of rotation provides harmony with environment and satisfies man's need for independence and stability. Adam remarks, " 'There's nothing but what's bearable as long as a man can work' " (p. 99). Even the hard work of suffering has its place in the universal

[25] Pritchett, p. 92.
[26] *The Victorian Frame of Mind* (New Haven: Yale Univ. Press, 1957), pp. 242, 251.

scheme: "Deep unspeakable suffering may well be . . . the initiation into a new state," a state "full of new awe and new pity" (p. 357). It is not accidental that the phrase "hard work," like a dominant chord, is one of the most frequent in the novel, acting to modify the leisurely world of traditional pastoral.

When we turn to a representative passage from the novel in order to examine the way in which the author tells her story and creates a body of particularized life, we find ample evidence of George Eliot's pastoral art in the techniques she uses to represent her pastoral world; one of these, the technique of pastoral distance, will be examined in depth. Technique is of course method of presentation. As a novelist, George Eliot must choose from various alternatives of presentation in order to achieve the richest and most coherent meaning possible. The evaluation of technique is a means of judging the author's control over his material—his ability to shape his material into a meaningful experience for the reader. Because of the inclusiveness and the leisurely rhythm of the novel and because of George Eliot's alternation between dramatic, descriptive, and discursive methods, the quotation that follows is necessarily long. It is part of a scene in which the Poysers are on their way to church.

You might have known it was Sunday if you had only waked up in the farmyard. The cocks and hens seemed to know it, and made only crooning subdued noises; the very bull-dog looked less savage, as if he would have been satisfied with a smaller bite than usual. The sunshine seemed to call all things to rest and not to labour; it was asleep itself on the moss-grown cow-shed; on the group of white ducks nestling together with their bills tucked under their wings; on the old black sow stretched languidly on the straw, while her largest young one found an excellent spring-bed on his mother's fat ribs; on Alick, the shepherd, in his new smock-frock, taking an uneasy siesta, half-sitting, half-standing on the granary steps. Alick was of opinion that church, like other luxuries, was not to be indulged in often by a foreman who had the weather and ewes on his mind. . . .

"There's father a-standing at the yard-gate," said Martin Poyser. "I reckon he wants to watch us down the field. It's wonderful what sight he has, and him turned seventy-five."

"Ah, I often think it's wi' th' old folks as it is wi' the babbies," said Mrs Poyser; "they're satisfied wi' looking, no matter what they're looking at. It's God A'mighty's way o' quietening 'em, I reckon, afore they go to sleep."

Old Martin opened the gate as he saw the family procession approaching, and held it wide open, leaning on his stick—pleased to do this bit of work; for, like all old men whose life has been spent in labour, he liked to feel that he was still useful—that there was a better crop of onions in the garden because he was by at the sowing—and that the cows would be milked the better if he stayed at home on a Sunday afternoon to look on.

. . . . .

"Dood-by, dandad," said Totty, "Me doin to church. Me dot my netlace on. Dive me a peppermint."

Grandad, shaking with laughter at this "deep little wench," slowly transferred his stick to his left hand, which held the gate open, and slowly thrust his finger into the waistcoat pocket on which Totty had fixed her eyes with a confident look of expectation.

And when they were all gone, the old man leaned on the gate again, watching them across the lane along the Home Close, and through the far gate, till they disappeared behind a bend in the hedge. For the hedgerows in those days shut out one's view, even on the better-managed farms; and this afternoon, the dogroses were tossing out their pink wreaths, the night-shade was in its yellow and purple glory, the pale honeysuckle grew out of reach, peeping high up out of a holly bush, and over all an ash or a syca-more every now and then threw its shadow across the path.

There were acquaintances at other gates who had to move aside and let them pass: at the gate of the Home Close there was half the dairy of cows standing one behind the other, extremely slow to understand that their large bodies might be in the way; at the far gate there was the mare holding her head over the bars, and beside her the liver-coloured foal with its head towards its mother's flank, apparently still much embarrassed by its own straddling existence. The way lay entirely through Mr Poyser's fields till they reached the main road leading to the village, and he turned a keen eye on the stock and the crops as they went along, while Mrs Poyser was ready to supply a running commentary on them all.

. . . . .

"Why, goodness me," said Mrs Poyser . . . , "look where Molly is with them lads. They're the field's length behind us. How *could* you let 'em do so, Hetty? Anybody might as well set a pictur to watch the children as you. Run back, and tell 'em to come on."

Mr and Mrs Poyser were now at the end of the second field, so they set Totty on the top of one of the large stones forming the true Loamshire stile, and awaited the loiterers; Totty observing with complacency, "Dey naughty, naughty boys—me dood."

The fact was that this Sunday walk through the fields was fraught with great excitement to Marty and Tommy, who saw a perpetual drama going on in the hedgerows, and could no more refrain from stopping and peeping than if they had been a couple of spaniels or terriers. Marty was quite sure he saw a yellow-hammer on the boughs of the great ash, and while he was peeping, he missed the sight of a white-throated stoat, which had run across the path and was described with much fervour by the junior Tommy. Then there was a little greenfinch, just fledged, fluttering along the ground, and it seemed quite possible to catch it, till it managed to flutter under the black-

berry bush. Hetty could not be got to give any heed to these things, so Molly
was called on for her ready sympathy, and peeped with open mouth wherever she was told, and said "Lawks!" whenever she was expected to wonder.

Molly hastened on with some alarm when Hetty had come back and
called to them that her aunt was angry; but Marty ran on first, shouting,
"We've found the speckled turkey's nest, Mother!". . .

"Well, well, now come on," said Mrs Poyser, "and walk before father
and mother, and take your little sister by the hand. We must go straight on
now. Good boys don't look after birds of a Sunday." [Pp. 159–64]

Aside from its charm, what immediately strikes the reader about this
excerpt is George Eliot's uninhibited delight in the rural-pastoral world
she creates. The passages describing the natural world breathe an air
of ease and pastoral contentment. The relaxed opening paragraph, the
riotous beauty of the blossoming flowers, the excited boys amid the perpetual drama in the hedgerows: these convey to the reader her deep
sense of nostalgia.

The passage illustrates the way in which George Eliot's prose style
suits the pastoral world she creates. Throughout, she develops a strong
feeling of concreteness for the locality. The main effect of the passage
is created by the large number of concrete nouns: exceptionally few
adjectives blur its concreteness. As Dorothy Van Ghent has shown, the
novel sustains a massively slow movement and a leisurely inclusiveness,[27] which are created not by rigorous selection but by extensive use
of detail. Everywhere in the passage, we are made aware of objects and
their shapes, of landscape, of animals, of human physiognomy. The
scene has a definite spatial structure: our attention is directed from outline to outline over the farmyard and fields. Because every person or
animal or salient landmark receives attention, there is a sense of continual movement, a deliberately unhurried movement that captures the
rhythm of rural life. As Mr. Irwine remarks, " 'our farm-labourers . . .
take life almost as slowly as the sheep and cows' " (p. 80).

In structuring the scene, George Eliot divides the pastoral *topos* into
portions suitable for orderly observation. In the opening paragraph of
the quotation, the eye is specifically directed to a unit of the larger landscape—the farmyard—and then to the smaller units which compose
it: the chickens, the bulldog, the sunshine, the cowshed, the white ducks,
the old black sow, her piglet—and finally on sleeping Alick. We follow
the characters across field after field in the same manner. The feeling
for the landscape, for the sense of "place," is so strong and solidly executed that we do not question the authenticity of the rural-pastoral life
portrayed. Although we can remark the occasional excesses—the exu-
berant description of the flowers and birds in the hedgerows—the

[27] *The English Novel: Form and Function* (New York: Rinehart, 1953), p. 173.

passage builds powerfully the depth and detail of the pastoral world.

The entire scene is visually ordered. It is arranged according to George Eliot's perception of spatial relationships, of objects against a physical background of measurable distances. The language itself has primarily visual appeal, emphasizing sighted objects and verbs such as *watch, looked, sight, view, saw, looking, peeping.* The eye follows the progressive physical movement of the family, while the sentences and paragraphs of prose capture the leisurely pace of the Poysers' walk. The art perfectly mirrors the action. The human figures are carefully placed against the natural background. They are fitted into the landscape, and the human and the natural intermingle. Because of the constant physical landmarks (hedges, gates, stiles, lanes, and fields), the human figures, seen by the reader from outside the scene, are placed against, yet are always merging with, the land. Old Martin is "a-standing at the yard-gate" and "wants to watch us down the field" with his wonderful sight (the gentry must use eyeglasses to enjoy a similar scene). As we watch with Old Martin, the Poysers slowly disappear into the land and blend with their physical environment. The many gates that are opened and closed by the Poysers mark over and over the boundaries of the fields. The gates repeatedly stop them from leaving, hold them inside their natural surroundings of animal and plant life, and so they linger within, and "the loiterers" are permitted to enjoy themselves in play before catching up with the group.

The reader senses keenly the physical isolation of the farm, and yet its unity and order. In the passage, George Eliot emphasizes human and animal and plant equally; all are integrated and interpenetrated. The scene is harmonized within each paragraph. The ducks nestle together, the cows and horses stand together in groups, the speckled turkey hen sits on her nest, the flowers bloom brilliantly, the sun shines. Constant interchange occurs within the scene: the boys play with the birds, the Poysers press slowly onward over the soil commenting on the stock and the crops, the horses and cows (described familiarly as "acquaintances" and given vague human perception) gaze at the passing group, "extremely slow to understand that their large bodies might be in the way."

Proportionately, a considerable amount of the passage—and novel—employs dialect, one of the ways George Eliot achieves her remarkable regional solidity. The use of dialect creates a sense of a unique people; it individualizes them and renders their personalities. Not directly, but through the implications of the dialogue, do we learn their internal states of mind. Yet the characters are also treated collectively; the modern sense of isolation has not yet developed except in Hetty, for she "could not be got to give any heed" to her cousins and had no sympathy for their discoveries.

As the passage makes clear, George Eliot uses the omniscient point of view, and her novel reflects both the advantages and the disadvantages of this narrative method.[28] What we gain in thoroughness and depth of treatment—the massive leisureliness—we lose in immediacy. We participate, but at a distance, as observers. We are addressed, as readers, directly; we are told of Alick's opinion rather than hearing it expressed or inferring it. Part of the result is that the novel seems external. With the possible exception of Arthur and Hetty, we have not yet achieved full entry into the operation of the characters' minds. Their internal mental state is aimed at in a different way—through a character's spoken opinions and through evaluations and commentary by the author. A system of moral values is therefore presented directly, and our response to each character is guided by the author. Yet an advantage of the omniscient point of view is that it helps to distance the reader from the pastoral world and to make it seem remote in time—unrecoverable, like the Golden Age. But the main advantage is the possibility it offers of rendering an integrated world. The point of view that allows George Eliot to reveal all she wishes about the world she is creating, also builds easily the illusion of unity; and the freedom of the author's movement within a scene—the total coverage—creates the illusion of a full and rounded picture of Hayslope. Because it plays so crucial a role in the novel, the point of view that distances the narrator from her rural material needs careful analysis. Having touched on distance earlier, in a general way, we can now examine more precisely the various kinds of distance and their function in the novel.

One of the most telling sentences in *Adam Bede* proposes a clear relationship between distance and pastoral material: "The jocose talk of haymakers is best at a distance; like those clumsy bells round the cows' necks, it has rather a coarse sound when it comes close, and may even grate on your ears painfully; but heard from far off, it mingles very prettily with the other joyous sounds of nature" (p. 177). As we have seen, George Eliot employs many strategies in *Adam Bede* that help to create a pastoral world which is solidly imagined and powerfully recaptured in language: contrasts of city and country and of past and present, pastoral uses of nature and the *locus amoenus*, and a skillful choice of nostalgic detail. One of the most valuable of these strategies, though one of the hardest to analyze, is the strategy of distance. More precisely, as the quotation indicates, it is a strategy of the *proper* nar-

[28] See W. J. Harvey, "George Eliot and the Omniscient Author Convention," *Nineteenth-Century Fiction*, 13 (1958), 81–108, for a good discussion of the omniscient narrator.

rative distance for pastoral, that is, the distance proper for a sympathetic appreciation of country life. Essentially rhetorical in its persuasive intent, this strategy of pastoral involves various forms of narrative distance—spatial distance, temporal distance, and emotional distance.[29]

Although temporal distance is pervasive and vital and deserves brief illustration, in *Adam Bede* it is the technique of *spatial* distance that transforms fictional material directly into pastoral. Because this form of distance tends to be more variable than the others, and thus more valuable to study, I will focus my discussion largely on the relationship between spatial distance and pastoral. In contrast, so-called realism requires little distance from fictional material; and as we will see, violations of the proper narrative distance for pastoral will snap the bond of sympathy and transform a scene of potential pastoral into antipastoral, or harsh realism.

In *Adam Bede* both the characters and their rural environment depend on various forms of distance for the impression they make on the narrator and thus for the effect they have on the reader. From this statement, a number of rough generalizations can be formulated. (1) Landscape descriptions, generally remembered rather than observed and thus almost always pastoral, are in the novel more fully pastoral whenever the narrator is at a significant spatial distance from the scene (e.g., pp. 16f., 185, 237, 246, 249, 305, 430, 443). (2) The tenant farmers such as the Poysers and the better workmen such as Dinah and the Bede brothers, or the admired gentry such as Mr. Irwine and his mother— all of these characters, who form the human substance of the novel, generally need only temporal distance to make them pastoral; they do not require spatial distance. Even Hetty, unadmired by the narrator, can become pastoral at an oblique distance: *through* either Adam or Arthur, whose thoughts of Hetty are sympathetically recorded by the narrator, or through the use of mirrors. (3) Farm-laborers and the rougher work-

[29] Conceding the imprecision of the term *emotional distance*, I use it as a convenient amalgam of emotional and social and intellectual distance, and mean by it the reader's perception of the way the narrator feels and thinks. Unlike aesthetic distance, from which my terms should be distinguished, emotional distance has nothing to do with the objectivity essential to art. It reflects the mind of the imagined persona rather than of the author herself, and is gauged by tone. In *Adam Bede* the narrator's emotional distance is generally a function of social class: emotional distance increases (reducing sympathy) in proportion to the social distance the narrator moves from the social "center" formed by the tenant farmers and the admired gentry. Thus Squire Donnithorne on one side and the farm-laborers on the other are treated by the narrator with the greatest emotional distance, so that the novel's social center and its pastoral center therefore coincide, creating actually a narrow social range of pastoral material. We can conclude, then, that in *Adam Bede* the emotional distance proper to pastoral is little or none at all. For this reason I do not discuss it in detail.

men of Hayslope can become pastoral *only* at a spatial distance (e.g., pp. 177, 430, 432); at the other end of the social scale, the gentry, except for Mr. Irwine and his mother, are nonpastoral regardless of the distance employed by the narrator (e.g., pp. 106–19, 138–49, 169, 206f., 230f., 251f.). These generalizations can be illustrated efficiently with a few representative passages, passages that should clarify the relationship between pastoral and distance and also qualify the critical cliché that pastoral works require significant narrative distance in order to be pastoral. Of equal importance, the passages will hopefully illuminate the artistic method that George Eliot preferred when working in the pastoral genre.

The use of temporal distance as a technique of pastoral operates invariably and finds memorable expression in the narrator's recollection of the country dance. In its use of temporal distance, the quotation is nicely representative of the vision that dominates the entire novel:

Pity it was not a boarded floor! Then the rhythmic stamping of the thick shoes would have been better than any drums. That merry stamping, that gracious nodding of the head, that waving bestowal of the hand—where can we see them now? That simple dancing of well-covered matrons, laying aside for an hour the cares of house and dairy, remembering but not affecting youth, not jealous but proud of the young maidens by their side—that holiday sprightliness of portly husbands paying little compliments to their wives, as if their courting days were come again—those lads and lasses a little confused and awkward with their partners, having nothing to say— it would be a pleasant variety to see all that sometimes, instead of low dresses and large skirts, and scanning glances exploring costumes, and languid men in lackered boots smiling with double meaning. [P. 240]

As she does in her evocation of Old Leisure, the narrator, located in the present, contrasts the simple innocence of the remembered past with the sophisticated corruption of the present, using antithesis to heighten the contrast, and parallel *that*-structures to generate nostalgic emotion. Temporal distance, here as throughout, encourages a pastoral attitude to develop, an attitude that tends to simplify rural character by eliminating hints of perversity or sordidness.

Spatial distance, different and more subtle in the way it helps to create pastoral, involves a special form of seeing or hearing: at a distance, an object or a scene may impinge quite differently on the imagination. In a passage of landscape description, the narrator illustrates clearly the differences in perception created by distance from a scene, and then by close proximity to the same scene:

One likes to pause in the mild rays of the sun, and look over the gates at the patient plough-horses turning at the end of the furrow, and think that the beautiful year is all before one. . . . how green all the grassy fields are! and the dark purplish brown of the ploughed earth and of the bare branches is beautiful too. What a glad world this looks like, as one drives or rides along the valleys and over the hills! I have often thought so when . . . I have come on something by the roadside which has reminded me that I am not in Loamshire: an image of a great agony—the agony of the Cross. . . . surely, if there came a traveller to this world who knew nothing of the story of man's life upon it, this image of agony would seem to him strangely out of place in the midst of this joyous nature. He would not know that hidden behind the apple-blossoms, or among the golden corn, or under the shrouding boughs of the wood, there might be a human heart beating heavily with anguish. . . .

Such things are sometimes hidden among the sunny fields and behind the blossoming orchards; and the sound of the gurgling brook, if you came close to one spot behind a small bush, would be mingled for your ear with a despairing human sob. [Pp. 305–6]

The first part of the quotation, in which the narrator stands at a considerable distance from the scene, represents fairly a number of similar passages.[30] At a distance, the narrator ("George Eliot") sees blocks of color and broad outlines and harmony of effects rather than the exact but perhaps unpleasing details that less distance from the landscape might reveal. If, however, "you came close" to the joyous nature that the narrator frequently recalls, pastoral impressions would vanish and suffering would bare its pained face. Pastoral thus requires a *proper* distance—here, as often, a proper spatial distance from the novelist's rural material—if pastoral is to avoid concentrating on human anguish. That George Eliot frequently alternates anguish with pastoral points to the source of the novel's ambiguity of attitude—its attempt, roughly speaking, to fuse realism and romance, and to achieve a fuller portrait than a pure pastoral vision might allow.

The concept of proper distance is nicely imaged in chapter 53, critically one of the most interesting chapters in the novel. The narrator recalls old Kester's thatching: "if anything were his forte more than another, it was thatching; and when the last touch had been put to the last beehive rick, Kester, whose home lay at some distance from the farm, would take a walk to the rickyard in his best clothes on a Sunday morning, and stand in the lane, *at a due distance*, to contemplate his own thatching,—walking about to get each rick *from the proper point*

---

[30] John Paterson, despite his full and illuminating analysis of the novel's landscape ("Introduction," pp. xxiv–xxix), does not mention that what makes the landscape pastoral is the narrator's spatial distance from it. Because the technique of spatial distance controls the view of landscape and characters that we take with us from the novel, it is important, I think, to analyze technically *why* the landscape is pastoral.

of view. As he curtsied along . . . you might have imagined him to be engaged in some pagan act of adoration" (p. 432; my italics). The italicized phrases signify what happens consistently in the novel on a larger scale: the achievement of proper spatial distance assures the narrator's purest sympathy for a rural scene and results in a commemorative hymn. Here, for example, despite patches of mild caricature, the narrator unashamedly commemorates old Kester.[31]

That the narrator must *discover* the right distance for pastoral—the kind of distance she found in order to commemorate Kester—can be illustrated by the whole of chapter 53. The chapter provides a paradigm of the relationship, observable throughout the novel, between narrative distance and pastoral. Called "The Harvest Supper," chapter 53 has as much potential for pastoral treatment as any chapter in the novel; yet the narrator's attitude toward the scene turns curiously ambivalent: fondness mixes with distaste, compassion with satire and irony. As spatial distance gradually changes, emotional distance changes and, with it, the narrator's attitude. The chapter opens in the evening sunlight, for pastoral the most congenial of external conditions:

As Adam was going homewards, on Wednesday evening, in the six o'clock sunlight, he saw in the distance the last load of barley winding its way towards the yard-gate of the Hall Farm, and heard the chant of "Harvest Home!" rising and sinking like a wave. Fainter and fainter, and more musical through the growing distance, the falling dying sound still reached him, as he neared the Willow Brook. The low westering sun shone right on the shoulders of the old Binton Hills, turning the unconscious sheep into bright spots of light; shone on the windows of the cottage too, and made them a-flame with a glory beyond that of amber or amethyst. It was enough to make Adam feel that he was in a great temple, and that the distant chant was a sacred song. [P. 430]

The repetition of *distance* and its variants—*fainter and fainter, falling dying*, and *westering*—is not accidental, for the sacredness of the scene depends on Adam's distance from it.[32] We know from a passage quoted earlier that at close range the distant chant would ring coarse and grate upon the ears. But here the chant grows *more* musical as distance in-

---

[31] It is useful to compare the narrator's view of Eppie in the concluding chapter of *Silas Marner*: "Seen at a little distance as she walked across the church-yard and down the village, she seemed to be attired in pure white, and her hair looked like the dash of gold on a lily."

[32] To the chant as "sacred song" within "a great temple," we should compare similar phrases earlier in the novel: the Donnithornes' "sacred grove" and Mrs. Poyser's dairy as a "temple of cleanliness." Such imagery invests the novel's pastoralism with a religious dimension reminiscent of both Wordsworth and Renaissance pastoral.

creases. The repetition of long, slow -*ing* words (ten in all) marks the languorous rhythm, while the alliteration composes the music of the passage, with both music and rhythm creating a subtle and effective underscoring of the meaning. Using an analogy, we might say that the author's dependence on memory, itself a way of creating distance from direct observation, finds its equivalent in the narrator's fondness for spatial distance from the events she describes. In both cases, increasing distance softens the jagged edges and crude force of ugliness.

From this opening, in which distance brings pastoral into focus, the narrator moves to the Poysers' annual "supper" of plum pudding and roast beef. Engaged now in recording directly the habits and conversation of "those good farm-labourers," the narrator has no longer the benefit of spatial distance. As spatial distance vanishes, so does the scene's pastoralism. Without spatial distance, the narrator substitutes emotional distance, unfavorable to pastoral because of its tendency toward irony and criticism. Dismayed with close observation of the laborers, the narrator turns from a pastoral opening to a record of the supper that can only be termed antipastoral. If initially the scene makes "a goodly sight," the narrator focuses in the next sentence on the laborers' animality in eating and drinking (Tom Tholer takes to his meat as if it were "prey"). Although the Poysers are amused by the behavior of the laborers, the narrator winces: there is no distance to insulate and offer protection. Earlier in the novel, when a laborer comes out of his cottage to watch Dinah preach, the narrator detects his slouch and his "slow bovine gaze" *only because* he is "close at hand" (p. 17). Here, similarly, although we have already met Alick the shepherd, it is not until the narrator brings us close enough to see the ruddiness of his complexion that we learn that "his speech had usually something of a snarl in it" (p. 433) and that Alick and old Kester share none of the sentimental politeness of a Tityrus and a Meliboeus, shepherds in Vergil's first eclogue.[33] The narrator summarizes her varied descriptions with a statement that is both emotionally detached and intellectually distant, both objective and realistic: "The bucolic character at Hayslope, you perceive, was not of that entirely genial, merry, broad-grinning sort, apparently observed in most districts visited by artists. The mild radiance of a smile was a rare sight on a field-labourer's face, and there was seldom any gradation between bovine gravity and a laugh" (p. 433). The narrator's resolution, expressed earlier, to "tolerate, pity, and love

---

[33] It is worth noting that Hardy also alludes to Vergil's *Eclogues* when he recreates the shearing supper in *Far from the Madding Crowd*. A comparison of the two suppers is instructive: it shows that for Hardy spatial distance is not required for pastoral treatment of the laborers. Rendered even at close distance, the scene draws upon Hardy's warm sympathy.

... these more or less ugly, stupid, inconsistent people, whose movements of goodness you should be able to admire" (p. 151) clearly weakens. Throughout chapter 53 the narrator prefers not to examine the scene at close range, but to discuss the background of the scene (the origin of the harvest song) or to explain the personality and reputation of the laborers ("Tom Saft," Kester, Alick, Tim) or to focus on the more intelligent Mr. Craig and his political views (he is "a knowing fellow"). The narrator returns to the laborers only briefly before we learn that Adam, a reliable index of value in the novel, "had been longing to go" and that he was "resolute" in his intention to leave the harvest supper. At the beginning of the chapter, Adam feels "that he was in a great temple" when he hears at a distance the chant of "Harvest Home"; yet brought close, to the altar of the temple, within reach of the same laboring singers, Adam gladly exits at the close of the chapter. The sonorous organ tones have thinned to the discordant rasp of unlettered voices. Unlike the rustics who gather at Bathsheba's home in *Far from the Madding Crowd*, the laborers at the harvest supper appear foolish rather than charming, coarse rather than quaint, sordid rather than entertaining. In terms of technique, the key to the ambiguity of attitude is, I am convinced, distance—the narrator's spatial and temporal distance from the scenes of the novel. Hence the relationship between distance and the possibility of pastoral.[34]

We can conclude that the ambiguous pastoral quality in *Adam Bede* should be traced to the narrator's shifts from a narrative distance conducive to pastoral, to that distance conducive to a realistic or naturalistic presentation. The tension thereby created between one mode and another, though it causes uncertainties of tone, has the effect of persuading the reader to accept the novel's pastoralism as meaningful rather than escapist, significant rather than artificially pretty, since the novel's fictional world does not seem unreal. George Eliot believed that so long as fiction was based on real life, the sympathy generated by a pastoral treatment made life *more* real because it penetrated externals in order to show the inner life—thus obviating the criticism of irrelevance standard in most discussions of pastoral. Moreover, recognition that tenant farmers can be sympathetically portrayed without spatial distance, but

[34] In "George Eliot and the Climate of Realism," William J. Hyde quotes George Eliot's view that peasants (by which she means farm-servants and farm-laborers) are unsuited to complex artistic treatment, because their behavior is simple and coarse, " 'they are principally to be studied from without' " (*PMLA*, 72 [1957], 153). Hyde discusses perceptively the coarse animality of the peasants in George Eliot's novels, but valuable as it is, his essay perhaps oversimplifies *Adam Bede*. It is important, I think, to recognize that spatial distance controls the treatment of the farm-laborers in *Adam Bede*. They lend themselves to a naturalistic treatment at close range, but not at a distance.

can yet require temporal distance, lends only qualified support to the critical cliché that pastoral *requires* narrative distance: as we have seen in *Adam Bede* at least, some aspects of country life, in order to become pastoral, require more distance, and of a different kind, than other aspects. We can conclude, then, that the distance required to create pastoral is a variable: always, a *proper* distance is required. Along with various contrasts and a skillful selection of detail, the narrator's use of considerable spatial and temporal distance is highly congenial to a pastoral effect, since both kinds of distance are methods of softening coarseness and blurring minute details in order to create a unified impression of rural life, in order to make entirely persuasive the narrator's pastoral vision.

A representative passage and a close examination of distance have suggested the values that George Eliot discovers in rural Hayslope. In *Adam Bede* all of the characters partake of a common source of belief and sustenance: a small but integrated world. Because the connection is so close, so "organic," they are complete human beings only as they are represented fictionally within their microcosmic world. In a fragmented industrial society, by contrast, modern writers such as Lawrence and Joyce and Virginia Woolf have demonstrated that the individual is alienated from a common fund of tradition and belief and can therefore legitimately be portrayed alone, without a "community" context. The Poysers, on the other hand, are complete only as they relate to each other, to their farm, and to their community. Most of the novel offers a constant interplay of human relationships. Interchange and connection between individuals binds them into cohesion so that George Eliot stresses the gregariousness of the Bedes and the Poysers. Because the various family groups are tightly organized into the community, they create happiness out of their immediate surroundings.

We are most absorbed in the novel when it concentrates on Hayslope as microcosmic pastoral world, and we leave the pastoral world unwillingly. We are, in fact, more interested and absorbed in the ordinary life of Hayslope—it is this that George Eliot does best—than we are in the extraordinary events that occur outside the rural order: the murder of Hetty's child, Hetty's trial, her pardon. Though numerous critics have objected to the marriage of Adam and Dinah as an artificial happy ending, George Eliot's return to the pastoral world at the end represents a sense of balance established and calm restored, though we may perhaps agree that her matching of Adam and Dinah compromises their integrity.[35] The marriage is nevertheless the pastoral counterpart

---

[35] Henry James states best the argument against the marriage: "That his marriage at some future time was quite possible, and even natural, I readily admit; but that was matter for a new story" ("The Novels of George Eliot," in *Discussions of*

of the near-execution of Hetty in the industrial world and is again a way of implying value: the one offers new life, the other offers death. Hetty's deportation purges the most serious violator of the pastoral order. After exile and a fever, Arthur, however, is allowed to return to Hayslope, with clear possibilities of his rehabilitation in view.

From the present, George Eliot looks with the nostalgia characteristic of pastoral toward a happier time and place, where life is simpler and more meaningful and where an integrated community and a unified culture have not been displaced, where in Mr. Irwine's words " 'Men's lives are as thoroughly blended with each other as the air they breathe' " (p. 355). The novel's massive solidity documents rural-pastoral life with a precision scarcely matched in earlier novels—*The Vicar of Wakefield* or *The Heart of Midlothian*, for example—and perhaps unrivaled since. George Eliot's seriousness, her moral earnestness, her understanding of humanity, the uncompromising sincerity of attitude toward her fictional material—these are qualities which help to make her work a valuable rendering of rural experience. A great novel must be so executed that the observer is imperceptibly transformed into a participant by the power of the work to create a world that breathes autonomous life. It is such an autonomous pastoral world that George Eliot creates in *Adam Bede*. The depth of characterization and the range of character analysis, the "vertical" sense of the community, the densely cumulative detail, the inclusive and leisurely pace, the verisimilitude of the dialect—in short, the fully realized creation of a secluded pastoral world makes *Adam Bede* an impressive novel and makes George Eliot, in one critic's words, "the great novelist of the traditional sanctities of pastoral England."[36]

George Eliot, ed. Richard Stang [Boston: Heath, 1960], p. 4). The problem with the characterization of Dinah, which has disturbed most critics of the novel, is that we do not see Dinah suffering personal pain and thus we do not feel that she is fully human—that she quite achieves human proportions. Awareness of pain is one signal of depth in human character, and it is for this reason that Adam, in spite of his idealized qualities, is a successful character.

[36] Graham Hough, *The Last Romantics* (New York: Gerald Duckworth, 1947), p. xi.

Chapter 4

Silas Marner

"A Snug Well-Wooded Hollow"

DESPITE differences of emphasis, *Silas Marner* is a distillation of *Adam Bede*, a compressed and more artistic handling of similar elements of plot, theme, and characterization. In both novels a female's sexual indiscretion and a male's betrayal lie at the narrative center, while traditional community gatherings and salty topical dialogue weight the narrative center with regional solidity. The impressiveness of George Eliot's art consists of her using the universal situation as her focus, then surrounding the focus with incredibly rich layers of regional contextualization, like a hard seed surrounded by sweet fruit, to use one of her own figures. In both novels the regional elements gather force and authority, and ripen into marriage and a subsequent domestic idyll. Molly Cass is a Hetty whose baby lives; Arthur becomes Godfrey; Silas mutes the eccentric figure of Bartle Massey and follows Adam's change from hardness to fellow-feeling; the Poysers modulate into the lower-keyed Winthrops; while the village festivities invariably join together both the indiscretion and its social context.

Like much pastoral literature *Silas Marner* is sometimes written off, with a quick flourish of the pen, as a charming but slight work of en-chanted reminiscence. Thus Dr. Leavis in *The Great Tradition* brands it "that charming minor masterpiece."[1] What has been seldom re-marked, though, is the novel's quiet pastoralism (to use John Hol-loway's phrase),[2] which functions as a pointed critique of nineteenth-century industrial society and which provides an appropriate means for discovering and illuminating moral values. Embodying a common pas-toral pattern, the escape from modern industrialism to the rural life of the past brings ultimately a happiness and fulfillment that can, it seems, be discovered nowhere else. In much of the novel a lambent and radiant light casts a glow over rural life; and an air of good cheer and enjoy-

[1] F. R. Leavis, *The Great Tradition* (1948; rpt. New York: New York Univ. Press, 1964), p. 46.

[2] *The Victorian Sage* (1953; rpt. New York: Norton, 1965), p. 152. U. C. Knoepflmacher in *George Eliot's Early Novels* (Berkeley and Los Angeles: Univ. of California Press, 1968) also writes of "the pastoral world of *Silas Marner*" (p. 3) and of "the pastoral novel she had perfected in *Silas Marner*" (p. 5), although his use of the term *pastoral* does not form an essential part of his discussion.

ment hovers over many of the scenes—the brilliantly captured dialogue at the Rainbow, the Christmas festivities at the Red House, and almost the whole of Part II. By examining the pastoral elements of the novel, we can appreciate the work in its proper genre—less as a fable or realistic novel than as a pastoral novel that pictures a retreat into a secluded, circumscribed, traditional world where contentment can be won.

The structural pattern of *Silas Marner* links the novel to pastoral romance. The standard action of the pastoral romance, writes Walter R. Davis, follows the hero from the complex urban world to the simple natural world to the supernatural center, then out again, and shows the hero's disintegration in the chaotic outer circle, education in the pastoral circle, and reawakening at the sacred center.[3] The action of *Silas Marner*, though spaced over a long period of time, is remarkably similar. Accused of theft and jilted in love, Silas withdraws from the pain and corruption of urban life and escapes into the pastoral region of Raveloe, where he discovers another way of life that prepares him to reassess his embittered attitudes. The supernatural center of the pastoral region is Silas' cottage at the moment Eppie miraculously appears on the weaver's hearth. Under Eppie's direction Silas completes his education "with reawaken[ed] sensibilities," is reborn, and years later, as in the romance, departs for the urban world—only to find that the world he escaped had "disintegrated." Preferring now the sheltered pastoral region to the oppressive atmosphere of Lantern Yard, Silas returns to Raveloe. Thus the novel alters the pattern of pastoral romance by insisting on Silas' ultimate allegiance to the rural world. After Silas returns to Raveloe, another parallel with the traditional genre manifests itself in the marriage of the two pastoral peasants, Eppie and Aaron, and in the feast that celebrates their marriage (see chapter 1). The marriage reasserts the positive value that inheres in the rural order and, as we leave Raveloe, ties into unity the lives of the rustic characters.[4]

Important to any pastoral work is of course the sharp rural-urban contrast, which embodies the basic pastoral impulse to criticize urban society by locating value in remote areas. In *Silas Marner* we find also

[3] *A Map of Arcadia* (New Haven: Yale Univ. Press, 1965), p. 38.

[4] Ian Milner has discovered some notable parallels between *Silas Marner* and *The Winter's Tale*: "Up to the point of the child's discovery," he remarks, "the narrative has much in common with the pastoral romance of a lost child and foster-father such as Shakespeare drew upon for *The Winter's Tale*." Despite differences in their treatment, both Shakespeare and George Eliot treat the discovery of a child; both associate this discovery with gold; both portray a peasant rearing a foundling of higher birth; and both children marry not gentry but peasants ("Structure and Quality in *Silas Marner*," *Studies in English Literature*, 6 [1966], 722–23). One might add that Pastorella in *The Faerie Queene* (Book VI) is also reared by an old shepherd who is not her natural father.

the expected nature-art antithesis stemming from this contrast: simplicity is praised over complexity, and the natural is preferred to the artificial or man made. At the opening of the novel, we are not surprised to learn that "nothing could be more unlike his native town" (p. 20)[5] than Raveloe, hidden from the world and entirely self-sufficient. Lantern Yard and Raveloe are not connected in the highly organic way that contrasted geographical areas are connected in *Middlemarch*. The rural world, though not free from evil, is re-created largely in idyllic terms,[6] whereas industrialism assumes the grizzled outlines of a ferocious beast. When Silas and Eppie return to Lantern Yard years after Silas has departed, the city is strangely transformed: traditional landmarks have vanished in the wake of industrialism. " 'O, what a dark ugly place!' " exclaims Eppie on their arrival. " 'How it hides the sky! It's worse than the Workhouse. I'm glad you don't live in this town now, father.' " In place of the tiny chapel where Silas had worshipped, a large factory towers; and they are greeted by a "multitude of strange indifferent faces," all in a hurry (pp. 266–67). "Here and there a sallow begrimed face looked out from a gloomy doorway at the strangers, and increased Eppie's uneasiness" (p. 268). Because the city is envisioned as fearful and ugly, the rural world alone offers the possibility of fulfillment. If such passages display a rural point of view of urban or industrial life, the reverse point of view operates also and provides a different perspective, encouraging us to see, as often in pastoral, one way of life as a means of evaluating the other.

Contributing to the reader's awareness of the rural-urban or simplicity-complexity contrast is the novel's dominant point of view, which is complex, intellectual, and analytic, viewing the pastoral retreat of Raveloe from a critical perspective, avoiding easy praise of the narrow understanding of those who live in Raveloe, and refusing to ignore the flaws of their society. George Eliot speaks more than once of the "rude mind" of rustic folk. The "critical perspective" allows us however—in dialectical fashion—to sense the cultural value of an intellectual urban life such as George Eliot lived during the 1860s, a life that offers "perspective" as one of its benefits.[7] The impression of an objective urban onlooker emerges from the long expository introduction which prefaces the action. With the narrator, we look on as outsiders: "To the

---

[5] Parenthetical page numbers refer to George Eliot, *Silas Marner*, vol. IX in *The Works of George Eliot*, Cabinet Edition (Edinburgh and London: William Blackwood, n.d. [1868]).

[6] For a different view, see Henry Auster, *Local Habitations* (Cambridge: Harvard Univ. Press, 1970), pp. 177–94.

[7] Q. D. Leavis discusses the biographical stimulus for writing the novel in her fine introduction to the Penguin Edition of *Silas Marner* (1967), pp. 12, 34n, 40–42.

peasants of old times, the world outside their own direct experience was a region of vagueness and mystery"; or, the villagers of Raveloe, "honest folk, born and bred in a visible manner, were mostly not over-wise or clever—at least, not beyond such a matter as knowing the signs of the weather" (p. 4). The narrator explains the villagers to a reader who, without commentary, might not understand or sympathize with them. Again, the reader remains outside the particularized pastoral world of the novel when he learns that Nancy Lammeter "was not theologically instructed enough to discern very clearly the relation between the sacred documents of the past which she opened without method, and her own obscure, simple life" or when he learns that her religious theory was "pieced together out of narrow social traditions, fragments of church doctrine imperfectly understood, and girlish reasonings on her small experience" (pp. 231, 235–36). Nancy's character is analyzed from outside the sphere of Raveloe and in terms of a more complex, sophisticated method of determining value; she is judged according to an educated and responsible urban code that lies beyond the limits of her own culture. Although it diminishes the scope and significance of Raveloe in the reader's mind, such a point of view—which invites us to see Raveloe from without and from within—helps to link the novel to pastoral.

We have seen in an earlier chapter that George Eliot departs from the traditional conception of pastoral. Using Wordsworth as her model, she injects toil and a measure of unhappiness into the pastoral world and so, while retaining many of the traditional features of the genre, she aims toward greater realism in her representation of rural life. What exists clearly in the novel is an ambiguity in George Eliot's attitude toward her material, the sort of ambiguity we saw in *Lycidas*: the deeply felt impulse toward pastoral alternates with a keen sense of realism, and sympathy alternates with critical distance, in the same way that rural and urban points of view operate. Perhaps for this reason, the novel splits into two balanced halves. The plot dealing with Silas is generally pastoral in conception and execution, whereas the story of the Cass family is generally realistic. The pastoral attitude is played off against the realistic attitude, and it is this careful balancing of conflicting tendencies which gives the novel its distinctive tension.[8] Because of this allowance for greater realism, evil stations itself not only in the

[8] About the two plot strands Jerome Thale remarks that the "manner of the Godfrey story is very different from that of the Silas story—it is realistic where the Silas story is pastoral and fairy-tale-like" (*The Novels of George Eliot* [New York: Columbia Univ. Press, 1959], p. 59). See also Fred C. Thomson, "The Theme of Alienation in *Silas Marner*," *Nineteenth-Century Fiction*, 20 (1965), 82–83; and Auster, p. 189.

mushrooming industrial centers, but spreads its tentacles even into so sheltered a pastoral retreat as Raveloe. Thus we find in George Eliot's early novels the mixture of pastoral and realistic elements that Hardy inherits. The narrative tension that results is used to admirable artistic advantage by George Eliot. Examined minutely, the narrative reveals a tensive movement like that of the shuttle of a loom, tracing a uniform pattern between opposite poles of tension and release, anguish and hope; for example, Dunstan committing a crime in darkness and rain (ch. 4) juxtaposed to Silas' warm fire and anticipation of food (ch. 5); agony (ch. 5) opposed to conviviality (ch. 6) and conviviality opposed, then, to the investigation of the robbery (chs. 7–8); Godfrey's predicament (ch. 9) placed next to neighborly visits (ch. 10); and the New Year's Eve festivities (ch. 11) pitted against Molly's journey and death (chs. 12–13). George Eliot's use of narrative antithesis creates much interest and dramatic tension, reflecting not only the initial contrast between Lantern Yard and Raveloe but metaphorically extending the mechanics of the weaver's trade into the structuring principle of the novel.

The narrative is, we have said, told through the device of the double plot. One plot traces the history of Silas and Eppie; the other plot charts the lives of Squire Cass and his sons. When Silas Marner's close friend wished to marry Silas' fiancée, he falsely accused Marner of stealing the funds of their church. The church members prayed, drew lots, found Marner guilty, and suspended him from church membership. Stunned, Silas fled from Lantern Yard to Raveloe, where he became a weaver. His extreme thrift earned him the reputation of a miser until Dunstan Cass, son of the local squire, stole Silas' money and disappeared, thereby connecting Silas to the Cass plot. Godfrey, the best of Squire Cass's sons, had surreptitiously married an opium addict who bore him a daughter, but Godfrey in his shame refused to acknowledge them. One New Year's Eve, Molly Cass traveled toward the Red House to expose Godfrey as her husband. On the way, however, she died, and her child wandered into Silas' cottage. The two plots again merge. When Godfrey did not come forward to claim the child, Silas adopted her as his own and named her Eppie. In Part II the narrative moves forward sixteen years. Godfrey and his second wife Nancy decide to adopt Godfrey's natural daughter, but when they ask, Eppie refuses; instead she marries Aaron Winthrop, the Casses' gardener, and returns with Aaron to Silas' cottage where the three of them settle happily.

In the industrial world, then, Silas is robbed of a wife, his honest name, and his faith in God by the deceit of his closest friend. But evil, appearing also in the rural world, causes Silas to be robbed of his gold. There are yet other forms of robbery in Raveloe. When Godfrey Cass renounces his claim on the child, by refusing to identify himself as her father, he too is robbed—of fathering a child by his second wife. Nemesis operates even in the pastoral world. Yet evil in the novel is largely limited to the plot that treats the lives of the Casses. The plot that treats the rustics is surprisingly free from corruptive elements.[9] In fact, evil can be found everywhere but in the *locus amoenus* of Silas' once-empty cottage, where work gives way to love—when supernatural powers send Eppie to Silas' hearth—and then to a domestic idyll. The *locus amoenus* escapes evil because behavior there is premised on innocence. Because of the importance of innocence, the plot device common to pastoral novels, of the empty or abandoned cottage now occupied by persons in retreat, encourages in *Silas Marner* an asexual sequence of events rather than the sexual sequence evident in *Adam Bede* or *Lady Chatterley's Lover* or potentially in *The Woodlanders*.

But more important than the acknowledgment of evil, in demonstrating the change in attitude toward traditional pastoral, is the novel's heavy emphasis on work. The plot that traces the activities of Squire Cass and his sons reveals significantly few mentions of work. Instead, the characters who speak of work are usually Silas, Eppie, and Aaron Winthrop, characters who are linked together on this basis. Half of such citations refer to Silas himself, perhaps because Silas reflects most clearly the importance of work in the novel. The Victorian ethic of hard work, which George Eliot shares with her age, conflicts with the pastoral impulse toward leisure and freedom which also stimulates her imagination. Both motives exist in the novel: Silas works constantly yet he is in pastoral retreat. The convention of a toilless bower, popular in the pastoral genre, has perhaps been reversed. Yet it should be said that a holiday spirit of *pause* from work emerges from the novel as a whole. The lingering descriptions of the Rainbow dialogue and the Squire's party are especially memorable, and (interestingly) we see Silas, Eppie, and Aaron together not at work but on a Sunday afternoon or in the evening or on the day of the wedding. George Eliot's selection of such scenes contributes much to the novel's pastoralism.

For Silas work offers escape from pain. When he learns of the evil which had been visited upon him in Lantern Yard, "his first movement

[9] Leslie Stephen remarks of *Silas Marner* that "if we accept George Eliot's view, we have a kindly sympathy for the old order upon which she looked back so fondly. A modern 'realist' would, I suppose, complain that she had omitted, or touched too slightly for his taste, a great many repulsive and brutal elements in the rustic world. The portraits, indeed, are so vivid as to convince us of their fidelity; but she has selected the less ugly, and taken the point of view from which we see mainly what was wholesome and kindly in the little village community" (*George Eliot* [New York: Macmillan, 1902], p. 110).

after the shock had been to work in his loom. . . . He seemed to weave, like the spider, from pure impulse, without reflection. Every man's work, pursued steadily, tends in this way to become an end in itself, and so to bridge over the loveless chasms of his life" (pp. 22–23). Work is a dependable substitute for unpredictable affection. It offers a "refuge from benumbing unbelief" and gives purpose to life when human affection fails. Once Silas discovers that his money has been stolen by an intruder, he "tottered towards his loom, and got into the seat where he worked, instinctively seeking this as the strongest assurance of reality" (pp. 64–65). In both instances of loss, he turns to the loom "instinctively," "from pure impulse, without reflection," as a natural method of giving order to mental turmoil. Work functions as salvation from psychological distress. As in Hardy's novels, work is therapeutic, a means of reorienting oneself to the world, of prolonging life and assuring survival. If not pursued as an end in itself, work has the force of a moral imperative because it sustains emotional adjustment. When Silas has grown old, Godfrey Cass says to him:

> ". . . you've been a hard-working man all you life."
> "Yes, sir, yes," said Marner, meditatively. "I should ha' been bad off without my work: it was what I held by when everything else was gone from me." [P. 250]

But in *Silas Marner* work functions as more than therapy to relieve distress. Work offers a standard of value in the novel. The characters who are admired are industrious, are "the laboring people." This positive standard of work, by which the characters of the novel are appraised, can be recognized most clearly in Eppie's choice of Marner over Godfrey and Nancy Cass: " 'I can't think o' no other home. I wasn't brought up to be a lady, and I can't turn my mind to it. I like the working-folks, and their victuals, and their ways. And . . . I'm promised to marry a workingman, as'll live with father, and help me to take care of him' " (p. 259). From Mrs. Cass herself we learn that Aaron Winthrop, whom Eppie has promised to marry, is "very sober and industrious." We discover, on the other hand, that the characters drowned in idleness are either unhappy with themselves, such as Squire Cass, or are reclaimed by nature, such as Dunstan and Molly Cass. "Raveloe was not a place where moral censure was severe, but it was thought a weakness in the Squire that he had kept all his sons at home in idleness" (p. 34). Idleness, then, cannot be equated with pastoral *otium*. In *Silas Marner* idleness sows the seeds of death. Even Molly Cass is similarly afflicted with a variant of indolence: "she was enslaved, body and soul," to opium. Her enslavement, like Dunsey's to gambling and alcohol, draws her gradually into torpor. Thus when she sets out on her journey to the Red House, we learn that she had "lingered on the road, inclined by her indolence" (p. 165), and in a matter of hours death comes. In the terms of the novel, productive characters tend not to be specifically reclaimed by the forces of nature. The system of value created by the admired characters is inversely reinforced by the unadmired characters.

If the rural world of Raveloe is not identical to the world created by traditional pastoral, it nonetheless exhibits many elements of that world. The village of Raveloe is most clearly pastoral in its self-sufficiency and in its circumscribed geographical location. Because a circumscribed rural world is distant from the forces of upheaval, pastoral literature has long argued that contentment and peace of mind can best be pursued by escaping the ambition of city life and discovering a pastoral haven. In pastoral a circumscribed world often becomes a spiritual landscape, an imaginary world that expresses unfulfilled aspirations and images of rare beauty, a selection and thus a simplification of complex adult reality. In *Silas Marner* the rigorous and economical selection of details—the omission of minute descriptions of the ordinary villager and his daily life, descriptions we find in *Adam Bede*—makes a full portrait of Raveloe impossible. The details in *Silas Marner* usually focus on either the unusual or the communal: on Silas or the Casses; or on the local tavern or a festive party or the church or a wedding. To the degree that such a focus is a simplification, with the full reality of Raveloe supplied in the margins, by exposition, Raveloe represents a circumscribed pastoral world, hidden and aloof equally from political concerns or from the economic realities of buying and selling goods.

We learn immediately that "Raveloe was a village where many of the old echoes lingered, undrowned by new voices" and that "it was nestled in a snug well-wooded hollow, quite an hour's journey on horseback from any turnpike, where it was never reached by the vibrations of a coach-horn, or of public opinion" (p. 7). Entirely unlike Lantern Yard, Raveloe is a "low, wooded region, where [Silas] felt hidden even from the heavens by the screening trees and hedgerows. There was nothing here, when he rose in the deep morning quiet and looked out on the dewy brambles and rank tufted grass, that seemed to have any relation with that life centring in Lantern Yard" (pp. 20–21). The cumulative suggestions of a circumscribed, isolated world solidify when we learn later that "Raveloe lay low among the bushy trees and the rutted lanes, aloof from the currents of industrial energy and Puritan earnestness" (p. 33). Because Raveloe is hidden and enclosed, the two mutually exclusive geographical areas symbolize two opposed orders of experience—Raveloe leading ultimately to expanded and sensitive awareness of the moral worth of human relationships and especially of love as a redeeming force, Lantern Yard leading to a contraction of feeling into mechanical and centripetal activity. We find in Raveloe a pastoral (or semipastoral) world sheltered by trees and isolated from the rapidly changing industrial world outside, a pastoral world in which nature is bountiful to the point of "neglected plenty." Raveloe is not only "low" and hidden among the trees, but also low in its aspirations. It is an isolated agricultural village, not unlike the bowers of traditional pastoral in which the search for equilibrium and contentment seems uppermost. We are asked to discover this equilibrium not in shepherds playing their pipes or in amoebean song contests, but in festivity and work, Sunday services and neighborly companionship—in those regions of experience that draw out the fullest emotional response from both Silas and the narrator. Once the circumscribed pastoral world has become geographically precise, the mixture of communal *and* Hesiodic *and* purely pastoral elements is greatly enriched.

The correlation between isolation and lack of strife[10] is reinforced by the location of Silas' cottage at the Stone-pits. His cottage lies up a "lonely sheltered lane" so that there is a double isolation in the novel. Raveloe is sheltered from the world, and within this isolation, Silas' stone cottage is remote from the village. George Eliot explains that "the tender and peculiar love with which Silas had reared [Eppie] in almost inseparable companionship with himself" had been aided by "the seclusion of their dwelling" (pp. 218–19) and by their limited means of mobility. As long as human ties are not severed, the novel suggests that seclusion from the urban world closely corresponds to peace and happiness.

There is yet another technique that George Eliot uses skillfully to create a circumscribed pastoral world: the use of interlocking scenes rather than a straight or flat narrative line. When one character leaves for another character's home, the reader is shifted immediately to the character about to be visited, and is immersed in the action occurring there. The visiting character then arrives in the midst of that action. Though chronological time is actually preserved, the rhetorical effect is one of repeated backtracking or reversion. When Silas, for instance, leaves his cottage and sets out for the Rainbow tavern to tell of the robbery, we immediately shift to the jocular conversation within the Rainbow. Then after what seems a considerable lapse of time (because

[10] It is notable that although England is engaged in a war during the time of most of the novel, the inhabitants of Raveloe show little awareness of war. Instead, the militaristic backdrop emphasizes, by contrast, the remoteness and peaceful isolation of the village.

of the lengthy conversations), Silas at last reaches the Rainbow with his story. Again, when Silas discovers Eppie asleep on his hearth, the narrator shifts to the Red House to participate fully in the New Year's Eve festivities. As in the previous example, a considerable amount of time appears to elapse before Silas arrives at the Red House with the newly discovered child. Though the scenes technically observe chronological time, the effect is one of turning back the clock and of forming what we might call "loops" in the plot of the novel. Through the use of this technique, the rural world appears to be more tightly knitted than if the narrative had followed a single character—Silas, for example— without turning first to his destination in order to prepare the background for the scene. The use of this technique creates the sense of a tightly ordered past and, more important, the sense of turning constantly back into the past, as if to recover the Golden Age.

In addition to topographical location and narrative loops, the frequent mention of a rooted traditional past—a concern always important when traditional values are crumbling—contributes importantly to George Eliot's creation of a circumscribed pastoral world. In *Silas Marner* occur frequent suggestions of the continuity between past and present, and of the remoteness necessary to foster this continuity. The motif of remoteness and insulation sounds, we have seen, in the opening paragraphs of the novel. We are placed at once in "that far-off time [when] superstition clung easily round every person or thing that was at all unwonted." The peasants are "peasants of old times" (p. 4). The reader is placed at a great distance from the present, and this distance creates a strong sense of the remoteness of Raveloe, enabling the reader more easily (by means of this detachment) to compare small things to great. George Eliot's world is insulated both in time and in space.

When Silas, like romance heroes, escapes Lantern Yard to come to Raveloe, it seems fitting that he suffer discontinuity with his past. He has abandoned the world of unrest. After he settles in Raveloe, even searching for the once familiar herbs "belonged to the past, from which his life had shrunk away" (p. 31). But gradually Silas adjusts by means of human love to the new social order, and his life becomes "blent . . . with the life of his neighbors." The coming of Eppie assures his acceptance into the community because she forces him to seek out his neighbors for aid and advice. He breaks with his personal past in order to incorporate himself into the agricultural past, whose location and traditions have remained constant for centuries. Such a break signals a supreme gesture of conservatism because the rooted past absorbs a splintered fragment of the deracinated present. Silas travels "backward" in time in order to recover security and peace. It is what we might call a pastoral journey, since the pastoral novel locates value in isolated

rural regions of the past. Given enough time, Silas travels from disorder
into order, from disintegration into harmony and unity. Gradually, too,
he learns—as Hardy's villains never do—to connect past and present
through memory: "By seeking what was needful for Eppie, by sharing
the effect that everything produced on her, he had himself come to appropriate the forms of custom and belief which were the mould of
Raveloe life; and as, with re-awakening sensibilities, memory also reawakened, he had begun to ponder over the elements of his old faith,
and blend them with his new impressions, till he recovered a consciousness of unity between his past and present" (p. 213). Silas must come
to the rural world to recover this unity.

The repeated suggestions of a rooted past demonstrate George Eliot's
special concern for custom and village tradition. Custom and tradition
swell the circumscribed pastoral world, traditionally indeterminate,
with the pressures of history, so that pastoral and history merge. What
happens here, I think, happens in the pastoral novel as a whole. The
concern for tradition (part of the realistic framework intended for the
story) replaces the rigid song contest of the pastoral lyric or the elaborate disguises of the pastoral romance: tradition thus assumes the function of giving form to the characters' actions and verbal responses. The
repeated local gatherings, for example, lead the villagers—and the
narrator—to talk largely of communal and locally historical matters,
such as Mr. Macey's much-relished history of the Lammeter family or
the narrator's "vertical" description of the great dance; and Silas himself recovers his memory of past history as he recovers his ability to
verbalize his thoughts. Thus the most brilliant holiday celebration in
Raveloe was traditionally held at the Red House: "It was the great
dance on New Year's Eve that made the glory of Squire Cass's hospi-
tality, as of his forefathers', time out of mind" (pp. 133–34). When
Solomon Macey breaks with much spirit into the "Sir Roger de Cover-
ley," the couples "formed themselves for the dance, and the Squire led
off with Mrs Crackenthorp, joining hands with the rector and Mrs
Osgood. That was as it should be—that was what everybody had been
used to—and the charter of Raveloe seemed to be renewed by the
ceremony" (pp. 156–57). This renewal by ceremony, unlike the similar dance in *Daniel Deronda*, revitalizes orderly patterns of human
life, which confer upon Raveloe both stability and meaning. But such
age-old customs are expected in a family such as the Casses "that had
killed its own geese for many generations" (p. 134). And the doctor?
"Time out of mind the Raveloe doctor had been a Kimble; Kimble was
inherently a doctor's name" (p. 151).

Perhaps the most striking instance of inherited tradition occurs at
the conclusion of the novel. After Eppie's marriage to Aaron, we learn

that Silas and Eppie "had declared that they would rather stay at the Stone-pits than go to any new home" (p. 273). So alterations are made in the house to accommodate the larger family, thus preserving the domestic structure as well as the tradition of the family home. The new couple has no intention of leaving Raveloe for urban or industrial society. The decision to stay not only in Raveloe but in Silas' cottage as well is a triumph for tradition, for the rooted past and for its continuation, and anticipates the conservative plot resolutions of *Under the Greenwood Tree* and *Far from the Madding Crowd*. Earlier, Eppie had said to Silas: " 'But I don't want any change. . . . I should like to go on a long, long while, just as we are' " (p. 224). Although Aaron presses for change and although a marriage finally occurs, the marriage represents the least change possible while still ensuring the propagation of the rural community and the continuity of the domestic idyll. Because custom and tradition help to insulate Raveloe from change, the decision to remain at the Stone-pits is a symbol of triumph for humble rural life.

I said in an earlier chapter that city-country contrasts, the creation of a circumscribed pastoral world, and harmony between landscape and character were prime features of the pastoral novel. As it formed a convention of pastoral, nature was spontaneously bountiful, pastoral characters enjoyed a harmonious relationship with their natural rural surroundings, and the season was usually clement and positive. In *Silas Marner*, this attitude changes. Here, the pastoral characters continue to exist in harmony with nature, but the use of a spiritual landscape, which we find in Vergil and elsewhere, has in *Silas Marner* been barred. In a pastoral novel, dealing as it does with rural life, the uses of nature assume special significance because they offer us an index of the author's underlying view of the pastoral world he delineates and because the uses of nature help to illuminate the lives of the characters by showing their relationship to the natural world. In *Silas Marner* nature functions in several ways: to hide the pastoral community from the world beyond, to heighten its aesthetic qualities, to reclaim the characters who are indolent and morally corrupt, and to serve as a basis to which man can be compared in order to suggest his relationship to nature.

As we have seen, Raveloe is hidden in a snug and well-wooded hollow, hidden even from the sky by trees and hedgerows. Nature, in hiding Raveloe, also isolates the community from industrial infection, and the natural barriers of mountains and trees help to prevent urban invasion (Silas is the exception) and thus to preserve Raveloe's traditions and customs, its continuity with the past. If nature circumscribes with hills and dense trees, it also provides a setting of beauty for the pastoral world, an aesthetic context for human lives that would be impoverished if they were lived in "those barren parishes . . . inhabited by meagre sheep and thinly-scattered shepherds" (p. 6) to which the parish of Raveloe is contrasted. Eppie wants a flower garden for its beauty. She wants double daisies, and rosemary, bergamot, and thyme for their sweet fragrance. " 'It'll be a deal livelier at the Stone-pits,' " she remarks to Silas, " 'when we've got some flowers, for I always think the flowers can see us, and know what we're talking about' " (p. 209). After her marriage to Aaron, we learn that

> Eppie had a larger garden than she had ever expected there now. . . . The garden was fenced with stones on two sides, but in front there was an open fence, through which the flowers shone with answering gladness, as the four united people came within sight of them.
>
> "O father," said Eppie, "what a pretty home ours is! I think nobody could be happier than we are." [P. 273]

Though they will be accused of illustrating Ruskin's "pathetic fallacy," Eppie's personifications suggest a dialogue between man and nature. Nature actively participates in human life. Although the use of personification is unusual in George Eliot's early work, it suggests, as in the two instances above, a communication between man and nature that reinforces the unity and harmony characteristic of the pastoral world.

But beneath its outward beauty nature can also be indifferent or even malign, an idea which appears in embryonic form in George Eliot's early novels but which is not fully explored until it recurs in Hardy's fiction. Nature has therefore another function in the novel: to reclaim those who corrupt the pastoral community or bring suffering upon it. Before Dunstan is drowned in the stone pit, he boasts (ironically) to Godfrey, " 'I'm always lucky in my weather' " (p. 43). But after Dunstan has sold Wildfire, Dunstan rides the animal in a hunt and then into a sharpened stake, killing it. As he walks home, the narrow rutted lane grows slippery, with the mist "passing into rain." After he enters Silas' cottage and steals the gold, "the rain and darkness had got thicker, and he was glad of it. . . . So he stepped forward into the darkness" (p. 59). It is darkness that nature sets down over him like a veil, and darkness that the accumulated rain in the stone pit soon brings to Dunstan's consciousness as he drowns. When Silas returns to the cottage and discovers the robbery, he rushes to the door and pulls it open: "the rain beat in upon him, for it was falling more and more heavily. There were no footsteps to be tracked on such a night" (p. 65). "The rain had washed away all possibility of distinguishing foot-marks" (p. 91). Thus the natural world rapidly obliterates the physical traces of human evil.

Nature has obliterated Dunstan's tracks, then absorbed his body into its body. Nature has buried both Dunstan and the corrupting gold at the bottom of the pit, and has, as it were, attempted to restore pastoral innocence to Raveloe. As in Hardy's novels, nature assumes an active moral role. Thus Dunstan's journey, which began in insolent jest, gathers evil as it progresses, an evil mirrored in the natural world by the increasing darkness which reaches its height of intensity in the ulti-mate form of darkness—death. Nature, it would seem, has (in terms of the novel) a conscious mind which can initiate the reclamation process whenever that process is required to restore innocence to the pastoral community.[11]

Molly's death is similar. When she sets out for the Red House to expose Godfrey as her husband and as father of her child, snow begins to fall. The snow-covered lanes of Raveloe slow her journey and weaken her spirit. But opium offers comfort against snow and freezing wind. Wearily, she "sank down against a straggling furze bush, an easy pillow enough; and the bed of snow, too, was soft. She did not feel that the bed was cold, and did not heed whether the child would wake and cry for her" (p. 166). Death follows gently but quickly; her conscious-ness, like Dunstan's, is gradually absorbed into the earth, both of them lying against the earth's surface to die. When Silas reaches her, a natural burial has already begun, "with the head sunk low in the furze, and half-covered with the shaken snow" (p. 172).

Significantly, Molly sets out on her journey on New Year's Eve to complete "a premeditated act of vengeance." The natural world has completed its annual autumn death; and it brings an end, as well, to the evil forces that operate even in George Eliot's pastoral world. Thus the new year will begin in pristine freshness. The snow which covers Molly as she dies is "virgin snow." Later, Molly's death is explicitly related to the death of nature when George Eliot remarks, "the unwept death . . . seemed as trivial as the summer-shed leaf" (p. 184). In the old year, vengeance is reclaimed and buried, but a new life takes firm hold when Eppie wanders into Silas' cottage just as the new year bursts into existence. The snow had stopped falling, and the stars had come out in the sky in order for Eppie to find her way to Silas' cottage. The sugges-tion of a moral cycle is clear enough, and this suggestion indicates a renewal of the goodness, rather than the evil, of the world. At the same time that evil is destroyed in Dunstan and Molly, Eppie's "rebirth" brings happiness to Silas, who in turn is reoriented by his pastoral ex-periences and then fully absorbed into the community. The novel reas-

[11] Surprisingly, it is not so clearly Dunstan's *character* (as so often in George Eliot's work) which brings about his death and burial as it is a semiconscious force of nature—a force which anticipates the use of fate in Hardy's novels.

serts order and peace in the pastoral world and shows, in the marriage of Eppie and Aaron and in the purposeful workings of nature, the possibilities for renewal of pastoral happiness.

As Hardy pairs Fitzpiers and Mrs. Charmond in *The Woodlanders*, George Eliot skillfully joins Dunstan and Molly in the reader's mind by employing landscape to reflect character, even though this technique, used very frequently in pastoral, applies (in this case) negatively to unadmired characters. Dunstan and Molly are unacquainted companions in evil. Both follow the same physical and psychological path toward decease. Indolent yet momentarily swollen with vengeance, they walk slowly along the narrow Raveloe lanes. Before they reach their common destination of the Red House, they both run off the road near Marner's cottage. Within a short time, both die accidental deaths of drowning or freezing. In both cases George Eliot satisfyingly surrounds Dunstan and Molly with unfavorable weather conditions, the fog and rain and snow externalizing the moral blindness of both, so that landscape and character harmonize in just the way they do when, conversely, "the sunshine fell more warmly than usual" on the day of Eppie's wedding.

Nature, agent of beauty and a moral force, serves also as a basis of comparison for the separate human world. The kinship between man and nature finds continual expression in the novel. Yet seldom is nature visualized in terms of man because George Eliot, like Theocritus, did not imaginatively conceive of nature as subject to the ambiguities and complexities of human nature. Instead nature is used as the vehicle rather than the tenor of most figures. The process is frequently reductive. Man is reduced to the stature of lower forms because he is shown, through comparison, to be in some way *like* plants and animals. Although George Eliot's use of similes can be satirical and pejorative, still the closer man is reduced to the natural world, the more natural and instinctive he appears in terms of the novel. And provided he maintains communication with his fellow men, the more natural and instinctive he becomes, the happier he becomes since his actions are less complex and difficult. Frequently, for example, Silas Marner is characterized by animal and insect imagery. He is compared to a deer, a spider, an insect, a spinning insect, an ant, a calf, a toad, a rabbit, and a dog. All of these comparisons occur however in the first half of the novel, when Silas abandons the urban world to seek "an out-of-the-way country place." Because he breaks so sharply and unequivocally with his fellow man—even after he comes to Raveloe—George Eliot suggests through the imagery that he is reduced, in the first half of the novel, to the simple, mechanical existence of an animal or insect. She shows the reductive process actually occurring in Silas' life. After his flight from the industrial city, his adjustment to a new kind of life is at first like an animal's adjustment. Working without thought, he eats and sleeps instinctively: "He seemed to weave, like the spider, from pure impulse, without reflection." Hunger and routine chores help, along with weaving, "to reduce his life to the unquestioning activity of a spinning insect" (p. 23). When Eppie is sent to Silas, however, he is redeemed, comes into harmony with himself, and finds again his place among his fellow men. In the second half of the novel, then, the animal-insect imagery is gradually replaced by a sense of the communication and interdependence between man and nature. As Silas is gradually assimilated into the rural world, the texture of the novel becomes highly pastoral: "And when the sunshine grew strong and lasting, so that the buttercups were thick in the meadows, Silas might be seen in the sunny mid-day, or in the late afternoon when the shadows were lengthening under the hedgerows, strolling out with uncovered head to carry Eppie beyond the Stone-pits to where the flowers grew, till they reached some favorite bank where he could sit down, while Eppie toddled to pluck the flowers, and make remarks to the winged things that murmured happily above the bright petals" (p. 193). The reductive animal and insect imagery modulates finally into harmony and interpenetration among the flowers, the insects and birds, and humanity. The passage firmly establishes a dialogue between man and the animate world. The winged things murmur happily to Eppie; she and Silas listen for "some sudden bird-note"; and the total environment converges into an equilibrium full of pastoral charm.

In order to see how George Eliot creates a pastoral world in *Silas Marner*, it may be illuminating to examine a passage from the novel in which pastoral elements are unequivocally at work. Though the passage is perhaps representative only of the later part of the novel, when Silas has lost his antipastoral love of money, it indicates the direction toward which the novel tends as Silas, alienated and urban, gradually joins the rural order. The following scene, much like a tableau, occurs as Silas and Eppie depart from the old Raveloe Church on Sunday morning.

"I wish *we* had a little garden, father, with double daisies in, like Mrs. Winthrop's," said Eppie, when they were out in the lane; "only they say it 'ud take a deal of digging and bringing fresh soil—and you couldn't do that, could you father? Anyhow, I shouldn't like you to do it, for it 'ud be too hard work for you."

"Yes, I could do it, child, if you want a bit o' garden: these long evenings, I could work at taking in a little bit o' the waste, just enough for a root or two o' flowers for you; and again, i' the morning, I could have a turn wi' the spade before I sat down to the loom. Why didn't you tell me before as you wanted a bit o' garden?"

"*I* can dig it for you, Master Marner," said the young man in fustian, who was now by Eppie's side, entering into the conversation without the trouble of formalities. "It'll be play to me after I've done my day's work, or any odd bits o' time when the work's slack.

. . . . .

"There, now, father, you won't work in it till it's all easy," said Eppie, "and you and me can mark out the beds, and make holes and plant the roots. It'll be a deal livelier at the Stone-pits when we've got some flowers, for I always think the flowers can see us and know what we're talking about. And I'll have a bit o' rosemary, and bergamot, and thyme, because they're so sweet-smelling; but there's no lavender only in the gentlefolks' gardens, I think."

"That's no reason why you shouldn't have some," said Aaron, "for I can bring you slips of anything; I'm forced to cut no end of 'em when I'm gardening, and I throw 'em away mostly. . . . there's never a garden in all the parish but what there's endless waste in it for want o' somebody as could use everything up.

When Aaron turned back up the village, Silas and Eppie went on up their lonely sheltered lane:

Eppie was now aware that her behaviour was under observation, but it was only the observation of a friendly donkey, browsing with a log fastened to his foot—a meek donkey, not scornfully critical of human trivialities, but thankful to share in them, if possible, by getting his nose scratched; and Eppie did not fail to gratify him with her usual notice, though it was attended with the inconvenience of his following them, painfully, up to the very door of their home.

But the sound of a sharp bark inside, as Eppie put the key in the door, modified the donkey's views, and he limped away again without bidding. The sharp bark was the sign of an excited welcome that was awaiting them from a knowing terrier, who, after dancing at their legs in a hysterical manner, rushed with a worrying noise at a tortoise-shell kitten under the loom, and then rushed back with a sharp bark again, as much as to say, "I have done my duty by this feeble creature, you perceive"; while the lady-mother of the kitten sat sunning her white bosom in the window, and looked round with a sleepy air of expecting caresses, though she was not going to take any trouble for them.

. . . . .

Silas sat down now and watched Eppie with a satisfied gaze as she spread the clean cloth, and set on it the potato-pie. . . .

Silas ate his dinner more silently than usual, soon laying down his knife and fork, and watching half-abstractedly Eppie's play with Snap and the cat, by which her own dining was made rather a lengthy business. Yet it was a sight that might well arrest wandering thoughts: Eppie, with the rippling radiance of her hair and the whiteness of her rounded chin and throat set off by the dark-blue cotton gown, laughing merrily as the kitten held on with her four claws to one shoulder, like a design for a jug-handle, while Snap on the right hand and Puss on the other put up their paws towards a morsel which she held out of the reach of both—Snap occasionally desisting in order to remonstrate with the cat by a cogent worrying growl on the greediness and futility of her conduct; till Eppie relented, caressed them both, and divided the morsel between them. [Pp. 207–12]

This is a highly pastoral scene. In creating a domestic idyll, George Eliot is concerned to show the pastoral simplicity and freedom, the humor and the leisure, of the humble rustic life at the Stone-pits. Together, the garden and the isolated cottage replace the bower of traditional pastoral; and work is conceived not as the peasant's hard task but as pleasurable. The scene reminds us of the Poysers on their way to church, illustrating as they go the interdependence of plant, animal, and human worlds, or of Giles and Marty planting trees in *The Woodlanders*. Here, with flowers and animals as companions, Silas and Eppie reveal similarly the essential unity of various levels of life.

The scene opens with discussion of a garden. Yet the garden is not to be the vegetable garden we might expect in a rural area but a flower garden, catalogued in pastoral fashion, that will provide touches of beauty. As in portraits of the Golden Age—Vergil's in the fourth eclogue, e.g.—nature is exuberantly fertile in Raveloe, and parish gardens bear profusely. In its natural wealth, its innocence, and its harmony between man and nature, Raveloe is like Hayslope and other circumscribed pastoral regions—Mellstock in *Under the Greenwood Tree*, Weatherbury in *Far from the Madding Crowd*, Little Hintock in *The Woodlanders*, Nethermere in *The White Peacock*, and Wragby Wood in *Lady Chatterley's Lover*.

Yet unlike the leisure of traditional pastoral, work is required to tend this abundant natural growth. In traditional pastoral the earth produces spontaneously: no gardening is needed. But there is little *otium* implied in this scene, for rich topsoil must be hauled, the ground spaded and raked, the flower beds made, the holes dug, and the new slips planted and watered. Yet such work is not arduous or dreaded; rather, Eppie and Aaron and Silas work willingly to prepare the garden. "It'll be play to me after I've done my day's work," remarks Aaron. To the pastoral characters, work is not task but pleasure, and this fact calls into question the rigid distinction between work and *otium* usually insisted on by theorists of pastoral, for work offers satisfactions similar to those offered by leisure. Working with the soil is praised by George Eliot, as it is by Hardy and Lawrence after her, because it results in the creation of beauty, the meaningful use of time, and direct communion with the natural world. In *Silas Marner*, as in traditional pastoral, the aesthetic triumphs over the utilitarianism of the georgic.

The close relationship between the pastoral characters and the natural world is again made clear when Silas and Eppie, on the way up their sheltered lane, meet the donkey. Not only does Eppie gratify him with her usual notice, but the donkey appears to understand humanity. In an unusual attribution, the donkey possesses the human power of thought and emotion, and is not scornful but thankful to share in human trivialities. We do not see the donkey as a beast of burden but as a participant in human activity. Like the flowers, the donkey seems to understand his surroundings. Although the suggestion of animal and plant perception is sentimental, it has the effect of narrowing the normal distance between the human world and the animal-and-plant world beneath it. This narrowing creates an intimacy between the pastoral characters and their environment, a correlation between spiritual and physical, that is typically pastoral. This narrowing process sustains the intimacy between man and nature that underlies George Eliot's treatment, analyzed earlier, of the deaths of Dunstan and Molly.

As Silas and Eppie approach the door of the cottage, the interaction between animal and human continues. The brown terrier, a "knowing" terrier, almost speaks to Silas and Eppie. The kitten's mother, a "lady," expects caresses; but as though capable of deliberate thought, she disdains to seek them. Later, Snap remonstrates the cat "on the greediness and futility of her conduct." The enlarging or "additive" process clearly at work here reverses the reductive process that prevails in the early part of the novel. The animals, because they are like humans, seem more significant than ordinary animals. They are, instead, communicating companions, like animals in Theocritus and Vergil; as a result the emphasis falls on the high degree of satisfying communication between the human and animal worlds.[12] The agent of this communication is Eppie, who has helped Silas to seek assimilation into the rural order and who has "come to link him once more with the whole world. There was love between him and the child that blent them into one, and there was love between the child and the world—from men and women with parental looks and tones, to the red lady-birds and the round pebbles" (p. 200). What flashes forth in the scene as a whole is the unity and harmony of life at the Stone-pits. This life is symbolic of the larger life of the village itself, excluding only the Cass family, which is openly acknowledged to be atypical. The Casses possess wealth along with the

---

[12] In *The Green Cabinet* (Berkeley and Los Angeles: Univ. of California Press, 1969), Thomas G. Rosenmeyer remarks (p. 138) that animals in pastoral are typically companions. They help man adjust to a larger natural environment.

complexities and problems that wealth brings, and are for this reason nonpastoral. The only threat to the equilibrium of the pastoral community arises from the turbulence and disorder engendered by those who are neither humble nor poor. Silas and Eppie and Aaron and the other humble characters in the novel have little money, and Silas spends little of what he earns. Unlike the Squire and his sons, they are neither wealthy nor idle nor proud. Their unwillingness to aspire for wealth and position leads them toward innocence and happiness, as it did pastoral shepherds of old. Searching not for power or fame, they reject ambition. " 'I don't think I shall want anything else when we've got a little garden,' " Eppie says, and the narrator remarks: "people in humble stations" are often happier "than those brought up in luxury" (p. 202).

In pastoral literature a concern with the role of luxury, or money, has always been of underlying interest as one ingredient in the dialectic between city and country. Silas moves from a nonpastoral to a pastoral condition with the loss of his money, and when Godfrey Cass grows penitent near the end of the novel, we discover that the old Squire's inheritance has been divided among his several sons. Thus within the moral structure of the novel, loss or lack of money is equated with happiness. The inverse relationship between money (or property) and happiness is of course central to the pastoral ideal. In one sense George Eliot offers a rejection of the Victorian preoccupation with money and materialism that we find in Dickens, Thackeray, or Gissing by looking to the agricultural past in which solid relationships with family and the natural world counted for more than power or money. Such an insular world, if inarticulately perceived by the rustic mind, was yet intelligible. The failure to sustain the traditional agricultural way of life has, in the twentieth century, showed only more clearly its virtues, virtues nostalgically re-created in *Silas Marner*. If today the novel seems almost as slight as Hardy's *Under the Greenwood Tree*, it is because nostalgia for the traditional past brings more charm than piercing analysis to the artistic treatment of human life. Yet the intelligence and insights of *Silas Marner* are easily underrated. In *Daniel Deronda* or *Middlemarch*, George Eliot, moving closer to the present, saw rootedness disappear, as did Hardy in his novels of the 1890s. But those novels, all of them philosophically weightier, are animated much less fully by the pastoral ideal and so sacrifice the subtle art by which charm, saved from sweetness by realistic details, is made permanently interesting. *Under the Greenwood Tree* well sustains the charm and artistry of *Silas Marner*, but in its substitution of humor for analysis, Hardy's novel comes much closer to the achievement typical of the pastoral tradition.

Chapter 5

Under the Greenwood Tree
"Music, Dancing, and the
Singing of Songs"

BY 1840, when Thomas Hardy was born in Higher Bockhampton, Dorset, the industrialization that Eppie saw in Lantern Yard had progressed with vigor. But in the Dorset of Hardy's youth, the agricultural community, despite its low wages and poverty, seemed richly satisfying and permanent. As a child Hardy came to the conclusion that he wanted "to remain as he was, in the same spot, and to know no more people than he already knew"[1] Similarly, Hardy's father, established in the family home, refused to migrate to another area even when relocation would have served his economic interests. Often accompanied by his father and his uncle, Hardy regularly offered the rural community his musical talent at weddings, christenings, and parties—always without charge. But the coming of the railroad in the 1850s began to efface the familiar patterns and customs. A harvest home that Hardy watched as a child "was among the last at which the old traditional ballads were sung, the railway having been extended to Dorchester just then, and the orally transmitted ditties of centuries being slain at a stroke by the London comic songs that were introduced" (*Life*, p. 20). In 1862 Hardy himself, like George Eliot earlier, migrated to London to continue his study of architecture, "getting immersed in London life" (*Life*, p. 41). His emotional commitment to the rural world, however, was very powerful, and in 1867 he returned to Dorset to "go into the country altogether" (*Life*, p. 53). His return "completely restored" his health, which had deteriorated in the city, but he traveled back to his parents' home "with very different ideas of things." He perceived then that contrasting experiences of city and country "seemed to afford him abundant material" for fiction (*Life*, p. 56). Shortly afterward he witnessed the severe agricultural depression of 1874–79 (and at intervals thereafter), attended by the consequent and regrettable migration of agricultural laborers and their families. "The schoolmaster was leaving the village, and everybody seemed sorry," begins *Jude the*

---

[1] Florence Emily Hardy, *The Life of Thomas Hardy* (New York: St. Martin's, 1965), p. 16. Further references to this work have been placed in the text.

Obscure. The number of laborers in England and Wales declined from well over a million in 1871, when Hardy began his first pastoral novel, to less than three-quarters of a million in 1901, shortly after he had abandoned fiction.[2] Hardy's youthful attachment to country people and country ways, his subsequent experience of a different and less appealing mode of life (a "mechanical and monotonous existence" he called it— *Life*, p. 56), coupled with his great love of Vergil and Shakespeare and poetry—all of these forces guided Hardy toward the pastoral novel. The spectacle of a slowly depopulating countryside and the philosophical effects of a Darwinian view of nature, however, reduced the potential for pastoral: such pressures damaged the pastoral ideal of benevolent nature and "community" to which Hardy was powerfully drawn even though they simultaneously intensified his nostalgia for a dying culture. *The Woodlanders*, in particular, while still remaining a pastoral novel, measures the extent to which Hardy's conception of pastoral was damaged by changing social, economic, and philosophical conditions.

Under the Greenwood Tree (1872) is above all a work of fiction that can profitably be studied as a pastoral novel. Although realistic details frequent its pages, the novel praises rural life in lyrical tones and maintains a nostalgic quality. Its peasants are stylized and charming, and its love story peaceful and idyllic. Set in the past, its world proves self-sufficient and relatively isolated from urban culture. To be sure, critics have not been reluctant to use the term *pastoral*, although they have not discussed the pastoralism of the novel in any sustained fashion. Irving Howe, for example, calls *Under the Greenwood Tree* "a pastoral or prose idyll of English country life."[3] Walter Allen sees the novel as a "delightful pastoral," and Richard C. Carpenter observes that in *Under the Greenwood Tree* "the pastoral atmosphere is maintained with complete consistency."[4] The purpose of this essay is to examine *Under the Greenwood Tree* as a pastoral novel: to reveal its relationship to traditional pastoral—especially *As You Like It*—and, more important, to analyze in depth the qualities that create its pastoral atmosphere.

In Thomas Hardy's novels the pastoral impulse manifests itself not

[2] See Merryn Williams, *Thomas Hardy and Rural England* (London: Macmillan, 1972), ch. 1, on the migration of agricultural laborers.

[3] *Thomas Hardy* (London: Weidenfeld & Nicolson, 1968), p. 45.

[4] Allen, *The English Novel* (New York: Dutton, 1954), p. 289; Carpenter, *Thomas Hardy* (New York: Twain, 1964), p. 47. Lord David Cecil calls the novel a "pastoral idyll" in *Hardy the Novelist* (2d ed. [London: Constable, 1954], p. 26).

only in *Under the Greenwood Tree* but in *Far from the Madding Crowd* and *The Woodlanders*. These novels are pastoral because they reveal a sharp rural-urban or simplicity-complexity contrast, a rural perspective on urban life, intense nostalgia for a Golden-Age past, a withdrawal from sophistication and industrialization that implies criticism, patient creation of a pastoral world, and, altering tradition, a sympathetic realism that achieves verisimilitude yet softens rural coarseness to make country life palatable to urban society. Recent criticism, having broadened the term *pastoral* to include certain eighteenth- and nineteenth-century novels, has encouraged us to take a fresh look at some neglected rural fiction and to revaluate its merits.[5]

Irving Howe has commented that major novelists like Balzac, Faulkner, and Hardy—we might add Dickens, Thackeray, and Lawrence to the list—require the image of a simpler past in order to make explicit their criticism of contemporary society. Defining Hardy's pastoral fiction as a recollection of country life by a man stationed at some remove from the life he describes, Howe remarks:

> Pastoral has usually been the product of a high culture turning away from a surfeit of experience and, through a posture of simplicity, seeking to regain essential truths. But Hardy's pastoral impulse is quite different: it does not involve a yoking together of literary sophistication and a stylized defense of peasant values. While neither an aristocratic poet stooping to a moment of purity nor an actual shepherd recalling the events of his past, Hardy is, if anything, somewhat closer to the shepherd than to the aristocratic poet; at the very least, he has known shepherds.[6]

This is a valuable statement, in particular because of the rarity of comments on pastoral fiction. The idea of judging the troubled present by the distant Golden-Age past and, thereby, of either implying or stating a criticism of life is one of the features both of Renaissance pastoral and of Hardy's pastoral fiction. For Hardy to evoke the collective experience of a rural past still warm and vivid implies his penchant for the Golden-Age criterion used in pastoral to judge sophisticated urban life.

Hardy's form of pastoral is not synonymous with traditional pastoral; and Howe is right to say that Hardy's version shuns the artificiality of conventional pastoral. In Hardy's pastoral novels we do not feel the self-conscious distancing of traditional pastoral. Starting with Wordsworth,

[5] See Robin Magowan, "Pastoral and the Art of Landscape in *The Country of the Pointed Firs*," *New England Quarterly*, 36 (1963), 229-40; Howard Anderson, "A Version of Pastoral: Class and Society in *Tristram Shandy*," *Studies in English Literature*, 7 (1967), 509-29; Joseph M. Duffy, Jr., "Another Version of Pastoral: *Oliver Twist*," *ELH*, 35 (1968), 403-21; Robert C. McLean, "*The Bostonians*: New England Pastoral," *Papers on Language and Literature*, 7 (1971), 374-81.

[6] *Thomas Hardy*, pp. 45-46.

realism has crept in during the nineteenth century to reduce considerably, but not entirely, the distance between the author and his peasant-
shepherd. The shepherd and his natural setting are taken literally rather
than figuratively. The change in traditional pastoral shows largely in
Hardy's ability to combine realistic situations and details with the pastoral impulse. Elements of pastoral, in other words, are not expected by
Hardy's audience; they are necessary to express the delicate balance that
Hardy maintains between his nostalgia for an unchanging culture of
genuine charm and his direct observation of real country people. Pastoral as convention has yielded to pastoral as artistic necessity, the kind
of necessity Theocritus felt when he inaugurated the genre. Although
its attitude toward the genre differs from typical Renaissance attitudes,
Hardy's novel succeeds superbly in recovering the pastoral atmosphere
of Shakespeare's Arden—its lyricism, its light humor, and its romantic
complication.

We find the first and most obvious connection between *Under the
Greenwood Tree* and traditional pastoral in the title of the novel. The
title comes from a song in Shakespeare's pastoral comedy *As You Like
It*. Amiens, attending the banished Duke, sings:

> Under the greenwood tree
> Who loves to lie with me,
> And turn his merry note
> Unto the sweet bird's throat,
> Come hither, come hither, come hither.
> Here shall he see
> No enemy
> But winter and rough weather.
>
> [II.v.1–8]

> Who doth ambition shun,
> And loves to live i' the sun,
> Seeking the food he eats,
> And pleased with what he gets,
> Come hither, come hither, come hither.
> Here shall he see
> No enemy
> But winter and rough weather.
>
> [II.v.39–46]

Shakespeare's song reflects a number of pastoral elements: the singing
of songs, the carefree life, the rejection of ambition, and the call to
escape into an idyllic world. Through Hardy's use of Shakespeare's
pastoral song, we can expect *Under the Greenwood Tree* to manifest a
kinship to other elements of traditional pastoral.

We enter the novel, as in *The Woodlanders*, through a dark and lonely lane, covered by branches of trees densely interlaced. The hamlet of Mellstock, lying in isolation outside the gates of the world, offers the image of seclusion fundamental to literature motivated by the pastoral impulse. Love dominates the novel as it dominates Renaissance pastoral drama, and complex love entanglements resolve into a festive wedding. Moreover, the dominant tone or mood of the novel is, like the mood of much pastoral drama, comic: ironic, wryly humorous, light-hearted, and affectionate.

But a strong undercurrent of elegiac feeling, first introduced into the pastoral mode by Vergil, also flows through the novel.[7] In *Under the Greenwood Tree* this feeling takes the form of regret for a changing agricultural order, of nostalgic sympathy for the Mellstock choir, and of fond details of rural culture. In his preface to the novel, Hardy strikes the appropriately elegiac note: "One is inclined to regret the displacement of these ecclesiastical bandsmen by an isolated organist" (p. vii).[8] This elegiac feeling is aroused by the tension, common to pastoral, between rural and urban life. In *Under the Greenwood Tree* tension springs also from the conflicts between new and old, between refinement and simplicity, between art and nature, which Hardy vividly embodies in the collision of the Mellstock choir with Mr. Maybold's fashionable new organ.

Like *Silas Marner* or *The Woodlanders*, the novel has two main plot strands—one embodying the collision of traditional and modern, and the other illustrating the tortuous path of romantic love. The love story comprises the second part of the novel; the choir and its activities make up the first. The Mellstock church choir has for centuries played and sung the music for the Sunday morning church service. On Christmas Eve it has made annual visits to all the families in the parish and has evolved into an important cultural institution in an area traditionally remote from urban influence. But with the death of the old vicar, young Vicar Maybold arrives in the hamlet of Mellstock to furnish spiritual leadership. At the same time Miss Fancy Day, a schoolteacher of high scholastic attainment and many new notions, comes to Mellstock. In a short while, not one but three men fall in love with Fancy, a girl clever, beautiful, and vain—and a coquette who relishes the attentions of all three suitors.

Dick Dewy, first to fall, is honest, simple, and faithful—a true country boy. Mr. Shiner is a wealthy farmer; and Mr. Maybold, last to make

---

[7] See Erwin Panofsky, "*Et in Arcadia Ego*: Poussin and the Elegiac Tradition," in *Meaning in the Visual Arts* (Garden City, N.Y.: Doubleday, 1955), pp. 299–304.

[8] Parenthetical page numbers refer to Thomas Hardy, *Under the Greenwood Tree*, Wessex Edition (London: Macmillan, 1912).

known his romantic inclinations, is an urban figure. The vicar's love for Fancy spurs him to think of installing her (with Mr. Shiner's urgent support) into the newly created position of church organist. The venerable choir is then given until Michaelmas to "make room for the next generation." Soon, Vicar Maybold proposes marriage to Fancy and she accepts, without of course telling him that she is already secretly engaged to Dick. Soon repenting her hasty answer, she retracts the acceptance. Mr. Shiner having been earlier rejected, the aisle is at last clear for Fancy and Dick. So they marry.

The conflicts evident in the novel, then, are those between tradition and innovation, simplicity and sophistication. Innovation encroaches on parish tradition in the double form of a new vicar and a new school-teacher. With them they bring "the inauguration of a new order of things" (p. 177). The vicar brings a zealous sense of duty and a new organ. Fancy brings not only her education and her musical training but fashionable styles and a disregard of tradition. She insists, for example, on wearing muslin to church and on curling her hair: " 'But I will . . . wear my curls!' " (p. 135). Caught between modernism and tradition, she finds her position uneasy. When Fancy inaugurates the organ music, she appears with curls and a feathered hat; but only bonnets had ever before appeared in Mellstock Church. By defying humble rural traditions, Fancy and Maybold arouse the conflicts in the novel and generate the tension necessary to give the novel interest and a meaningful resolution.

The immediate effect of the arrival of Fancy and Maybold is the displacement of the established choir. The clash is made poignantly clear when Michael Mail says to the choir, " 'People don't care much about us now! I've been thinking we must be almost the last left in the county of the old string players?' " (p. 24). The death of the old choir is indeed foreshadowed at the opening of the novel by the responses that Hardy records to the Christmas hymns sung by the choir. Annually the choir has faithfully made its rounds of the village, but the three responses that Hardy shows are either abnormally delayed (Fancy and Maybold) or angry and negative (Mr. Shiner). When Fancy has inaugurated the "new order" with her stylish apparel and new organ music, Hardy makes clear the view that we are to take toward the change: "The old choir, with humbled hearts, no longer took their seats in the gallery" but "stood and watched the curls of hair trailing down the back of the successful rival. . . . After a few timid notes and uncertain touches her playing became markedly correct, and towards the end full and free. But, whether from prejudice or unbiassed judgment, the venerable body of musicians could not help thinking that the simpler notes they had been wont to bring forth were more in keeping with the simplicity of their old church than the crowded chords and interludes it was her pleasure to produce" (pp. 177–78). The final tumid phrase "it was her pleasure to produce" is perfectly elevated to evoke the contrast between the organist and the established musicians. Through such phrases Hardy carefully controls our attitude toward his theme of tradition-versus-innovation.

A complementary conflict, demonstrating directly the pastoral tension between city and country, is the class conflict between Fancy's urban standards and Dick's traditional rural standards, which are openly preferred. In the same way that Bathsheba speaks of Gabriel and that Mr. Melbury speaks of Giles, Fancy's father speaks to her of " 'that penniless Dick o' thine' " who " 'isn't good enough for thee' " (p. 172). Fancy's thoughts are often similar. She cries to Dick: " 'I love you always; and those times when you look silly and don't seem quite good enough for me—just the same, I do, Dick!' " (p. 139). The urban standard she has adopted while away for her education motivates her dissatisfaction. As in the case of Grace Melbury in *The Woodlanders*, this standard has in part alienated Fancy from the rural simplicity of her father's cottage. In her letter of retraction, she writes to Maybold: " 'It is my nature—perhaps all women's—to love refinement of mind and manners; but even more than this, to be ever fascinated with the idea of surroundings more elegant and pleasing than those which have been customary. . . . Ambition and vanity they would be called; perhaps they are so' " (p. 189). *Refinement, elegant, ambition,* and *vanity*—these are the characteristic terms by which Hardy describes and evaluates the figures whose attachments are urban rather than rural. The qualities implied by these terms, though attractive, are openly opposed to the modesty, generosity, honesty, and faithfulness of Dick Dewy. This class conflict expresses itself most pointedly in Mr. Day's speech to Dick when Dick asks for the hand of Fancy: " 'I live in such a miserly way,' " he says, so that " 'if any gentlemen, who sees her to be his equal in polish, should want to marry her, and she want to marry him, he shan't be superior to her in pocket. Now do ye think after this that you be good enough for her?' " Dick modestly turns away, "wondering at his presumption in asking for a woman whom he had seen from the beginning to be so superior to him" (p. 164). The same protean situation recurs in *Far from the Madding Crowd* and *The Woodlanders*—the rejection of the rural world because it lacks money and education. The situation haunted Hardy. Yet the dialogue offers only two points of view, and neither is that of the implied author outside the novel. We discover the author's commentary near the conclusion when Hardy describes Fancy's eyes as "too refined and beautiful for a tranter's wife; *but, perhaps, not too good*" (p. 201; italics mine). Hardy implies the attitude, supported by the entire novel, that we are to take toward the rural-urban conflict: refinement improves the surface of life but decreases moral worth by imposing upon a character a seemingly false set of values. The pastoral mode (though at times ironically) tends always to place its faith in simplicity rather than complexity of character; in perspective, Hardy suggests, Fancy and Dick are equals.

Although the problem that the rural-urban conflict introduces is of course resolved in the marriage of Fancy and Dick, the wedding itself reveals best the pastoral tensions in the novel. Again Hardy controls our view through his diction so that our sympathies incline toward custom and tradition. (Hardy's subtlety becomes clearer if we contrast his approach to that of another novelist treating the same themes: in *The Bride of Lammermoor* Scott presents the clash between old and new in a heightened and melodramatic form, without hope of compromise.) Fancy insists that Dick dress in respectable clothes. Appropriately, he appears at the wedding in "a painfully new coat of shining cloth, primrose-coloured waistcoat, hat of the same painful style of newness," with hair cut to "an unwonted shortness" (pp. 200–201). Since the repetition of *painful* to describe newness is pejorative, Hardy guides us away from modernity. Through similar resonances in the novel, we come surely to accept Hardy's viewpoint and to favor, perhaps nostalgically, the traditional, the tried, the stable. Although rural life is invaded by refined urban standards, the tensions between rural and urban resolve largely within the confines of the rural world. The organ is introduced, but other customs remain intact. After the wedding, the tranter says:

"... we shall march two and two round the parish."
"Yes, sure," said Mr. Penny: "two and two: every man hitched up to his woman, 'a b'lieve."
"I never can make a show of myself in that way!" said Fancy, looking at Dick to ascertain if he could. . . .
"Respectable people don't nowadays," [added] Fancy. "Still, since poor mother did, I will." [Pp. 201–2]

The superficially respectable falls at the feet of custom and tradition, reflecting at least a partial triumph for rural stability. But after agreeing to the customary two-by-two promenade around the parish, Fancy balks again:

"The proper way is for the bridesmaids to walk together," suggested Fancy.
"What? 'Twas always young man and young woman, arm in crook, in my time!" said Geoffrey, astounded. [Pp. 203–4]

At last Fancy agrees to " 'have it the way mother had it' . . . and the couples moved along under the trees, every man to his maid" (p. 204).

Thus Fancy again reconciles herself to rural custom and is reabsorbed into the rural order. Stability is reestablished because the influence of the urban world has been resisted.

What is especially interesting, however, is the parallel between the pattern of alternating responses to Fancy's objections and the similar pattern in *As You Like It*, when the sojourners in Arden define "what 'tis to love" (V.ii.82–122). Silvius says, "It is to be made of sighs and tears; / And so am I for Phebe." Phebe replies, "And I for Ganymede." Orlando replies, "And I for Rosalind." And Rosalind replies, "And I for no woman." A similar pattern, of a statement followed by parallel replies, occurs three times more in the same scene. If Shakespeare's comic method is to pose statements around which cluster a series of responses, Hardy's method is to place an objection at the dramatic center of a scene, then to offer a series of rebuttals which dissolve the conflict. When Fancy objects that *she* cannot march around the parish, four parallel replies silence her objection:

> "Why, we did when we were married, didn't we, Ann?" said the tranter; "and so do everybody, my sonnies."
> "And so did we," said Fancy's father.
> "And so did Penny and I," said Mrs. Penny. . . .
> "And so did father and mother," said Miss Mercy Onmey. [Pp. 201–2]

A second objection, that properly the bridesmaids should walk to church together, arouses another chorus of parallel replies. Both Shakespeare's scene and Hardy's scene occur in relation to marriage ceremonies, either forthcoming or past; and both involve a group of celebrants. The matrimonial pairing of couples in Shakespeare's Arden—Orlando with Rosalind, Oliver with Celia, Phebe with Silvius, and Touchstone with Audrey—finds a clear counterpart in Hardy's coupling of Fancy and her father, followed by six other couples, all on their way to the marriage ceremony. Such parallels as these and others, along with the novel's title, are perhaps too striking to be coincidental, and suggest that *As You Like It* influenced the design of Hardy's novel.

When we move from the first half of the novel, dominated by the choir, to the second half, dominated by the love story, we move from one element to its apparent antithesis. The death of the choir balances the birth and growth of human love. Yet the two halves or plots of the novel, representing two separate themes, closely interconnect. The plot describing the choir shows definite change—the transformation of the old social order into the new; the plot developing the love story shows the absorption of the new social order into the old. Like Becky Sharp or Silas Marner or Grace Melbury, Fancy Day is the valence between two plots. The two plots in *Under the Greenwood Tree* assume the shape of two cones—one inverted and narrowing downward, the other uninverted and narrowing upward into closure. Because the sacrifice of the choir is antiphonally answered by the reabsorption of Fancy into the rural order, the two opposing changes complement and balance each other to give the novel structural stability and thematic coherence.

Since the vision of the pastoral genre reveals the harmony between man and his environment, one device in particular—the skilful use of nature and nature's cycles—helps to develop the respective themes of both halves or plots of the novel. Both halves begin in winter, with our entrance into Mellstock. Although the plot describing the fall of the choir is resolved on Michaelmas, evoking autumnal dissolution, the plot developing the love story begins also in winter but carries the action into spring, suggesting that the new life which love produces will survive. Hardy's use of the seasons functions to reinforce the two major themes: the death of the old, and the birth and survival of new love. The half of the novel charting the love that develops between Fancy and Dick is a simple story that runs a fairly straight course to marriage. Because it is so tightly fused with the rural year, the love story is impressively illuminated by the commentary that the natural world indirectly makes upon it, a commentary that illuminates at the same time that it guides our response to the characters and to the themes they develop.

Hardy extends the functional settings used by earlier Victorian novelists, Dickens or Trollope or George Eliot, by his manipulation of nature to define character. In addition to the thematic use of the seasons, nature indirectly comments on the love story through Hardy's use of the seasons as his structural design. He arranges the chapters of the novel into four parts: "Winter," "Spring," "Summer," and "Autumn," followed by a brief conclusion that embraces the spring wedding and its festivities under the greenwood tree. The love story mirrors this seasonal framework in much the same way that the love story of *Daphnis and Chloe* mirrors the cycle of the seasons. The growth of love between Fancy and Dick follows roughly a seasonal structure: in winter the conception and birth of love at the Dewys' Christmas party, in spring the growth of love, in summer the engagement between the lovers, in autumn the near-death of love when Fancy accepts the vicar's proposal, then in the following spring the marriage and birth of wedded love. Like the circular seasonal movement, the plot of the novel also follows a circular movement by following the various lovers—Dick, Mr. Shiner, Vicar Maybold, and Dick again—as they are attracted to and then rejected by the plot center, Fancy.

Hardy's use of weather—particularly the use of rain—shapes our response to the development of love with special effectiveness. The use of rain as commentary is concentrated in a single section of the novel— the section where Maybold proposes marriage to Fancy and where, to our surprise, she accepts his proposal. The chapter "Into Temptation," opening with an autumn rain, shows Fancy alone in the schoolroom, sitting upon a windowsill: "As the evening advanced here she perched herself, as was her custom on such wet and gloomy occasions, put on a light shawl and bonnet, opened the window, and looked out at the rain" (p. 179). Dick arrives, then leaves. Shortly Maybold appears in the rain under an umbrella "of superior silk" and then offers marriage. Just before Fancy's affirmative reply, there is a "surging of the rain against the window-panes, and then Fancy spoke, in a faint and broken voice" (p. 183). The rain hammers out a vicarious groan and foreshadows the effects that Fancy's imminent reply will bring. If it is reading too much into the scene to say that nature sheds tears for her hero Dick, we might still with justice say that the rain almost succeeds in drowning out Fancy's unfaithful words.

The next day Maybold writes a letter to his friend in Yorkshire, accepting an offer of an exchange of livings. Maybold wants to leave Mellstock (" 'Of course we would not live here, Fancy' ") because he has no rooted attachment to the village. As he departs on foot to post the letter, the rain continues in a different form: "It was a foggy morning, and the trees shed . . . noisy water-drops" (p. 185). When he learns from Dick of Fancy's earlier commitment, he stops—bewildered—on the bridge and is again associated with water imagery:

He saw—without heeding—how the water came rapidly from beneath the arches, glided down a little steep, then spread itself over a pool in which dace, trout, and minnows sported at ease among the long green locks of weed that lay heaving and sinking with their roots towards the current. At the end of ten minutes spent leaning thus he drew from his pocket the letter to his friend, tore it deliberately into such minute fragments that scarcely two syllables remained in juxtaposition, and sent the whole handful of shreds fluttering into the water. Here he watched them eddy, dart, and turn, as they . . . gradually disappeared from his view. [Pp. 187–88]

The heaving and sinking of the green locks of weed image the vicar's own current of feelings—feelings that are washed away in the form of minute fragments of a letter. Nature provides a physical profile of Maybold's state of mind. If we view the river as the accumulated rain, then a form of rain swallows the vicar's dream of marriage to Fancy and carries it to oblivion. The uses of rain and water have, however, already suggested the doom of their brief affair. Thus the commentary on the alliance between Fancy and Maybold is controlled almost as much by nature as it is by the narrator's voice.

In addition to seasonal design and functional weather, nature comments on the course of love between Fancy and Dick through Hardy's skillful handling of bees, the traditional symbol of a happily integrated community. In the section "Spring," Dick's love for Fancy is continuously threatened by the vicar's feelings. At the height of Dick's perplexity, his father asks him to transport two swarms of their bees to the vicar's capricious mother, "who had just taken into her head a fancy for keeping bees" (p. 117). The bees, symbol of productivity and happiness, are in essence carried from Dick to the vicar—here, the vicar's former home—so that the stability of the rural world seems precarious, challenged. Later in the novel Fancy returns to Yalbury Wood to help her father, who had earlier smothered some hives, with the honey-taking. The death of the bees forebodes unhappiness for Dick and Fancy, for Mr. Day soon rejects Dick's proposal to marry the village schoolteacher. Hardy's treatment of the bees guides our response to the lovers and prepares us for their plight.

After Mr. Day's change of heart, the bees must be resurrected—must in some way be returned to Dick—before the reader feels that the marriage is approved within the moral framework provided by the novelist. Accordingly, Dick's best man comes just before the wedding ceremony to announce that Dick will be a little late because "the hive o' bees his mother gie'd en for his new garden swarmed jist as he was starting, and he said, 'I can't afford to lose a stock o' bees; no, that I can't, though I fain would; and Fancy wouldn't wish it on any account'" (p. 198). Just as the rebirth of the hive symbolizes the rebirth of Rome in Book IV of the *Georgics*, so the fruitful new "life" that the swarming bees will create serves as a proleptic image of the new life that Fancy and Dick embark on. Shortly, Dick arrives. Who would have thought

"That my bees should ha' swarmed jist then, of all the times and seasons! ... And 'tis a fine swarm, too: I haven't seen such a fine swarm for these ten years."
"A' excellent sign," said Mrs. Penny, from the depths of experience. "A' excellent sign."

.   .   .   .   .

"Well, bees can't be put off," observed the inharmonious grandfather James. "Marrying a woman is a thing you can do at any moment; but a swarm o'bees won't come for the asking." [Pp. 200–201]

The swarming of a new hive of bees signifies a rebirth of stability, a resurgence of hope, a means of revealing the pastoral vision of man in harmony with his surroundings. The swarming at so propitious a

moment is a positive sign for the betrothed couple as well as for Mellstock as the larger social order to which the couple attach themselves.
Mrs. Penny, representing the folk perception and probably Hardy's
own view, says it best: "A' excellent sign." We believe her just as we
believe Geoffrey Day's unhesitating remark that Dick is a "genuine wise
man" to attend to his bees before he attends to his wedding.

At the conclusion we see that the rural order is reassured, although
it changes: Fancy is reabsorbed, but so has her organ-playing been accepted; Maybold is alienated from the Mellstock villagers, but so has
the choir been turned out to pasture. The wedding of course puts the
final seal of validity on the rural order, makes it finally intact. Even at
the wedding nature provides the thematic and moral framework for
our deeper understanding of the surface action by commenting obliquely
on the marriage. Here is the wedding party on the way to church: "Now
among dark perpendicular firs, like the shafted columns of a cathedral;
now through a hazel copse, matted with primroses and wild hyacinths;
now under broad beeches in bright young leaves they threaded their
way" (p. 204). The description, appropriately idealized and rhetorically heightened by the use of anaphora, implies the author's strong
sanction of the wedding.

A similar pastoral atmosphere dominates the final chapter, "Under
the Greenwood Tree," which shows the culmination of the love story
I have analyzed. The title of the chapter, like the title of the book,
comes from *As You Like It* and refers to the unspoiled joys of life that
the exiled court finds "under the greenwood tree." Roughly representative of the novel, this chapter is a paradigm of the whole and manifests
a strong bond with traditional pastoral.

The point in Yalbury Wood which abutted on the end of Geoffrey Day's
premises was closed with an ancient tree, horizontally of enormous extent,
though having no great pretensions to height. Many hundreds of birds had
been born amidst the boughs of this single tree; tribes of rabbits and hares
had nibbled at its bark from year to year; quaint tufts of fungi had sprung
from the cavities of its forks; and countless families of moles and earth-
worms had crept about its roots. Beneath and beyond its shade spread a
carefully-tended grass-plot. . . .

All . . . the guests gathered on the spot, where music, dancing, and the
singing of songs went forward with great spirit throughout the evening. The
propriety of every one was intense, by reason of the influence of Fancy, who,
as an additional precaution in this direction had strictly charged her father
and the tranter to carefully avoid saying "thee" and "thou" in their conversation, on the plea that those ancient words sounded so very humiliating to
persons of newer taste; also that they were never to be seen drawing the
back of the hand across the mouth after drinking—a local English custom

of extraordinary antiquity, but stated by Fancy to be decidedly dying out among the better classes of society.

While the dancing progressed, the older persons sat together under the tree, told stories, and "at intervals surveyed the advancing and retiring couples," who danced reels, hornpipes, and other country dances until time for the indoor supper.[9] After the meal, Dick prepares to take the bride to his new cottage near Mellstock. To his query "How long will you be putting on your bonnet, Fancy?" comes the reply:

"Only a minute."
"How long is that?"
"Well, dear, five."
"Ah, sonnies!" said the tranter, as Dick retired, "'tis a talent of the female race that low numbers should stand for high, more especially in matters of waiting, matters of age, and matters of money."

·   ·   ·   ·   ·

Amid a medley of laughter, old shoes, and elder-wine, Dick and his bride took their departure side by side in the excellent new springcart which the young tranter now possessed. The moon was just over the full. . . .
"Fancy," he said, "why we are so happy is because there is such full confidence between us. Ever since that time you confessed to that little flirtation with Shiner by the river (which was really no flirtation at all), I have thought how artless and good you must be to tell me o' such a trifling thing, and to be so frightened about it as you were. It has won me to tell you my every deed and word since then. We'll have no secrets from each other, darling, will we ever?—no secret at all."
"None from to-day," said Fancy. "Hark! what's that?"
From a neighbouring thicket was suddenly heard to issue in a loud, musical, and liquid voice—
"Tippiwit! swe'e'et! ki-ki-ki! Come hither, come hither, come hither!"
"O, 'tis the nightingale," murmured she, and thought of a secret she would never tell. [Pp. 206–11]

In this brief wedding chapter, we breathe the fragrance of leisure and festivity, and are reminded of the final sunny chapters of *Silas Marner*. Under the ancient and enormous "greenwood" tree gather both the old and the young of the village. The tree, which Douglas Brown calls the symbol of the continuity of generations,[10] has served many forms of

9 Cf. lines 15–20 of Goldsmith's *Deserted Village*, which uses very similar images:
    How often have I blessed the coming day,
    When toil remitting lent its turn to play,
    And all the village train, from labor free,
    Led up their sports beneath the spreading tree,
    While many a pastime circled in the shade,
    The young contending as the old surveyed.
10 *Thomas Hardy*, 2d ed. (London: Longmans, 1961), p. 42.

life, both animal and plant, and now it spreads its protective shade over the celebration of the marriage between Fancy and Dick. The circular journey of love has in the final chapter contracted into the circular form of the country dance and has precipitated into marriage. Similarly the forest of trees at the opening of the novel has contracted into a single, highly functional tree. The novel, then, converges upon a single scene which draws all loose threads into tight resolution. Thus the movement of the novel is from broad to narrow: the novel opens with a mixture of rural and urban elements—the Mellstock choir beside Fancy and Maybold—then gradually strips off urban influences until, in the final scene, those influences are largely rejected. The novel retreats symbolically away from the urban world and its influences so that we are left at the close with a bucolic, pastoral scene of great charm.

If Hardy at times strains for effects, with awkward similes and quirks of style, and if he sometimes fails to develop a scene, as in the account of the wedding supper, his strengths are more evident—a subtle and varied humor, an expressive use of dialect, and an authentic rendering of rustic life. Typical of the ironic humor in the novel are the exchanges between the men on a recurrent theme in Hardy's fiction: female folly. The humor is often clever, sometimes stylized to the point of artificiality, as in the tranter's reply that with the female race low numbers stand for high "in matters of waiting, matters of age, and matters of money." Though only stylized peasants speak with such pithy skill, often enough the humor is realistic. We think of the characteristic sweating of the Dewy family or of Thomas Leaf, the amiable village idiot. Lord David Cecil has written that "Hardy's humour . . . is traditional. Like the characters who are its subject, it descends directly from Shakespeare and the Elizabethans."[11] But surely Mrs. Poyser is as much as Bottom a literary predecessor for the humor of Hardy's peasants, a humor that ranges widely—from the farce of the tranter and Maybold hunting a dropped pen, to caricature of Leaf, to satire on Fancy, to sly irony toward the love story. Modernity, of course, but Fancy in particular, is ridiculed gently, affectionately, with the weapon of irony. In the quoted scene, such stilted phrases as "so very humiliating to persons of newer taste" or "stated by Fancy to be decidedly dying out" reveal Hardy's humor.

Our concluding glimpse of the couple shows them making a final journey—this time to their new cottage. The use of the moon and the nightingale to accompany them shows Hardy falling back on conventional devices of romance. Yet he employs the devices not sentimentally but ironically and satirically to offer a smiling, biting commentary on

---

[11] *Hardy the Novelist*, p. 94.

Fancy's artfulness, on her concealed affair with the vicar. It is this kind of commentary that saves the novel, throughout, from lapsing into a sentimental glorification of pastoral life. The repetition of "come hither" directly quotes, of course, the pastoral song that Amiens sings in the Forest of Arden. One might be tempted to argue that the nightingale is calling the newlyweds to love; but the artistic juxtaposition of the bird's loud voice and Fancy's necessarily qualified remark forces us to conclude that through the nightingale nature, in fact, mocks Fancy's deception and pronounces her, at the close, morally inferior to the villagers of the rural world she has joined.

One critic has pointed out that "undoubtedly Hardy meant the denouement to have something of the tone of Shakespearian comedy . . . and, by concluding with the traditional 'assembly-scene' in which a marriage takes place and in which rustic revelry has its fling, and where the possibility of sorrow is quite forgotten, he achieved this effect."[12] But it is as much to the point at least to mention not only the idyllic, pastoral elements of the final scene but also its antipastoralism. The pinch of realism that the nightingale provides in order to close the novel punctures the pastoral scene in a way that reminds us again of *As You Like It*, with the play's balancing of the realistic Audrey and William against the polished Arcadians Phebe and Silvius, and with its frequent parody and satire by Touchstone and Jaques. The four marriages at the close of *As You Like It* anticipate Hardy's treatment of Dick and Fancy's marriage. Duke Senior says:

> Play, music! And you, brides and bridegrooms all,
> With measure heaped in joy, to the measures fall.
>
> [V.iv.184–85]

Then the dancing begins, but not before Jaques has added his salty humor to protect the conventional ending of pastoral comedy from turning into pure idyll. We see in this play perhaps the root of the modified version of traditional pastoral that we have examined in *Under the Greenwood Tree*—the version in which real elements are judiciously combined with such pastoral elements as stylized peasants, rustic charm, sympathetic nature, and an atmosphere of idyll.

What, we might well ask, is the significance of a novel that is usually considered slight but charming, an early work whose scope is too narrow to allow a full rendering of universal human situations? Part of its significance lies in its artistic merit per se, its ability to create a pastoral

12 Carpenter, pp. 46–47.

world. The artistic execution of that world may occasionally be unsure, but in this regard the novel simply shares the uneven quality of Hardy's novels. As important as its artistic merit is the fact that it announces the basic themes, situations, character types, imagery, and landscape descriptions of the two pastoral novels that follow it: *Far from the Madding Crowd* (1874) and *The Woodlanders* (1887).

Under the Greenwood Tree is a preliminary sketch for *Far from the Madding Crowd*, using the same structure of vivid rural scenes organized around the seasonal year, the same character types, and many of the same techniques of portraiture, humor, and imagery. Hardy announces the theme of rural-urban conflict in *Under the Greenwood Tree*, then develops it in *Far from the Madding Crowd* and *The Woodlanders*. In each case, rural integrity triumphs in the reader's mind over urban superficiality and materialism. The conflict between the values of the urban world and those of the rural world is, for example, especially evident in the conflicting attitudes toward education. In *Under the Greenwood Tree*, Mr. Day wants Fancy to marry outside the rural world because she is educated. In *Far from the Madding Crowd*, one reason Bathsheba rejects Oak's proposal of marriage at the opening of the novel is that "I am better educated than you." In *The Woodlanders* the same situation occurs: Mr. Melbury insists on Grace's education, then on her marrying a man of comparable attainment. But in *The Woodlanders* Hardy allows Melbury's dream to materialize, then records the bitter result of Grace's marriage to an urban figure. The situations in both *Under the Greenwood Tree* and *The Woodlanders* are the same, but in *The Woodlanders* the treatment is more troubled, less hopeful of the outcome when urban and rural collide.

In addition to the theme of rural-urban conflict, *Under the Greenwood Tree* announces techniques that Hardy will use more powerfully and with greater range of suggestion in later novels. The use of trees in *Under the Greenwood Tree* (the title of the novel suggests Hardy's special interest) is fully exploited in *The Woodlanders*, where trees continuously seclude the pastoral world and mirror the sufferings of the characters. The skillfully thematic use of rain is employed again in both *Far from the Madding Crowd* and *The Woodlanders* to comment on the characters and to act as a plot agent. The effective uses of nature are, throughout Hardy's pastoral novels, a primary source of their appeal.

In Fancy and Dick and Maybold, we find prototypes of the main characters who appear in the later pastoral novels. Fancy, for instance, is the typical stereotyped coquette (as her name suggests) who balances indecisively between rural and urban inclinations. Bathsheba Everdene in *Far from the Madding Crowd* is a more powerful, better realized portrait of the same figure. In *The Woodlanders* a paler, more perplexed version appears in Grace Melbury. Similarly, Dick, whose character reminds us of the sturdy integrity of Adam Bede and Aaron Winthrop, anticipates Gabriel Oak and Giles Winterborne in his simplicity, honesty, ready acceptance of work, altruism, and faithfulness. All three figures are cut from the same imaginative pattern. Each of the three waits patiently for the girl he loves to accept him in marriage, but their roles of patient fidelity are rewarded less decisively with each novel. Moreover the patient male figures grow progressively less compromising in each novel: Dick readily bends his will to Fancy's when new ideas challenge old; on the other hand, Oak's moral sense allows only limited flexibility when his ideas conflict with Bathsheba's (as in the case of her alliance with Boldwood); but Giles is unable to compromise his moral standards and his sense of propriety: and his lack of flexibility becomes a cause of his premature death. With increasingly reduced vigor, the movement of the three figures is away from rural vitality and resilience.[13]

In Vicar Maybold we have the prototype of the outsider who intrudes upon the serenity and tradition of the rural world. As a character type, Maybold is divided in *Far from the Madding Crowd* into the urgent but unsuccessful lover, Boldwood, and the destructive urban invader, Troy. The romantic and effusive impulses of Maybold and Boldwood (the similarity of names suggests the similarity of function) are in *The Woodlanders* turned into the passionate outpourings of Mrs. Charmond; on the other hand, the disruptive impulses of Maybold and Troy harden into the villainy of Fitzpiers. The intrusive, unadmired characters become more deeply disliked with each novel, whereas the admired characters grow less hopeful about the perpetuation of the rural order. Because the character types and character groupings within these three novels are similar (in some ways identical), the same kinds of situations arise in each novel. The differences between them spring up in the varying resolutions to these situations. In each successive novel, the treatment of theme and character grows more serious and fuller, but more elegiac and darker.

Thus the structural pattern of the three novels is similar, with *Under the Greenwood Tree* announcing the pattern of the novels to follow. Fancy and Dick are blessed with marriage at the close, thereby reinforcing the stability and endurance of the rural world. In *Far from the Madding Crowd* the growth of love between Bathsheba and Oak is, after long delay, sanctioned by marriage. Happiness and serenity are

---

13 For a full discussion of this idea, see John Holloway, "Hardy's Major Fiction," in *From Jane Austen to Joseph Conrad*, ed. Robert C. Rathburn and Martin Steinmann, Jr. (Minneapolis: Univ. of Minnesota Press, 1958), pp. 234–45.

restored only after turmoil and destruction have scarred the rural world. The close is peaceful, yet won with hardship. In *The Woodlanders* the pastoral atmosphere sours at the close; instead of a marriage between Giles and Grace (which we might expect according to the pattern of the two earlier novels), Grace marries the urban intruder Fitzpiers, and in the final pages Hardy allows the natural world to reclaim Giles, the child of the earth. Although Fancy and Bathsheba are reabsorbed into the natural world, Grace is alienated from it through her education and her marriage. Unrewarded at the close, Marty South is left alone to murmur an elegy over Giles's grave. The weddings in *Under the Greenwood Tree* and *Far from the Madding Crowd* become, in *The Woodlanders*, a pastoral elegy and a joyless marriage. At this point the pastoral world has been unmistakably abandoned to be replaced with the soiled landscape of *Tess* and *Jude*. After *The Woodlanders* we must wait for D. H. Lawrence's *The White Peacock* to find another full-length expression of the pastoral impulse.

Under the Greenwood Tree was Hardy's first pastoral novel, whose stylized perfection has made it a minor masterpiece in a neglected genre.[14] Though its prose may at times turn rough and though detailed evocation of setting and depth of character may sometimes disappear and therefore disappoint, such failures are small beside the skillful integration of setting, plot, and theme; the skillful rendering of the nuances of dialect and character; and the creation of a unique pastoral world—an integrated human community deep in the past and still untouched by the twin evils of industrialism and materialism. Equally important, *Under the Greenwood Tree* anticipates in theme, character, and technique the more impressive and more substantial achievements, *Far from the Madding Crowd* and *The Woodlanders*. If *Under the Greenwood Tree* is not a great novel, we can agree with Irving Howe (p. 102) that it is "Hardy's finest pastoral."

[14] Albert J. Guerard calls it Hardy's "most perfect work of art" (*Thomas Hardy* [1949; rpt. Norfolk, Conn.: New Directions, 1964], p. 5).

Chapter 6

Far from the Madding Crowd
"Pastoral King"

IN A LETTER to Leslie Stephen, Hardy explained that his new novel was to be "a pastoral tale with the title of *Far from the Madding Crowd*" in which "the characters would probably be a young woman-farmer, a shepherd, and a sergeant of cavalry."[1] Hardy succeeded in his early intention of writing "a pastoral tale" in two respects. He wrote a novel about sheep and shepherds, the traditional pastoral subject; but he also wrote a novel at least partly in the traditional manner, by portraying rural life nostalgically and by stressing its beauty rather than its coarseness. The numerous pastoral scenes weave a solidly rural texture that has the smell of hay and the feel of fleece, and Hardy's knowledge of the agricultural world expresses itself in richly connotative prose that frequently crystallizes into poetry. Reminiscent and idealized, the result is a charming interpretive account of rural society.

Yet the falsification and artificiality of traditional pastoral have been rigorously excluded from Hardy's account. In *Far from the Madding Crowd* (1874) there is no perpetual summer, no frolicking sheep, no piping shepherds who live without care. Instead, there are many realistic details of actual rural life: sheep die, storms threaten, shepherds have misfortunes both "amorous and pastoral," peasants work, and unhappiness and despair are spattered over the second half of the story. Before the novel's essential realism, prettiness disappears. As William J. Hyde has shown, "a selective and discriminating use of the actual always forms the basis of [Hardy's] portraits."[2] Because these realistic details are not usually found in traditional pastoral literature, it is true that Hardy's novel is not traditional pastoral, but a modified version of traditional pastoral in which the manner and the underlying attitudes of pastoral are still present but in which real details of rural life form the substance of the work. Hardy's purpose, that is, was not to give a precise transcript of real rural life, but rather to select and to heighten those features which form a vital pattern of comprehension and mean-

[1] Florence Emily Hardy, *The Life of Thomas Hardy* (New York: Macmillan, 1962), p. 95.
[2] "Hardy's View of Realism: A Key to the Rustic Characters," *Victorian Studies*, 2 (1958), 56.

ing and which embody the value of what he saw as a pastoral world apart from urban society.[3]

The title of the novel is a typically pastoral title that introduces us to the pastoral framework in which the novel is written. It refers to the peasants in Thomas Gray's "Elegy Written in a Country Churchyard" (1751) who are praised for living "Far from the madding crowd's ignoble strife" and in "the cool sequester'd vale of life." As the title indicates, the setting of the novel is an area remote from an urban world, much like the settings of traditional pastoral. We have escaped the city for "the horizons and landscapes of a partly real, partly dream-country," Hardy said in his preface to the novel. In this remote setting we find that the ancient occupation of sheep-raising and its attendant rural tasks are still pursued. Lambing, washing the sheep, grinding the shears, shearing the sheep, the shearing-supper and entertainment, protecting and harvesting the crops, the harvest supper and dance, and the annual sheep fair—all are traditional "pastoral" tasks that form the foundation of the shepherd's life.[4] The shepherds and other peasants of the novel form a rural order nearly as old as the land itself, an order which preserves both ancient customs and the traditional agricultural way of life. It is a way of life, Hardy wrote, for which "the indispensable conditions of existence are attachment to the soil of one particular spot by generation after generation" (p. xxii).

In *Far from the Madding Crowd*, the center of the pastoral world is Gabriel Oak, often called "Shepherd Oak" in Weatherbury. From his childhood, Oak had "assisted his father in tending the flocks of large proprietors" (p. 10); and since sheep-tending was Gabriel's specialty, as it was with the shepherds of traditional pastoral, he is both knowledgeable and skilled in handling sheep. We see an equally strong con-

---

[3] For a full discussion of the question of Hardy's realism, see Hyde's article (n. 2 above): 45–59. He concludes in his study, however, that "a survey of some of the social and economic history of nineteenth-century English rural life will at times confirm Hardy's observations but will at the same time suggest the 'real' peasant beside whom Hardy's carefully chosen specimens must have appeared idealized to some of his contemporaries. Such a survey will encounter two major impressions that Hardy usually leaves out of focus: the animal nature of the peasant and the economic suffering of his lot" (p. 48).

[4] In the novel Hardy actually uses the word *pastoral*, as perhaps we might expect, in its earliest historical sense of relating to the life of shepherds and their sheep (*OED* 7:542). He speaks for instance of "the serious turn pastoral affairs seemed to be taking" (p. 23), "A Pastoral Tragedy" (p. 30), "his modest elevation as pastoral king" (p. 35), and "his misfortunes, amorous and pastoral" (p. 38). Parenthetical page numbers refer throughout to *Far from the Madding Crowd*, ed. Richard L. Purdy, Riverside Edition (Boston: Houghton Mifflin, 1957).

nection with traditional pastoral in Oak's prized flute, whose dulcet notes often "beguile a tedious hour." In countless poems of traditional pastoral, the use of the flute is the same. While Oak is in Casterbridge searching for a job as shepherd, "he drew out his flute and began to play 'Jockey to the Fair' in the style of a man who had never known a moment's sorrow. Oak could pipe with Arcadian sweetness, and the sound of the well-known notes cheered his own heart as well as those of the loungers" (p. 36). For a moment, Oak becomes a piping shepherd out of the *Idylls* of Theocritus. But only for a moment, because Oak, in contrast to conventional shepherds, has recently experienced "misfortunes, amorous and pastoral." His life, though idealized, is essentially that of a real shepherd.

Another connection with traditional pastoral is that of plot complication. In *Far from the Madding Crowd* intricate romantic relationships form the action in the foreground of the novel. Such a complicated plot was a standard device of Elizabethan pastoral romances and pastoral dramas such as Sidney's *Arcadia*, Greene's *Menaphon*, Lodge's *Rosalynde*, Shakespeare's *As You Like It*, and the woodland scenes of *A Midsummer Night's Dream*. The most commonly used device to create plot complication was, Hallett Smith has shown, the situation of "cross-eyed Cupid" in which A loves B, B loves C, C loves D, and D loves A.[5] In *Far from the Madding Crowd* it is no surprise to find a similar complication of the plot. At the opening of the novel, Gabriel Oak falls suddenly in love with Bathsheba Everdene, but Bathsheba rejects his hasty proposal of marriage only to find herself sudden heir to her uncle's sheep farm in the village of Weatherbury. She has risen, she believes, far above the humble Shepherd Oak. An anonymous and impulsively mailed valentine, with the message "MARRY ME," stirs a flaming passion in Bathesheba's neighbor, Mr. Boldwood. When he discovers that Bathsheba is the sender, he promptly offers marriage. Bathsheba, however, is but momentarily attracted to the older man. Instead, she meets by accident a handsome soldier on her farm, and a swift and passionate attraction develops between them. Bathsheba does not know that Sergeant Troy has seduced her youngest servant, Fanny Robin, and has failed to marry her. So all too soon, Bathsheba marries Troy. But when Fanny and her baby are discovered dead at the Casterbridge workhouse, Bathsheba discovers as well her husband's role; and their union is

---

[5] *Elizabethan Poetry* (Cambridge: Harvard Univ. Press, 1952), pp. 17–18. In addition to romantic confusion, the disguises in *Far from the Madding Crowd* also link the novel to traditional pastoral. We see Sergeant Troy disguised at the sheep fair, then disguised again at Boldwood's Christmas party. When Bathsheba and Troy pass Fanny Robin on the road to Casterbridge, they do not at first recognize her because her haggard condition disguises her true identity.

blasted forever. Sergeant Troy then disappears. His disappearance spurs
Boldwood to renew his romance with Bathsheba, who views her suitor
with pity and shame yet without ardor. When Troy appears unexpec-
tedly at Boldwood's Christmas party, the older man (whose passion for
Bathsheba approaches insanity) shoots Troy dead, then gives himself
up to imprisonment. No barriers then remain between Bathsheba and
Gabriel Oak. Bathsheba's pride has been humbled through her experiences, and Oak is now entirely acceptable to her. A quiet marriage between "these two sensible persons" closes the novel.

It will be illuminating to schematize the romantic attachments among
the characters in two diagrams. As figure 1 demonstrates, plot complication in *Far from the Madding Crowd* is achieved by double romantic

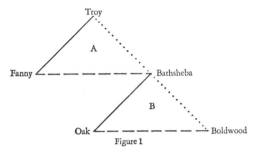
Figure 1

triangles that are connected by Bathsheba, who provides a link between
rural and urban worlds as her affection alternates between Oak and
Boldwood on the one hand and Troy on the other. To resolve the plot
complication, the tensions represented by the two triangles must be
dissolved during the course of the narrative. When the dotted side of
each triangle (representing infatuation) dissolves, the broken side
(representing competition between suitors) must also dissolve. The
triangular relationships among the five characters then collapse, leaving
only the emotional bonds represented by the two solid lines: Bathsheba
and Oak are, in this world, united in marriage; and Fanny and Troy
are, in the world beyond, united in death. (Boldwood, in his insanity,
hovers *between* life and death.) At the close of the novel, order and
unity are thus reestablished.

The two triangles also demonstrate two separate outcomes to the
same kind of romantic dilemma, the dilemma of two in love with one.
In the first version of the dilemma, schematized by triangle *A*, the rural
world is betrayed and then destroyed by urban forces: Fanny dies because Troy lacks moral fidelity. In the second version of the dilemma,
represented by triangle *B*, the rural world is sanctioned by the outcome
of the unstable triangular situation: for his fidelity, Oak is rewarded

with Bathsheba. Thus Hardy is able to offer alternate resolutions to similar conflicts within the framework of a single novel. These alternate resolutions perhaps suggest an ambiguity in Hardy's attitude toward rural life because they offer what we might call a "real" solution and a "pastoral" solution to the matrix of plot difficulties. Yet only the "pastoral" solution, which supports rural life, also supports the preservation of human life. And because this solution—the gradual emergence of friendship into love between Bathsheba and Oak—occurs within the pastoral order, it has immediate relevance to our purpose of studying the pastoral world which Hardy creates.

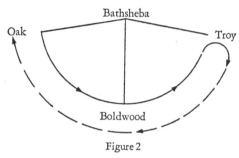

Figure 2

Figure 2 schematizes the narrative movement of the novel, a movement that takes the form of a pendulum arc with Bathsheba as its pivotal center. The pendulum is set into motion by Bathsheba's mercurial feelings, which move in succession from Oak to Boldwood to Troy, then back to Boldwood and finally back to Oak. Most important, the pendulum is kept in motion during much of the novel by the lure of the urban world. Bathsheba moves from one suitor to the next—from Oak to Boldwood, then from Boldwood to Troy—on the basis of their increasing urban attraction. The swinging pendulum does not reverse its movement until the symbol of urban values, Sergeant Troy, is found to be, in Hardy's words, "a trickster." Thus we move from the true bond of feeling between Bathsheba and Oak, to the false bond between Bathsheba and Boldwood, to the superficial and impermanent bond which springs up between Bathsheba and Troy. The course of love must then be retraced—from Troy to Boldwood to Oak—until genuine feeling reasserts itself in the form of marriage. As in the traditional comic pattern, we find the romantic difficulties serenely resolved within the framework of the pastoral world.

In a plot formed of romantic difficulties, elements of folly and thus of comedy are important.[6] Bathsheba's "misdirected ingenuity" in mail-

[6] Donald Davidson calls *Under the Greenwood Tree* and *Far from the Madding Crowd* "rural comedies." These novels are, he writes, "essentially comedy, joyful and

ing the valentine to Boldwood initiates a series of foolish actions in the
novel. Because she is at the structural or plot center (as Gabriel Oak
is at the thematic center), Bathsheba's foolish actions spread outward
and affect the other characters—Oak's sudden proposal of marriage, for
example, or Troy's momentary infatuation, or his impulsive gift to her
of a family watch, or Boldwood's senseless neglect of his farm and
crops. The major characters frequently speak of folly and of actions
that are erratic and wild. Bathsheba regrets the "sheer idleness," the
"trifling trick" of mailing the valentine and wishes she "had never
stooped to folly of this kind." Boldwood's passion for Bathsheba is a
"wild infatuation"; " 'I am weak and foolish,' " he tells Gabriel; " 'the
very hills and sky seem to laugh at me till I blush shamefully for my
folly' " (p. 181).

Such folly, of course, relates the novel to the comic pattern of romantic entanglement, resolved in marriage, which we find traditionally
in pastoral drama and pastoral romance. Although the middle segment
of the novel turns somber in tone, the novel begins and ends as comedy.
The happy ending, symbolized by the marriage of Bathsheba and Oak,
reasserts the order and harmony with which the novel opens; and in
this respect, the novel is structured on the pattern of *Adam Bede, Silas
Marner*, and *Under the Greenwood Tree* before it. The mixture of
comic and serious elements can be observed in the two plot solutions
that Hardy offers to the double-triangle entanglements we have examined: one solution is marriage within the Weatherbury rural order;
the other, union or "marriage" in death. Thus part of the novel is
traditional in its comic-pastoral conception and execution; part is tragic
and modern. Later, Hardy separates the two strains in his fiction. In
Tess of the d'Urbervilles and *Jude the Obscure*, the tragedy suffocates
the idyllic and traditional pastoral view and reveals a rural order that
is reminiscent no longer of the Golden Age. Here the charm is eclipsed
and the beauty has burned to ash. In *Far from the Madding Crowd*,
however, comic elements still dominate much of the plot, and these
elements help to tie the novel to traditional pastoral.

Far from the Madding Crowd, like *The Woodlanders*, is perhaps unusual in that it disconnects rather easily into "plot" and "theme," into
the surface action and the poetic Wessex background of peasants, seasonal work, landscape, and rural festivities that make up the thematic

---

almost idyllic" ("The Traditional Basis of Thomas Hardy's Fiction," *Still Rebels,
Still Yankees and Other Essays* [Baton Rouge: Louisiana State Univ. Press, 1951],
pp. 58–59).

materials of the novel.[7] These materials embody the novel's meaning, its underlying system of value. They also embody the highest reaches of Hardy's creative imagination and evoke in the reader the fullest imaginative response. In *Far from the Madding Crowd* this thematic strand (as opposed to the plot strand) gathers up what are probably the most significant aspects of the novel: the explicit conflict between rural and urban; the nostalgic portrayal of the country virtues of humility, integrity, and stoicism; the integrated and idealized community of peasants; and the fascinating natural world over which the country people move and work. These elements, rather than the surface plot, comprise the achievement of the novel.

As we have seen, critics generally agree that a fundamental element of pastoral is the rural-urban contrast, a contrast that takes the derivative forms of nature versus art, past versus present, and simplicity versus refinement and complexity. An innocent virtue found in a remote location has, from the beginning of pastoral, implied a corrupt sophistication in the present. The contrast between rural and urban is frequently noticed in the novel, primarily to show the superiority of the wholly rural Gabriel Oak to the urbanized Sergeant Troy. Bathsheba, for example, cannot penetrate to Sergeant Troy's hollowness because "Troy's deformities lay deep down from a woman's vision, whilst his embellishments were upon the very surface; thus contrasting with homely Oak, whose defects were patent to the blindest, and whose virtues were as metals in a mine" (p. 166). The contrast is one of appearance with reality, of outside with inside. The essence of the contrast is in the different qualities that vision discovers when it penetrates to a man's heart: whereas Troy's urban deformities are uncovered, Oak's country virtues are revealed. Simple country life has no need of the surface appearances that the complexity of city life demands.

A similar rural-urban contrast emerges when Troy moves into Bathsheba's ancient house near Weatherbury. Significantly, Troy ("the erratic child of impulse") wants to change the *surface* of the house, to embellish it with a modern appearance, to obliterate its ancient features:

[7] Joseph Warren Beach in *The Technique of Thomas Hardy* (1922; rpt. New York: Russell & Russell, 1962) has parallel comments on the novel: "The second stage in Hardy's progress was marked by the discovery of 'Wessex,' that old world of dream from which the characters speak to us, in grave or humorous tone, but ever with a mellow sweetness, like the flutes and oboes of the Pastoral Symphony. The first employment of this charm in a story of depth and passion was in *Far from the Madding Crowd*" (pp. 17–18). Later he adds: "One would like to know whether, in designing this novel, the author started with a plot and added a setting, or started with the setting. He conceived the idea of a pastoral idyll, in which he should bring together the greatest possible number of country scenes and occupations such as, taken together, would amount to a reconstruction of his ideal 'Wessex'" (pp. 50–51).

"A rambling, gloomy house this," said Troy, smiling. . . .

"But it is a nice old house," responded Gabriel.

"Yes—I suppose so; but I feel like new wine in an old bottle here. My notion is that sash-windows should be put throughout, and these old wainscoted walls brightened up a bit; or the oak cleared quite away, and the walls papered."

"It would be a pity, I think."

"Well, no. . . . I am for making this place more modern, that we may be cheerful whilst we can." [Pp. 209–10]

The old must, in Troy's opinion, be resurfaced to *look* fashionable. Yet Gabriel, we learn, was "not only provokingly indifferent to public opinion, but a man who clung persistently to old habits and usages, simply because they were old" (p. 293). His predilection for the old and the traditional suggests that his character will be similarly durable. The merely fashionable fails to arouse Oak's interest. When Boldwood asks him to tie his neckerchief, Oak knows no "late knot in fashion." For Oak the impermanent and the fashionable are the antithesis of the recurrent cycles of the natural world which he follows in his labor.

The novel's tension between city and country is exemplified most pointedly in Bathsheba. Although for a time she is proud, even supercilious because of her education and her inheritance of Weatherbury Upper Farm, Bathsheba's is still a "simple country nature, fed on old-fashioned principles." Her attraction to the modern urban principles that Troy represents is part of what Boldwood calls her "woman's folly indeed!" or what Hardy himself calls "the element of folly distinctly mingling with the many varying particulars which made up the character of Bathsheba Everdene" (p. 165). She fails to recognize, even when warned by Oak and Boldwood, that Troy's complex urban standards are alluring but deceiving to simple country natures: "Though in one sense a woman of the world, it was, after all, that world of daylight coteries and green carpets wherein cattle form the passing crowd and winds the busy hum; where a quiet family of rabbits or hares lives on the other side of your party-wall, where your neighbour is everybody in the tything, and where calculation is confined to market-days. Of the fabricated tastes of good fashionable society she knew but little, and of the formulated self-indulgence of bad, nothing at all" (pp. 165–66). Only gradually does she learn to throw off fabricated tastes and return "fresh as spring" to her affection for Gabriel. The rural world is conceived by Hardy to be both innocent and good. The contrast in the novel between city and country is so emphatically heightened in Bathsheba because the urban world signifies for Hardy an attractive but an essentially artificial and evanescent life that is merely veneered with complexity.

But it is Gabriel Oak who embodies, cumulatively, what are for Hardy the characteristic virtues of rural life: its integrity and humility, its stoicism and stability, its rewarding labor, its love for the traditional, and as in all pastoral, its deep sympathy with the world of nature. Throughout, Oak functions as a standard of value at the center of the novel. We can measure the other characters according to how closely they approach him in character. Those who approach his character (Bathsheba and the peasants of Weatherbury) are rewarded in terms of the world created by the novel; those who do not are purged.

Oak, for instance, is "generous and true"; his character is one of "outspoken honesty." He is humble "with the humility stern adversity had thrust upon him" (p. 43). If poverty comes to him suddenly, in the form of a pastoral disaster, he accepts it stoically.[8] When his erring dog chases the sheep to their death at the bottom of a cliff, "all the savings of a frugal life had been dispersed at a blow; his hopes of being an independent farmer were laid low—possibly for ever" (p. 33).[9] After the death of the sheep and the departure of Bathsheba, "Gabriel was paler now. His eyes were more meditative, and his expression was more sad. He had passed through an ordeal of wretchedness which had given him more than it had taken away. He had sunk from his modest elevation as pastoral king into the very slime-pits of Siddim; but there was left to him a dignified calm he had never before known, and that indifference to fate which, though it often makes a villain of a man, is the

[8] It might be argued that Oak is contradictorily presented as poor and humble, yet also ambitious. Even though he has temporarily "lost in the race for money and good things" (p. 169), Oak *appears* to be ambitious for wealth and power when he resents Bathsheba's " 'right to be her own baily [bailiff] if she choose—and to keep me down to be a common shepherd only' " (p. 96). He says to Bathsheba, " 'don't suppose I'm content to be a nobody. I was made for better things' " (p. 170). Hardy himself answers the objection when he observes that Oak "did not covet the post [of bailiff] relatively to the farm," but "in relation to [Bathsheba], as beloved by him and unmarried to another, he had coveted it" (p. 133). In other words, Oak wants to strengthen the bond between himself and Bathsheba, not to accumulate wealth and power as a goal in itself. It is, however, true that Bathsheba and Oak are, at the conclusion, humble but in no sense poor. There is likely some ambiguity in Hardy's mind between pastoral humility and poverty (distinctly rural) and economic ambition and success (distinctly urban). Theodore Holmes, in a discussion of Hardy's poems, illuminates the ambiguity: "The stricture and importance of Hardy's work derives at once from the contradiction that lies at its center. The poems are never able to lay the ghost of the urban initiative for success and progress . . . because Hardy was never able to turn his back on this world. His whole life turned on the attempt to make his way in the world about him, to the extent that he put off his true artistic efforts for a generation while he used his vocation to secure his earthly means" ("Thomas Hardy's City of the Mind," *Sewanee Review*, 75 [1967)], 298).

[9] Compare Luke 8.3 as a possible literary source for this scene: "The herd ran violently down a steep place into the lake, and were choked."

basis of his sublimity when it does not" (p. 35). To Oak's humility is added the tenacity and endurance that lead to a stoical outlook. Pastoral happiness must be found within the range of this outlook, within this limited angle of vision. Traditional pastoral happiness is thus modified by a frank awareness of anguish. Gabriel's stoicism results from his immense inner strength conflicting with such accidental circumstances as losing Bathsheba and his sheep. Essentially, a wall is formed between the two forces to prevent the outer accident from detroying the inner strenth. Thus Oak becomes "a man whom misfortune had inured rather then subdued" (p. 227). Because Boldwood cannot erect a similar psychological wall to protect his character, he sinks into insanity.

Bathsheba is different. She is the only character who changes and matures. In the course of the novel, Bathsheba develops the same strength that Oak possesses at the outset. Early, she spends much time lamenting the position into which her vanity and folly have plunged her; but as her pride stumbles on misfortune, she matures, grows silent, and learns to bear her sorrows alone. "Her original vigorous pride of youth had sickened" (p. 287), "her exuberance of spirit was pruned down," and "the severe schooling she had been subjected to had made Bathsheba much more considerate than she had formerly been of the feelings of others" (p. 294). Only then does she reassess her values, and begin to appreciate Gabriel Oak. She appreciates him because her maturing attitudes gradually come into unison with his own seasoned outlook:

What a way Oak had, she thought, of enduring things. Boldwood, who seemed so much deeper and higher and stronger in feeling than Gabriel, had not yet learnt, any more than she herself, the simple lesson which Oak showed a mastery of by every turn and look he gave—that among the multitude of interests by which he was surrounded, those which affected his personal well-being were not the most absorbing and important in his eyes. Oak meditatively looked upon the horizon of circumstances without any special regard to his own standpoint in the midst. That was how she would wish to be. [P. 260]

The barrier that comes between them is pride. As in pastoral romance, where characters retreat from courtly pride to country humility, the death of Bathsheba's pride soon brings a peace of mind strikingly similar to that which shepherds of traditional pastoral enjoyed, except that in *Far from the Madding Crowd* calm is won through hardship. Again, traditional pastoral is fortified with a recognition of real human difficulties. But the final effect is the same: tranquility within a pastoral setting. The marriage between Bathsheba and Oak celebrates the calm they have achieved.

Even more than his humility and endurance and stoicism, Oak's intimate relationship with the natural world, in demonstrating another sterling virtue of rural character, reveals an element of pastoral that should be stressed: the interaction of nature and man, the reflection of landscape in mind and of mind in landscape. Throughout the novel the descriptions of nature, and of man within nature, call upon Hardy's acute sensitivity to rural sights and sounds—to the distinctive habits of animals and earth and sky. When Oak senses the approach of the powerful August storm in chapter 36, Hardy describes vividly the changes that begin to occur in nature. The August night was dry, sultry, sinister: "the sheep had trailed homeward head to tail, the behavior of the rooks had been confused, and the horses had moved with timidity and caution." [10] Thunder now threatened. Soon Gabriel left the stack-yard of Weatherbury Upper Farm and

proceeded towards his home. In approaching the door, his toe kicked something which felt and sounded soft, leathery, and distended, like a boxing-glove. It was a large toad humbly travelling across the path. Oak took it up, thinking it might be better to kill the creature to save it from pain; but finding it uninjured, he placed it again among the grass. He knew what this direct message from the Great Mother meant. And soon came another.

When he struck a light indoors there appeared upon the table a thin glistening streak, as if a brush of varnish had been lightly dragged across it. Oak's eyes followed the serpentine sheen to the other side, where it led up to a huge brown garden-slug, which had come indoors to-night for reasons of its own. It was Nature's second way of hinting to him that he was to prepare for foul weather.

Oak sat down meditating for nearly an hour. During this time two black spiders, of the kind common in thatched houses, promenaded the ceiling, ultimately dropping to the floor. This reminded him that if there was one class of manifestation on this matter that he thoroughly understood, it was the instincts of sheep. He left the room, ran across two or three fields towards the flock, got upon a hedge, and looked over among them.

They were crowded close together on the other side around some furze bushes, and the first peculiarity observable was that, on the sudden appearance of Oak's head over the fence, they did not stir or run away. They had now a terror of something greater than their terror of man. . . .

This was enough to re-establish him in his original opinion. He knew now that he was right, and that Troy was wrong. Every voice in nature was unanimous in bespeaking change. [Pp. 214–15]

---

10 Compare Vergil's *Georgics*, I.311–92, for a lengthy parallel description of an autumn storm, including similar natural signs that warn the farmer of the storm's approach—e.g., a calf looks up at the sky and snuffs the wind with apprehensive nostrils. The influence of Vergil on Hardy remains to be explored.

Like many passages in the novel, this one documents Hardy's specific and detailed knowledge of natural processes—a knowledge far exceeding that displayed in George Eliot's early novels. Yet this knowledge is transmuted into fiction; it is not mere technical or didactic information, but knowledge that assumes evocative and poetic significance. The passage demonstrates, in particular, the intimate relationship that Oak enjoys with nature. Oak understands animal pain and natural phenomena. He can read nature accurately. He and "the Great Mother" understand each other, they communicate. He reminds us of Giles Winterborne planting trees in *The Woodlanders*. Both men are nature's sons, children of the earth who are in harmony with the seasons and cycles of the natural world. Both renounce what Ruskin calls the "Goddess of Getting-on" in favor of immersing themselves in the animal and plant life of the agricultural sphere.

Because Oak is "an intensely humane man," he does not kill the toad or the snail or the spiders as would Sergeant Troy, whose sword pierces a caterpillar in chapter 28.[11] Hardy's phraseology is significant. He does not make the objective statement, "it was Nature's second way of hinting foul weather," but writes instead: "It was Nature's second way of hinting *to him* that *he* was to prepare for foul weather." The diction reveals subtly the special position that Oak holds in the rural world—a position generally shared by the other rustics in the novel. In this scene Troy, on the other hand, is more interested in the harvest entertainment than in protecting the crops from the storm; he has no understanding of the agricultural world because he is essentially an outsider who wants to exploit the rural world for the income it can provide. Thus when he plants flowers on Fanny's grave, nature exerts a moral force and immediately floods them out with rain, rejecting his efforts to repent.[12] If the characterization of Oak helps to create a pastoral world, Hardy's use of landscape to reflect Oak's mental or emotional perspective further illustrates Oak's intimate relationship to nature and illustrates as well Hardy's control of a subtle but effective pastoral technique.

In most novels landscape provides setting and may also reflect theme, as it does in *Bleak House* or *The Portrait of a Lady*. But seldom in Victorian novels does landscape fulfill both of these functions and also reflect the mind of a single character. In *Far from the Madding Crowd* mind and landscape are—with the exceptions of Bathsheba's entry into the swamp of ferns and chapter 28 describing the sword-exercise—

[11] Compare Troy's treatment of Bathsheba's horse a few pages later: Troy completed his sentence "by a smart cut of the whip round Poppet's flank, which caused the animal to start forward at a wild pace" (p. 232).

[12] For a full discussion of Hardy's use of nature in the novel, see Howard Babb, "Setting and Theme in *Far from the Madding Crowd*," ELH, 30 (1963), 147–61.

causally linked, the one determining the other. As yet unrecognized by critics of the novel, the observation that Gabriel's mind and mood determine the novel's landscape further documents both Oak's central ethical position and Hardy's exceptional art. Examples of this singular correlation abound. In chapter 1 Oak, witnessing Bathsheba's confrontation with the gatekeeper, becomes "piqued" at her indifference to him (p. 8). In the next few paragraphs a "desolating wind" raises its voice to a "grumbling . . . moan," then to a wail, then to a tender sob (pp. 8–9). In chapter 2 Oak, alone in his shepherd's hut, plays his flute with contentment before immersing himself in his outdoor work and, thus, becoming conscious of the "charm in this life he led." When he returns, the interior of the hut appears "cosy and alluring"; the fire, "reflecting its own genial colour upon whatever it could reach, flung associations of enjoyment even over utensils and tools" (p. 11). The mellow glow on external objects expresses, like a mirror reflection, Gabriel's internal contentment. In chapter 3 Gabriel, amused by Bathsheba's deft acrobatics on the pony and innocently confiding to her his secret knowledge, "deeply offended her" and so engenders his own "great regret" (p. 18). This regret is immediately projected onto the landscape. The next paragraph reveals freezing afternoon weather and then heavier frost with evening: the rimy air whips into Gabriel's hut. Falling asleep without ventilating the fire, Oak nearly suffocates from the smoke before Bathsheba discovers him and saves his life. In noticing that Gabriel's intense regret manufactures a landscape of bitter frost and suffocating smoke, we can see Hardy's typical fictional procedure of moving from internal emotion to external equivalent. Inside the hut Bathsheba arouses Oak's life-long interest in her, and it is here that he first feels "the secret fusion of himself in Bathsheba" (p. 30); as in other pastoral novels, action inside a secluded hut initiates an emotional change, a deep commitment of person to person. Without the encounter in the hut, "the acquaintanceship might . . . have ended in a slow forgetting" (pp. 18–19), comments the narrator.

If this pastoral procedure controls the landscape in the early chapters, it explains virtually all of the striking and highly expressive landscapes that appear later in the novel. Bathsheba's initial rejection of Oak's proposal of marriage (ch. 4), in spite of the scene's stylized and uncertain humor, reverberates throughout the novel as an emotionally destructive act. Oak's romantic misfortune, cutting and painful, immediately discovers its equivalent in two ruined landscapes, both of them apprehended with power and vividness: the still-life picture of the dead and dying ewes strewn over the floor of the chalk-pit (ch. 5) and—heightened now because of the death of the sheep and because of Oak's failure at the Casterbridge hiring fair—the dynamic picture

of the burning straw-rick (ch. 6) in which bits of straw "were con-
sumed in a creeping movement of ruddy heat, as if they were knots of
red worms, and above shone imaginary fiery faces, tongues hanging from
lips, glaring eyes, and other impish forms, from which at intervals
sparks flew in clusters like birds from a nest" (p. 40). Although the
novel, like a pastoral poem, shows nature's involvement with the sufferings of her hero, Hardy's procedure is more subtle than that of most
pastoralists: Oak's mental landscape transfers the emotional intensity
of what is *thought and felt* to the landscape that Oak *sees*, and thus
structures the length and the quality of that landscape description. The
key to Hardy's artistic method lies in our seeing that what Gabriel feels,
the novelist sees. This harmony between mind and landscape generates
the power to structure the external landscape into a form analogous to
mental experience.

The same sequence of mind followed by a landscape equivalent occurs—this time in a positive form—in chapters 14, 15, and 19. Gabriel,
now well established on Bathsheba's farm, bustled "vigorously from
place to place," looking altogether "an epitome of the world's health
and vigour" (pp. 90, 93). The visual equivalent reveals Gabriel, in the
warmth of Warren's Malthouse, nursing the sickly lambs to "a sleek
and hopeful state" (p. 99) and then, at his next appearance, washing
the sheep within a landscape entirely compatible with his happiness
(see below). Chapter 20, however, different in its effects, records a
quarrel between Bathsheba and Oak that is climaxed by Oak's dismiss-
al from the farm, after which chapter 21 immediately records "troubles
in the fold": having broken into a field of young clover, the unhappy
sheep display to the anxious onlookers bodies "fearfully distended."
Subtly, Hardy shows Gabriel's mind almost wholly determining the
artistic representation of the agricultural landscape.

In what, finally, best exemplifies this curious and striking narrative
procedure, chapter 35 traces the collision of Gabriel's hidden hope with
Bathsheba's marriage to a handsome soldier. This collision metamorphoses into Oak's corpselike face and then into Oak's fierce disdain, "his
face turning to an angry red," and then at last into the sinister and lurid
night a few paragraphs later. If my contention is accurate, so decisive
a blow as Bathsheba's impetuous marriage to an unworthy suitor, a
marriage that may forever imprison Gabriel's love, should create an
enormous disturbance in the landscape. Chapters 36 and 37, in fact,
follow immediately, evoking the signs of "foul weather" and then the
terrible lightning and the "diabolical sound" of repeated thunder. In its
lavish development and heightened use of sensory detail, this scene,
among the most brilliant in the novel, surpasses earlier or later uses of
landscape in registering shock. Without delay, Hardy transfers Ga-

briel's extreme mental turmoil into a landscape alive with destructive energy.[13] A flash of stunning light strikes "with the spring of a serpent and the shout of a fiend," and a later flash slices a tree "down the whole length of its tall, straight stem" (pp. 220, 222). With considerable artistic precision, moreover, Hardy carefully regulates the flow of mind into landscape. When Bathsheba, who has joined Gabriel atop an uncovered rick, hints at renewed feeling in words such as " 'Gabriel, you are kinder than I deserve. I will stay and help you' " (p. 222), immediately the lightning dies to a soft shimmer. And with her apology for marrying Troy and her tender solicitude toward Gabriel, the lightning and thunder dwindle to an earnest rain that is dismissed by the narrator in a single summary paragraph (p. 225). The earlier tension in the landscape disappears with Oak's soothed state of mind, "cheered [now] by a sense of success in a good cause" (p. 226).

The conversion of a character's mind into landscape description, soldering nature to man in the reader's mind, illustrates a typical pastoral procedure that is well suited to Hardy's mind and art. The equivalency between Oak and the landscape helps create the impression of unity which the novel leaves so powerfully behind; it provides, too, additional evidence for seeing Oak at the moral center of the novel and shows, contrary to prevailing opinion, that Hardy generally imagined nature not as a *character* but as a *function* of character. Especially, this technique of equivalency commands our admiration for Hardy's ability to express—as Dickens does—the inner life of his characters in complex and subtle ways, yet in ways that do not sacrifice the impression of an external world precisely observed. In the treatment of Oak and in his intricate relationship to landscape, we see part of the way in which Hardy creates a pastoral world. The other part consists of communal scenes of rural activity.

The discussion illustrating Oak's harmony with nature leads us to consider the distinctly rural life of the novel. We can best consider it

[13] My view of the storm differs from the views of Howard Babb or Jean Brooks. Babb argues: "Perhaps the power of the storm is supposed simply to mark nature's outrage as it answers Troy's obtuse claim. But the violent unnaturalness of the event . . . strikes me rather as nature measuring in its own fashion the ascendancy that the civilized Troy has gained on Bathsheba's farm" (p. 158). Brooks argues similarly that Troy's sword, which he uses as an instrument of deception and destruction, "places him as a human agent of cosmic dissonance" (*Thomas Hardy: The Poetic Structure* [London: Elek, 1971], p. 170). She sees the storm, therefore, as a reflection of Troy's drunken revel. But to see the storm as a delayed reflection of Gabriel's emotional state fits the storm, without distortion, into the recurrent *pattern* of landscape uses.

through analysis of three great pastoral scenes that form what we may call "the shearing-cycle": the sheep-washing, the sheep-shearing, and the shearing-supper. The reasons for examining such a cycle are several. The three scenes, occurring early in the novel, set the rural tone of the whole and show the distinctive character of rural life. They supply the country rhythm that provides a background for the surface plot—a background of useful agricultural work that provides a moral standard against which the plot action of the foreground can be assessed. The scenes also reveal Hardy's theme of the contrast between rural and urban worlds which lies at the center of the pastoral genre. But above all they reveal Hardy's art by demonstrating the way he creates for the reader the solid substance, the reality of a pastoral-agricultural world.

The first and briefest scene of the shearing-cycle is the sheep-washing, in which the sheep are prepared for shearing:

The sheep-washing pool was a perfectly circular basin of brickwork in the meadows, full of the clearest water. To birds on the wing its glassy surface, reflecting the light sky, must have been visible for miles around as a glistening Cyclops' eye in a green face. The grass about the margin at this season was a sight to remember long—in a minor sort of way. Its activity in sucking the moisture from the rich damp sod was almost a process observable by the eye. The outskirts of this level water-meadow were diversified by rounded and hollow pastures, where just now every flower that was not a buttercup was a daisy. The river slid along noiselessly as a shade, the swelling reeds and sedge forming a flexible palisade upon its moist brink. . . . A tributary of the main stream flowed through the basin of the pool by an inlet and outlet at opposite points of its diameter. Shepherd Oak, Jan Coggan, Moon, Poorgrass, Cain Ball, and several others were assembled here, all dripping wet to the very roots of their hair, and Bathsheba was standing by in a new riding-habit—the most elegant she had ever worn—the reins of her horse being looped over her arm. Flagons of cider were rolling about upon the green. The meek sheep were pushed into the pool by Coggan and Matthew Moon, who stood by the brink, thrust them under as they swam along, with an instrument like a crutch. . . . They were let out against the stream, and through the upper opening, all impurities flowing away below. Cainy Ball and Joseph, who performed this latter operation, were if possible wetter than the rest; they resembled dolphins under a fountain, every protuberance and angle of their clothes dribbling forth a small rill. [Pp. 109–10]

Scenes such as this recur frequently in the novel and invest it with a rural rhythm that few English novels have captured. Hardy locates the sheep-washing pool in the midst of an active, animated nature, which manifests its own life just as the separate life of the sheep is implied in the growth of their wool and just as the separate human movement reveals its own order and purpose. The three kinds of life exist in harmony. Our sense of this harmony increases when we observe that the pool for washing the sheep reflects the lighted sky, thereby suggesting interaction and unity. The birds in flight see the pool's surface as an eye; a visual exchange occurs. And more. The eye is an eye "in a green face." The personification causes the meadow to take on a human dimension, so that the eye of the meadow and the eyes of the birds watch each other. To complete the interpenetration, the grass around the pool is similarly "a sight" for the human eye to watch and remember; as Hardy says, the absorption process "was almost a process observable by the eye." All three components of nature "see": they visualize the active processes of the others. This visual interpenetration creates for the reader the impression of a harmonious and vital background against which the agitated surface action is caught.

We then see the men and the animals and the water mingling together in the sunshine. The yearly ritual forms part of the permanent agricultural fiber that gives the novel its sense of myth, of primeval ceremony. Near the pool, but isolated on its bank, is Bathsheba. Her pride, insistently mentioned, sets her clearly apart. In her new clothes, she attempts to be elegant. She is in opposition to the men and the sheep, for they are meek, natural. They are like the "large toad humbly travelling across the path" in an earlier passage. Only the human world shows pride; more specifically, only those who attempt to reach beyond the ritual sphere are guilty of pride and suffer its bitter fruit. It is only when she emerges into meekness and humility that Bathsheba joins again the agricultural world to which she fundamentally belongs.

In the very next paragraph Boldwood arrives; "Bathsheba immediately contrived to withdraw," and the two of them move significantly away from "the splashing and shouts of the washers above" (p. 110). Hardy's choice of "contrived" is perfect to suggest the unnaturalness of the pair (and their romance) as they leave a scene of great naturalness and simplicity. They move both literally and figuratively away from the springs of rural activity. Bathsheba and Boldwood draw near the annual rite but are not immersed; instead, their unhappiness turns to despair. Once the foolish passion for Bathsheba controls him, Boldwood neglects his husbandry and never again returns to the rural world. And it is only intense suffering that drives Bathsheba into a swamp of ferns, into the center of the inner pastoral circle of Weatherbury, where she can be morally regenerated through calm self-analysis—achieving "a freshened existence" (p. 267)—in order to reenter society as Gabriel's wife.

Fuller and richer in texture, the second scene of the shearing-cycle is the great one of the sheep-shearers at work in Bathsheba's medieval

barn. Here the value attached to the rural order crystallizes into dia-
mondlike luminosity:

It was the first day of June, and the sheep-shearing season culminated,
the landscape, even to the leanest pasture, being all health and colour. Every
green was young, every pore was open, and every stalk was swollen with
racing currents of juice. God was palpably present in the country, and the
devil had gone with the world to town. Flossy catkins of the later kinds,
fern-sprouts like bishops' croziers, the square-headed moschatel, the odd
cuckoo-pint,—like an apoplectic saint in a niche of malachite,—snow-
white ladies'-smocks, the toothwort, approximating to human flesh, the
enchanter's night-shade, and the black-petaled doleful-bells, were among
the quainter objects of the vegetable world in and about Weatherbury at
this teeming time; and of the animal, the metamorphosed figures of Mr. Jan
Coggan, the master-shearer; the second and third shearers, who travelled in
the exercise of their calling, and do not require definition by name; Henery
Fray the fourth shearer, Susan Tall's husband the fifth, Joseph Poorgrass the
sixth, young Cain Ball as assistant-shearer, and Gabriel Oak as general
supervisor. . . .
They sheared in the great barn, called for the nonce the Shearing-barn,
which on ground-plan resembled a church with transepts. . . .
One could say about this barn, what could hardly be said of either the
church or the castle, akin to it in age and style, that the purpose which had
dictated its original erection was the same with that to which it was still
applied. Unlike and superior to either of those two typical remnants of
mediaevalism, the old barn embodied practices which had suffered no muti-
lation at the hands of time. Here at least the spirit of the ancient builders
was at one with the spirit of the modern beholder. Standing before this
abraded pile, the eye regarded its present usage, the mind dwelt upon its
past history, with a satisfied sense of functional continuity throughout—a
feeling almost of gratitude, and quite of pride, at the permanence of the
idea which had heaped it up. The fact that four centuries had neither proved
it to be founded on a mistake, inspired any hatred of its purpose, not given
rise to any reaction that had battered it down, invested this simple grey
effort of old minds with a repose, if not a grandeur, which a too curious
reflection was apt to disturb in its ecclesiastical and military compeers. For
once mediaevalism and modernism had a common standpoint. The lanceo-
late windows, the time-eaten arch-stones and chamfers, the orientation of
the axis, the misty chestnut work of the rafters, referred to no exploded
fortifying art or worn-out religious creed. The defence and salvation of the
body by daily bread is still a study, a religion, and a desire.
To-day the large side doors were thrown open towards the sun to admit
a bountiful light to the immediate spot of the shearers' operations, which
was the wood threshing-floor in the centre, formed of thick oak, black with
age and polished by the beating of flails for many generations, till it had
grown as slippery and as rich in hue as the state-room floors of an Eliza-

bethan mansion. Here the shearers knelt, the sun slanting in upon their bleached shirts, tanned arms, and the polished shears they flourished, causing these to bristle with a thousand rays strong enough to blind a weak-eyed man. [Pp. 125–27]

This is a scene of great significance because it documents lucidly Hardy's case for the rural world. The prose, if occasionally clumsy, is vivid and dense, and as a whole the scene makes a deep impression on the reader of a strongly rooted past.

From the opening paragraph, a single sentence stands out forcefully: "God was palpably present in the country, and the devil had gone with the world to town." Here Hardy's preference, often enough implied, is made explicit; and as in all forms of pastoral, a criticism of urban life is suggested. Within the country, the paragraph reveals, the life of the natural world is as important as the human life that moves in and out of the landscape. The quaint variety "of the vegetable world in and about Weatherbury" is specified in convincing detail. Each variety has its own separate identity and importance. Moreover, the names of the plant varieties recall human correspondences: the moschatel is "square-headed," the cuckoo-pint is like a saint, "ladies'-smocks" and "doleful" bells abound, and the toothwort approximates "human flesh." In contrast to the identification of the plants, two of the shearers "do not require definition by name." The two orders of life seem equal in rank. Curiously, too, the eight plants balance the eight shearers in a kind of harmony of complements that prepares us for the harmony of the barn and its shearers in a later paragraph. The two kinds of lives—natural and human—are fused into one; on the other hand, the novel leads us to feel that the urban world is cut off from this natural life and that it exists as a rootless and isolated form of life, unsatisfying without sustenance from the natural world.

The famous third paragraph, dealing with the purpose and function of the ancient barn, underlines the essential ideas that provide the foundation of the novel: the ideas of continuing purpose, unchanging practices, "functional continuity" through history, harmony of past and present, massive stability through time. Together, these ideas enforce Hardy's claim for the superiority of rural life. The paragraph, marred only by its tendency toward exposition rather than evocation, shows the probable influence of George Eliot's early work, where such passages are frequent. The beholder's objective contemplation of the building breaks up into a series of subjective reflections on the building's history to produce a miniature essay on the barn.

We return in the fourth paragraph to the evocation of the sheep-shearing. The whole scene inside the shearing-barn is radiant with illumination, and the polished floor is as sturdy and substantial as the shepherds who work upon it. In its way the barn floor is equal to its urban counterpart, the state-room floors of an Elizabethan mansion; yet it is one notch better: the "beating of flails for many generations" is implicitly compared to the lavish dancing on state-room floors. The difference is one of purpose: entertainment is of a separate order of activity from "the defence and salvation of the body by daily bread." The one is fundamental and significant—continuously purposeful; the other, trivial.

The rural-urban contrast at the heart of the pastoral genre is, of course, a major theme in the novel and is effectively, often subtly, embodied in pastoral scenes such as this one. The paragraph that follows is an integral part of the same shearing scene and manifests again Hardy's attitude toward the distinctions between rural and urban life. Hardy says of the shearing scene:

> This picture of to-day in its frame of four hundred years ago did not produce that marked contrast between ancient and modern which is implied by the contrast of date. In comparison with cities, Weatherbury was immutable. The citizen's *Then* is the rustic's *Now*. In London, twenty or thirty years ago are old times; in Paris ten years, or five; in Weatherbury three or four score years were included in the mere present, and nothing less than a century set a mark on its face or tone. Five decades hardly modified the cut of a gaiter, the embroidery of a smock-frock, by the breadth of a hair. Ten generations failed to alter the turn of a single phrase. In these Wessex nooks the busy outsider's ancient times are only old; his old times are still new; his present is futurity.
>
> So the barn was natural to the shearers, and the shearers were in harmony with the barn. [P. 127]

In his ideas on the function of time, Hardy pierces to the center of the contrast between rural and urban. In cities time is an enemy, for it demands rapid changes with a high degree of regularity—styles, theories, interests, tastes. But the rustics view time as a companion because it brings only slight changes to their occupations, traditions, habits, clothing, language, and architecture. Time scarcely affects their culture; and in comparison with cities Weatherbury does seem immutable, without "marked contrast between ancient and modern." Wessex works in harmony with time; London races dissonantly against time. The closer man is to the seasons, the earth, the animals—the more time is a benign force. In Wessex, culture merges *with* time; in London, culture changes as rapidly as time itself and thus becomes submerged in its own impermanence. The peasants of Wessex have discovered the pattern in change; their urban counterparts, only that time changes all. As the shearing scene proves, the agricultural world is continuous in its processes, and it is for this reason, above all, that "the barn was natural to the shearers, and the shearers were in harmony with the barn."

Later we find that the contrast between past and present, found often in pastoral, is strikingly supported by the description of Sergeant Troy, the embodiment in timeless Weatherbury of the rapidly fluctuating urban world: "He was a man to whom memories were an incumbrance, and anticipations a superfluity. Simply feeling, considering, and caring for what was before his eyes, he was vulnerable only in the present. His outlook upon time was as a transient flash of the eye now and then: that projection of consciousness into days gone by and to come . . . was foreign to Troy. With him the past was yesterday; the future, tomorrow; never, the day after" (p. 146). Troy's view of time is a heightened form of the urban view which Hardy has given us earlier. Memories in Weatherbury are never an incumbrance, but a source of pleasure—folk tales, local anecdotes, and family histories such as the maltster relates to Oak. Troy's outlook upon time "as a transient flash of the eye now and then" identifies the source of his isolation from the heart of Weatherbury life and implies criticism. Troy's flashing sword is the perfect symbol of his impermanence. He is shackled to time because he is at the mercy of the present and its vagaries. It is such transience that Hardy has in mind when he speaks in his preface of the gift of rootedness which is assured by "attachment to the soil of one particular spot by generation after generation" (p. xxii). But if Troy lives for the moment only, the barn and the church are the exact antithesis since they represent the control of time, of life; they regularize the lives of the peasants by providing stability and a connection with permanence. Everything that is "modern," Hardy discovered, has the opposite function; and for this reason modernism is the chief source of misery in the novel.

From the sheep-shearing and the barn and from their continuity through time, we turn to the final scene of the shearing-cycle, the charming and idyllic shearing-supper. Building cumulatively on the two earlier scenes, the shearing-supper leads from work to festivity and from one type of continuity to another. Like the other scenes, it too reveals the pastoral atmosphere that imbues the novel:

> For the shearing-supper a long table was placed on the grass-plot beside the house, the end of the table being thrust over the sill of the wide parlour window and a foot or two into the room. Miss Everdene sat inside the window, facing down the table.
>
> . . . . . .
>
> Supper being ended, Coggan began on his own private account, without reference to listeners:—
>> I've lost my love, and I care not,
>> I've lost my love, and I care not;

I shall soon have another
That's better than t'other;
I've lost my love, and I care not,

This lyric, when concluded, was received with a silently appreciative gaze at the table, implying that the performance . . . was a well-known delight which required no applause.

"Now, Master Poorgrass, your song!" said Coggan.

"I be all but in liquor, and the gift is wanting in me," said Joseph, diminishing himself.

"Nonsense; wou'st never be so ungrateful, Joseph—never!" said Coggan, expressing hurt feelings by an inflection of voice. "And mistress is looking hard at ye, as much as to say, 'Sing at once, Joseph Poorgrass. . . .'"

"Now, Joseph, your song, please," said Bathsheba from the window.

"Well, really, ma'am," he replied in a yielding tone, "I don't know what to say. It would be a poor plain ballet of my own composure."

"Hear, hear!" said the supper-party.

Poorgrass, thus assured, trilled forth a flickering yet commendable piece of sentiment, the tune of which consisted of the key-note and another, the latter being the sound chiefly dwelt upon. This was so successful that he rashly plunged into a second in the same breath. . . .

.   .   .   .   .

But the singer could not be set going again . . . and tranquillity was restored by Jacob Smallbury, who volunteered a ballad as inclusive and interminable as that with which the worthy toper old Silenus amused on a similar occasion the swains Chromis and Mnasylus, and other jolly dogs of his day.

It was still the beaming time of evening, though night was stealthily making itself visible low down upon the ground, the western lines of light raking the earth without alighting upon it to any extent, or illuminating the dead levels at all. The sun had crept round the tree as a last effort before death, and then began to sink, the shearers' lower parts becoming steeped in embrowning twilight, whilst their heads and shoulders were still enjoying day, touched with a yellow of self-sustained brilliancy that seemed inherent rather than acquired.

The sun went down in an ochreous mist; but they sat, and talked on, and grew as merry as the gods in Homer's heaven. Bathsheba still remained enthroned inside the window, and occupied herself in knitting, from which she sometimes looked up to view the fading scene outside. The slow twilight expanded and enveloped them completely before the signs of moving were shown.

. . . Liddy brought candles into the back part of the room overlooking the shearers, and their lively new flames shone down the table and over the men, and dispersed among the green shadows behind. . . .

Next came the question of the evening. Would Miss Everdene sing to them the song she always sang so charmingly—"The Banks of Allan Water" —before they went home?

After a moment's consideration Bathsheba assented, beckoning to Gabriel, who hastened up into the coveted atmosphere.

"Have you brought your flute?" she whispered.

"Yes, miss."

"Play to my singing, then."

She stood up in the window-opening, facing the men, the candles behind her, Gabriel on her right hand. . . .

In addition to the dulcet piping of Gabriel's flute Boldwood supplied a bass . . . which threw her tones into relief. The shearers reclined against each other as at suppers in the early ages of the world, and so silent and absorbed were they that her breathing could almost be heard between the bars; and at the end of the ballad, when the last tone loitered on to an inexpressible close, there arose the buzz of pleasure which is the attar of applause. [Pp. 134–38]

This, like the others, is a highly pastoral scene. The idyllic quality is unmistakable. At every juncture, peace and contentment color the prose. The dominant impression of the scene is one of merry but serene harmony. The shearers are caught during a time of relaxed enjoyment and good-natured fun. The mood is tranquil, warm, and gently idealized; the portrait is nostalgic.

The singing of songs after the shearing-supper is a traditional form of entertainment which binds the present to the past. Hardy, in fact, explicitly links the shearing-supper here to suppers "in the early ages of the world." Yet past and present are linked in another sense too—a literary sense. For Hardy compares the shepherd-singers here to the shepherd-singers of traditional pastoral by alluding to Vergil's sixth eclogue, where "old Silenus amused on a similar occasion the swains Chromis and Mnasylus." [14] The parallel to traditional pastoral is highly significant because it shows Hardy's conscious awareness of working within the pastoral tradition. The singing of songs, for instance, is found throughout pastoral literature; and in the alternation of the various singers, we can hear strong overtones of the traditional singing contest. To make the link with traditional pastoral a solid and convincing

[14] Specifically, Hardy has in mind lines 13–28 of Vergil's *Eclogue* 6: "The lads Chromis and Mnasyllos saw Silenus lying asleep in a cave, his veins swollen, as ever, with the wine of yesterday. Hard by lay the garlands, just fallen from his head, and his heavy tankard was hanging by its well-worn handle. Falling on him—for oft the aged one had cheated both of a promised song—they cast him into fetters made from his own garlands. . . . Smiling at the trick, he cries: 'Why fetter me? Loose me, lads; enough that you have shown your power. Hear the songs you crave; you shall have your songs, she another kind of reward.' Therewith the sage begins. Then indeed you might see Fauns and fierce beasts sport in measured time, then stiff oaks nod their tops" (*Virgil*, Loeb Classical Library, tr. H. Rushton Fairclough [Cambridge: Harvard Univ. Press, 1965], I, 43–44).

one, we need have only the "dulcet piping" of Gabriel's flute—the shepherd's traditional instrument—to accompany Bathsheba's plaintive ballad.

In his description of the shearing-supper scene, Hardy is fascinated by illumination. The warm glow of sunny evening descends upon the scene, glazing it with mellow affection. As the "yellow of self-sustained brilliancy" fades over the horizon, the shearers are gradually "steeped in embrowning twilight."[15] With night, they are enveloped completely, only to have Liddy bring another kind of illumination to the scene— the "lively new flames" of the candles. Once again we see the shearers in terms of a soft, mild illumination, which is the reflection of the author's feelings toward them. The evening light becomes a kind of symbol for the mood or tone of the scene, a physical representation of an attitude of idealization and nostalgia. After the singing and the "buzz of pleasure," the light is withdrawn and the scene breaks up into darkness.

We see the scene not only in terms of the human drama but in terms of nature's drama as well: the singers exchange ballads while the sunlight modulates first into darkness and then into candlelight. The two kinds of scenic changes are complementary; they occur together in a kind of harmony. And harmony, again, is the chief impression of a scene where the shearers in friendship "reclined against each other as at suppers in the early ages of the world," a scene endlessly recurrent through the centuries of agricultural work. The shearers are the same, the supper and singing the same, the humor the same. The years have changed, but time has left no stain where men are in touch with the permanence and self-sufficiency of the agricultural world. The idealized tranquillity of the shearing-supper scene—and of all the pastoral scenes —reasserts the value of the agricultural world and reassures its stability.

In this chapter we have observed in detail the pastoral qualities of *Far from the Madding Crowd*: the idyllic, yet frequently realistic, treatment of sheep and shepherds; the similarity of the plot to the plots of pastoral romance and pastoral comedy; the dominant rural-urban contrast; the intense nostalgia for the rural past; the creation of a remote pastoral world; and the cycle of scenes from pastoral life which give us a full view of Hardy's means of creating the pastoral atmosphere that surrounds the novel. This atmosphere is the result, as Henry James long

[15] Hardy's description of the shearers singing in the gathering twilight is strikingly similar to the final five lines of *Eclogue* 6: "All the songs that of old Phoebus rehearsed . . . these Silenus sings. The re-echoing valleys fling them again to the stars, till Vesper gave the word to fold the flocks and tell their tale, as he set forth over an unwilling sky" (ibid., ll. 82–86). Compare also the close of *Eclogue* 2: "and the retiring sun doubles the lengthening shadows" (l. 67).

ago observed, of "a certain aroma of the meadows and lanes—a natural relish for harvestings and sheep-washings."[16] Or in the words of a more recent critic, "*Far from the Madding Crowd* at its best creates a pastoral world of antique simplicity, a fitting background for . . . faithful shepherds and glamorous faithless soldiers."[17]

The novel expresses, often eloquently, the beauty and simplicity of nineteenth-century rural life. If the negative aspects of country life are seldom treated, the poetry and charm of pastoral life nonetheless remain. And if an aura of idealization and nostalgia wafts gently through the pages of the novel, it is because the ancient agricultural life was so quickly vanishing. Many of the greatest scenes in the novel—Oak reading the sky on Norcombe Hill, the sheep-shearing, the shearing-supper, the covering of the ricks before the storm, and the harvest supper —these recapture magnificently, and with insight, the regular rhythm of country life which offered meaningful work, tradition, and an organic relationship with the natural world. Hardy saw those virtues as the most significant loss in our transformation from a rural to an urban-industrial way of life. If the factory replaced the farm, then as Hardy found, so must spiritual impoverishment replace the traditional means of binding man successfully to his surroundings. *Far from the Madding Crowd* recaptures some of the sweet poetry of order at a moment before transformation begins. The pattern of country life, at its least, imposed regularity and order on human instability; at its best, it provided a meaning and a set of traditional beliefs which a later age has been hard pressed to provide.

[16] "Far from the Madding Crowd," *The Nation*, 24 Dec. 1874, p. 424.

[17] Albert J. Guerard, *Thomas Hardy* (1949; rpt. Norfolk, Conn.: New Directions, 1964), p. 74.

Chapter 7

The Woodlanders

"Arcadian Innocents"

PUBLISHED thirteen years after *Far from the Madding Crowd* and
fifteen after *Under the Greenwood Tree*, Thomas Hardy's *The
Woodlanders* (1887) possesses a texture and tone quite unlike that of
his earlier pastoral novels. If they are on the whole charming and idyllic,
The Woodlanders is gloomy and ironic. If they express full confidence
in the strength of the pastoral world to sustain itself, *The Woodlanders*
expresses doubt and anxious melancholy, reflecting perhaps Hardy's interest in Schopenhauer's *The World as Will and Idea.* Urban intruders
expand their number and assert a bludgeoning force. Pastoral figures,
turning stoical, move nearer the realism of the georgic. Yet this is not
the complete case. *As a story*, the novel was Hardy's favorite;[1] and I
believe that its underlying pastoralism made it his favorite story. Set in a
secluded and umbrageous pastoral haven, the woodland world of Little
Hintock harbors "Arcadian innocents" (p. 290), "self-contained lives"
(p. 24), a "prodigally bountiful" earth, and "gorgeous autumn landscape[s]" (p. 212); it reveals delight in work (p. 68), the language
of "trees and fruits and flowers" (p. 341), and an "intelligent intercourse with Nature" (p. 340). From Mrs. Charmond's perspective, the
reader sees that "the world is so simple here!" (p. 246).[2] Using the
method typical of the modern pastoral novelist, Hardy brings together
a large number of pastoral motifs—a dispossession theme, elaborate
plot complication, spurned lover and chastity themes, integration of
setting and character, urban intrusions, and a pastoral elegy—and then
adds to these motifs realistic observation, work, and a tonal flavor alternating curiously between opposite poles of aging vinegar and sweet
cider. It is my contention that this blend of elements has been insuf-
ficiently understood by critics of the novel. No one has I think demon-

---

[1] Florence Emily Hardy, *The Life of Thomas Hardy* (New York: Macmillan,
1962), p. 185. "In after years he often said that in some respects *The Woodlanders*
was his best novel" (ibid.).

[2] Page numbers in parentheses refer to Thomas Hardy, *The Woodlanders*, St.
Martin's Library edition (London: Macmillan, 1958). It should be said that Robert
C. Schweik has questioned the fidelity of the text of the Wessex Edition to Hardy's in-
tention ("Current Problems in Textual Scholarship of the Works of Thomas Hardy,"
English Literature in Transition, 14 [1971], 239–46).

strated, or even quite understood, why the novel is pastoral, or especially
to what degree the novel is a pastoral novel. Critics have recognized
the novel as "a peculiar version of pastoral," to quote one, or a "special
version of Wessex pastoral," to quote another, without satisfactorily distinguishing the novel's pastoral from its nonpastoral elements—a failure
determined largely by an uncertain grasp of what constitutes the genre.
In the current welter of criticism of pastoral, this is not surprising. Pro-
posing to bridge the critical gap, I hope to show that despite its apparent
departures from the traditional genre, *The Woodlanders* is essentially a
pastoral novel, linked to tradition by its plot situations and by its controlling vision.[3]

The novel's pastoral motifs derive from both classical and Renaissance pastoral. The theme of eviction or dispossession of property,
realistic and threatening as it is, occurs twice in Vergil's *Eclogues* and
provides a model for realistic pastoral. (One of the first books Hardy
owned was Dryden's *Virgil*.) *Eclogue* 1, developing the tension between
otium and *discordia*, portrays Meliboeus preparing his exit from the
pastoral precinct of music and shady trees: "I'm driven from my home
place," he tells Tityrus.[4] But "you'll enjoy the longed-for shade, the
cool shade," he adds, troubled and amazed. A "foreigner" has appropriated Meliboeus' land. *Eclogue* 9 compresses the dispossession motif,
openly explored in *The Woodlanders*, into a few lines. Moeris cries:

> Oh, Lycidas, that I should have lived to see an outsider
> Take over my little farm—a thing I had never feared—
> And tell me, "You're dispossessed, you old tenants, you've got to go."
> We're down and out. And look how chance turns the tables on us.
>
> [ll. 2–5]

With equal force, this situation recurs in *The Woodlanders*: by chance,
Giles Winterborne is dispossessed of his ancestral home by a foreigner.[5]

---

[3] Discussions of the novel's pastoralism fall into three camps: those who view
the novel as unalloyed traditional pastoral (Robert Y. Drake, Jr., " 'The Woodlanders' as Traditional Pastoral," *MFS*, 6 [1960], 251–57); those who view the
novel as a fusion of realism and pastoral (George S. Fayen, Jr., "Hardy's *The Woodlanders*: Inwardness and Memory," *SEL*, 1 [1961], 81–100; William H. Matchett,
"*The Woodlanders*, or Realism in Sheep's Clothing," *NCF*, 9 [1955], 241–61;
Peter J. Casagrande, "The Shifted 'Centre of Altruism' in *The Woodlanders*," *ELH*,
38 [1971], 104–25; and Ian Gregor, "Hardy's World," *ELH*, 38 [1971], 274–93);
and finally those who believe that the critical emphasis should fall elsewhere than
on pastoral (Irving Howe, *Thomas Hardy* [London: Weidenfeld & Nicolson, 1968],
p. 102). My discussion assumes a place in the middle ground.

[4] *The Eclogues and Georgics of Virgil*, tr. C. Day Lewis, Anchor Books edition
(Garden City, N.Y.: Doubleday, 1964).

[5] Cf. Wordsworth's "Michael," lines 474–75, and the Saxtons in *The White
Peacock*. Both the *Eclogues* and *The Woodlanders* reflect historical situations of exile

A chance failure to renew the lifehold leases that John South held, leases passed from Winterborne's mother (a South) to his father and then to him, ends his tenancy in Little Hintock and much of his income, whereupon he must depart from Mrs. Charmond's estate. Robert Creedle explains: "the law ordains that the houses fall without the least chance of saving 'em into Her hands at the House" (p. 95). In this highly Vergilian novel, Hardy intensifies the realism he finds in Vergil's *Eclogues*: if Marty is dispossessed of her hair by Mrs. Charmond, Giles is dispossessed not only of his property but of his emotional ties to Grace as well; we shall return to Giles's emotional dispossession later.

The dispossession theme, though central, is not the only pattern of classical pastoral that attracted Hardy's imagination. Hardy fuses patterns from both Vergil and Theocritus. From Theocritus' *Idyll* 7 he takes the pattern of sophisticated urbanites who journey into the country and eventually return to the city, as the substance of his "intruder" plot. But Hardy's attitude toward the intruder plot is not positive like the Greek poet's; in every scene the narrator of the novel mistrusts the intentions of the sophisticated intruders, who practice deception and enjoy idle leisure. At the heart of his "rural" plot, on the other hand, one finds the pattern of Vergil's *Eclogues* 1 and 9—in which exile, dispossession, time, unrest, and hints of labor move into the foreground;[6] one finds also the elegiac pattern of *Eclogue* 5, a lament for the dead shepherd Daphnis. Hardy then welds together these pastoral patterns, or plots. Once they are recognized, the novel emerges as more *purely* pastoral than has heretofore been imagined. If he reorders and adapts the special conditions of the bower, his vision retains its strong pastoral bias.

More central to the action of the novel is the pastoral motif of extreme plot complication, a convention of Renaissance pastoral romance. Unlike the brief compass of pastoral poetry, the length of the pastoral novel requires the variety and tension supplied by a plot: a division of emotional loyalties of course quickly injects conflict and interest into a long fictional form. Robert Drake, following the lead of Hallett Smith, recognizes that the romantic ties of *The Woodlanders* fall into the Renaissance pattern of "cross-eyed Cupid" in which A loves B, B loves C, C loves D, and D loves A: Marty loves Giles, Giles loves Grace, Grace

from the land; see, e.g., L. P. Wilkinson, "Virgil and the Evictions," *Hermes*, 94 (1966), 320–24.

[6] Michael C. J. Putnam remarks: "A journey out of the country toward the city, instead of vice versa, is symptomatic of . . . far-reaching intellectual discrepancies between Virgil and Theocritus" (*Virgil's Pastoral Art* [Princeton: Princeton Univ. Press, 1970], p. 337).

loves Fitzpiers, Fitzpiers loves Mrs. Charmond.[7] The arrangement of emotional relationships progresses like links of a chain, from rural Marty to urban Mrs. Charmond, spanning nicely the distance between simplicity and sophistication, poverty and wealth, toil and idleness—a distance continually exploited in the novel. If the motif of plot complication reflects the novel's pastoralism, so does the motif of the rejected swain or constant lover, which Hardy uses with total seriousness to trace the parabola of Giles's short life. The motif, though it is especially clear in the *Aminta*, occurs in Guarini's *Pastor Fido*, Daniel's *The Queen's Arcadia* and *Hymen's Triumph*, Fletcher's *The Faithful Shepherdess*, Randolph's *Amyntas*, and Jonson's *Sad Shepherd*. In Tasso's pastoral romance the *Aminta* (publ. 1580), the woodlander Aminta, spurned by his beloved but too-modest Silvia, seeks his own death.[8] His pure constancy, heightened by rejection, leads him to a cliff in the woodland from which he leaps, yearning for death. Instead, his fall is broken and he is gradually restored to health by the repentant Silvia, who at last conquers her cruel modesty. Giles Winterborne, a constant but unaggressive lover, updates Aminta. Reserved and upright, honest and pure, he has loved Grace Melbury since childhood (he is "one who had always been true" [p. 212]), and until she leaves Little Hintock to acquire her education, she loves him in return. But her training and her travels modernize her outlook, they deracinate her loyalties. When she returns home at last, "she had fallen from the good old Hintock ways" (p. 47).

[7] Drake, p. 253; Smith, *Elizabethan Poetry* (Cambridge: Harvard Univ. Press, 1952), pp. 17–18. Suke Damson, whose loyalties divide between Fitzpiers and Tim Tangs, does not fit the pattern.

In fact, the plot diagram of Guarini's *Pastor Fido* (publ. 1590), perhaps the best of the Italian pastoral dramas, looks much like the plot diagram of *The Woodlanders*:

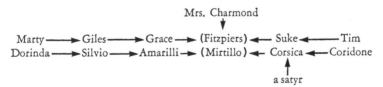

The plot centers (marked) of both works coincide; so do male and female participants. Giles and Silvio, both figures of the wood, coincide as the "constant lover" of pastoral tradition. Both works, like Tasso's *Aminta*, are tragi-comedies, although they differ in many respects, one being a drama, the other a novel.

[8] Cf. Thomas G. Rosenmeyer: "Throughout the later Renaissance, melancholy reigns supreme in the pastoral; death, exile, unhappy love are the important themes" (*The Green Cabinet* [Berkeley and Los Angeles: Univ. of California Press, 1969], p. 227).

Persuaded by her ambitious father that her training has rendered her "too good" for Giles, Grace discourages his attentions: " 'I am assured [marriage] would be unwise' " (p. 99). Giles, forced to "make the best of his loss" (p. 67), endures with feigned indifference her ensuing marriage to Dr. Fitzpiers and its collapse. Soon after hopes for a divorce collide with social law, Giles, living in exile in a hut near Little Hintock, takes sick. His fever "seemed to acquire virulence with the prostration of his hopes" (p. 303). When Grace, fleeing from her husband, seeks temporary refuge at Giles's hut, Giles's modesty allows him to expose himself, in a "strange self-sacrifice," much like Aminta's, to the cold damp. By the time Grace, herself a version of Silvia, overcomes her modesty, "cruel propriety" has, if only in part, felled her Giles (pp. 322–23). The rejected-swain motif, employed traditionally to show the cruelty of a beloved, permits Hardy to use Giles as his protagonist and to link the cruelty of love to larger social evils—divorce laws, urban invasion, and declining rural strength. We therefore see the pastoral bower from the innocent view within and from the sophisticated view without.

But parallel patterns reflect clusters of vertical weight rather than the horizontal complexity of verbal texture. Many pastoral elements appear in modern costume, and others, such as *otium*, undergo total metamorphosis.

Like many novels, *The Woodlanders* has both a male and a female protagonist. But unlike *Tom Jones* or *Pride and Prejudice* or *Adam Bede*, the two protagonists do not marry at the close of the novel. The relationship shared by Giles Winterborne and Marty South, like that between Catherine and Heathcliff or Jude and Sue, is more spiritual than sensual. Though Giles and Marty differ in some important respects from shepherds of classical or Renaissance pastoral, they are *pastoral* heroes. Giles bears the marks of pastoral in his innocence, altruism, honesty, relative poverty, intimate relationship with nature, chastity, humility, simplicity, meditativeness. To these we must certainly add his delight in his work. These qualities preserve *otium* or tranquillity, perhaps the most essential characteristic of the traditional pastoral lyric.

Living in "one of those sequestered spots outside the gates of the world," says Hardy, the inhabitants of Little Hintock exhibit "more meditation than action, and more listlessness than meditation" (p. 10): physical location and human response thus conjoin. Circumscribed by shady boughs—shade is the sine qua non of classical pastoral—and seldom in contact with the outer world of money and power, Giles and

Marty live pure, initially uncomplicated and tranquil lives. "Hardly anything could be more isolated or more self-contained than the lives of these two," remarks Hardy early in the novel (p. 24). A "reticent woodlander" (p. 124), Giles is "pure and perfect in his heart" (p. 333). Until his death, even Grace had not understood the "purity of his nature, his freedom from the grosser passions, his scrupulous delicacy" (p. 323). Marty South, solitary and sublime in character, possesses little of the narrative yet objectifies, with Giles, the novel's moral vision, its ethic of man and nature fusing harmoniously, each dependent on the other and linked together by an unwritten language. Hardy demonstrates this ethic in an important passage analyzing imaginatively the ideal relationship between Giles, Marty, and nature:

Marty South alone, of all the women in Hintock and the world, had approximated to Winterborne's level of intelligent intercourse with Nature. In that respect she had formed his true complement in the other sex, had lived as his counterpart, had subjoined her thoughts to his as a corollary.

The casual glimpses which the ordinary population bestowed upon that wondrous world of sap and leaves called the Hintock woods had been with these two, Giles and Marty, a clear gaze. They had been possessed of its finer mysteries as of commonplace knowledge; had been able to read its hieroglyphs as ordinary writing; to them the sights and sounds of night, winter, wind, storm, amid those dense boughs, which had to Grace a touch of the uncanny, and even of the supernatural, were simple occurrences whose origin, continuance, and laws they foreknew. They had planted together, and together they had felled; together they had, with the run of the years, mentally collected those remoter signs and symbols which seen in few were of runic obscurity, but all together made an alphabet. From the light lashing of the twigs upon their faces when brushing through them in the dark either could pronounce upon the species of the tree whence they stretched; from the quality of the wind's murmur through a bough either could in like manner name its sort afar off. They knew by a glance at a trunk if its heart were sound, or tainted with incipient decay; and by the state of its upper twigs the stratum that had been reached by its roots. The artifices of the seasons were seen by them from the conjuror's own point of view, and not from that of the spectator. [Pp. 340–41]

Hardy's generous use of anaphora ("They had been . . . had been . . . . They had . . . together they had . . . together they had. . . . From the . . . from the . . .") implies, rhetorically, his deep emotional commitment to the kind of interaction or "intercourse" between man and nature that functions for Hardy as an imaginative ideal. With hints of Platonism perhaps derived from Shelley, Hardy stresses the role of intelligent perception in penetrating the "finer mysteries" which may be hidden to the insensitive or the unsympathetic. Like Gabriel Oak, these two figures understand natural processes and readily decipher nature's alphabet.[9] As Grace says to Marty, "you and he could speak in a tongue that nobody else knew . . . the tongue of the trees and fruits and flowers themselves" (p. 341). Dispossessed of nature's language, Mrs. Charmond can hardly distinguish a beech from an oak. The knowledge, understanding, and sympathy with which Giles and Marty are able to approach nature allows them to form a unique, asexual alliance with nature: a marriage. Both renounce human sexuality: Giles is free from gross passion and at the hut observes a severe propriety; at the moonlit close, Marty "looked almost like a being who had rejected with indifference the attribute of sex" (p. 379). By embracing an "intelligent intercourse with nature" and by establishing a spiritual empathy between themselves, both characters illustrate the separation (frequent in pastoral) of sexual from spiritual love.

The intimacy of Giles and Marty with nature expresses itself not only in a conscious mental awareness of the interaction, but also in physical interaction with nature in the form of work. Normally the mention of work in pastoral is enough to shatter *otium*.[10] In this respect Hardy breaks with traditional pastoral to make an important change: in his treatment of rural life, he moves toward the georgic, ranking useful labor above *otium*. Traditionally, leisure and tranquillity merge in the bower. But in *The Woodlanders* Hardy splits them. To Giles and Marty he gives considerable tranquillity *and* work. To Mrs. Charmond and Grace, he gives idle leisure; to Fitzpiers, the pursuit of whim. Unlike

[9] Ian Gregor perceptively comments, however, that "Marty and Giles live within a world whose language is dying, and in consequence, it is a world which can no longer be made communicable. It becomes, as the final scene shows, a monologue to the dead" (p. 283). But Hardy makes clear in the final lines of *The Woodlanders* that Marty will continue, with Creedle as her assistant, to represent and to realize Giles's mythical absorption in natural processes. She will become Autumn's "sister" and, as such, will "communicate" her world. To say that "the old ways are exhausted" (Gregor, p. 283)—a point which Grace's final choice nicely illustrates—does not perhaps account for the future of meaningful work projected in the novel's last scene. Gregor would, I imagine, argue that the old ways can be expressed "only in the rigidity of gesture" (p. 284), an illuminating phrase. But I find that Fitzpiers' rhetorical effusions early and deceptive promises late, and Grace's taut insistence on following "the most correct and proper course" from beginning to end (p. 352), display an even greater rigidity of gesture than do Giles and Marty.

[10] "Whenever *labor* in whatever form, from physical action to the subtlest spiritual trials, challenges *otium*, it spells doom" (Putnam, p. 379). "But when the intrusion of *ponos* ['labor and pain'] becomes more than a minor counterpart . . . it is difficult to imagine that we continue to be dealing with a pastoral poem" (Rosenmeyer, p. 23).

traditional pastoral, leisure arouses, paradoxically, not *otium* but *negotium*—an emotional turbulence mild in Grace, pronounced in Fitzpiers, feverish in Mrs. Charmond.

For Giles and Marty, work is satisfying because it orders their world. Like Adam Bede, Giles "found delight" in his work (p. 68). Later, when Marty travels in the autumn with Giles's cider-press, she too will find satisfaction and purpose in her work. Early in the novel we find Giles and Marty preparing to plant trees:

> What he had forgotten was that there were a thousand young fir trees to be planted in a neighbouring spot which had been cleared by the wood-cutters, and that he had arranged to plant them with his own hands. He had a marvellous power of making trees grow. Although he would seem to shovel in the earth quite carelessly there was a sort of sympathy between himself and the fir, oak, or beech that he was operating on; so that the roots took hold of the soil in a few days. When, on the other hand, any of the journeymen planted, although they seemed to go through an identically similar process, one quarter of the trees would die away during the ensuing August.
>
> Hence Winterborne found delight in the work even when, as at present, he contracted to do it on portions of the woodland in which he had no personal interest. Marty, who turned her hand to anything, was usually the one who performed the part of keeping the trees in perpendicular position whilst he threw in the mould.
>
> .   .   .   .   .
>
> The holes were already dug, and they set to work. Winterborne's fingers were endowed with a gentle conjurer's touch in spreading the roots of each little tree, resulting in a sort of caress under which the delicate fibres all laid themselves out in their proper directions for growth. [P. 68]

That Giles and Marty work, as in the georgic, does not in any way negate the pastoral vision of man in harmony with nature. The "sympathy between himself and the fir, oak, or beech" differs little from the shepherd-piper teaching the woods to sing (Vergil's *Eclogue* 6, e.g.) or the trees lamenting the death of the shepherd-hero Daphnis. Like the pastoral piper, Winterborne enjoys a "marvellous power" over nature; like the piper, he is a "gentle conjurer." In the same way that nature in classical pastoral reciprocates by echoing the musician's melody, the roots, touched by Giles, "took hold of the soil in a few days."[11] True to the pastoral vision, moreover, delight in nature is divorced from money or personal gain: Giles, a minister of nature, had no "personal interest" to serve. Out of his delight springs a good measure of pastoral tran-

[11] See Phillip Damon, "Modes of Analogy in Ancient and Medieval Verse," *University of California Publications in Classical Philology*, 15 (1961), 282–90.

quillity. Later, Hardy expresses this idea of interaction between man and nature in mythological terms, using both anaphora and Grace's point of view: "He rose upon her memory as the fruit-god and the wood-god in alternation: sometimes leafy and smeared with green lichen, as she had seen him amongst the sappy boughs of the plantations: sometimes cider-stained and starred with apple-pips, as she had met him on his return from cider-making in Blackmoor Vale, with his vats and presses beside him" (p. 286). A Pan figure put to work, Giles, whether fruit-god or wood-god, is still the "conjurer" of the preceding passage— still the figure who has entered the heart of natural processes and who provides the *locus amoenus* with its divinity.

In another passage Giles's kinship (quite literally) to nature expresses itself in flashes of poetry, bathed with gentle feeling, that characterizes Hardy's pastoral fiction: "He looked and smelt like Autumn's very brother, his face being sunburnt to wheat-colour, his eyes blue as corn-flowers, his sleeves and leggings dyed with fruit-stains, his hands clammy with the sweet juice of apples, his hat sprinkled with pips, and everywhere about him that atmosphere of cider which at its first return each season has such an indescribable fascination for those who have been born and bred among the orchards" (p. 213). The quickest index to the depth of nostalgic "fascination" in this portrait is again the use of anaphora, a rhetorical scheme that Hardy regularly employs in passages to which he, or the implied author, commits himself emotionally. The identification of Giles with an organic process imaged as bountiful and benevolent achieves no simpler or purer form than it does here. The opening figure is instructive: a brother represents one's likeness or similarity; in this case the human figure manifests endless visual and gustatory parallels to nature. At one point Giles even assumes "the colour of his environment" (p. 156). If he is called a conjurer and a god, Giles is also, here, demythologized and brilliantly painted, the portrait seizing the whole man: seizing his internal beauty and innocence, and the external equivalents of his internal state. Hardy immerses him in the harvest, perfuming Giles's visual exterior with the redolent atmosphere of crops, much as Lawrence immerses George Saxton in the heavy perfume of the harvest field.

But if Giles delights in his work, Marty does not. His work is never tedious; hers is. Despite her absorption in natural occupations, she emerges as a realistic figure. This fact, in the way it distances the novel from pastoral, should not go unobserved. Skilled at her work and uncomplaining and heroic, yet poor and somber and sometimes listless, Marty South finds life "a hard struggle" (pp. 19–20); and as the novel opens, we find her working all night, making spar-gads for Melbury. As faithful to Giles as he is to Grace, Marty is "always doomed to sacrifice desire to obligation" (p. 153).[12] Stoic rather than epicurean, Marty approximates figures of the georgic, a genre in which the farmer, treated seriously, is glorified as he performs the hard tasks of planting or trimming trees or pressing apples into cider. The pastoral novel in the nineteenth century moves clearly in the direction of the georgic.

In *The Woodlanders* what Hardy does to pastoral is most interesting. We can discover a clue to his conception of modern pastoral in a phrase he uses to describe Marty's journey to Sherton Abbas. Her steadfast concentration, he says, "means purpose and not pleasure" (p. 37). For the pleasure or leisure he finds traditionally in pastoral, Hardy substitutes *purpose*—a purposive relationship with the natural world from which a livelihood, enjoyment, and emotional tranquillity are derived. The observation that purpose is moral and pleasure or leisure immoral can be readily illustrated in the novel.[13] The failure to find meaning through one's work is equated by Hardy, as by George Eliot, with moral and ethical failure. While Giles lived, Marty and Grace enjoyed "no anticipation of gratified affection" in their relationship with Giles. On the other hand, Hardy observes with dismay the tattooed marks of cloying leisure on Mrs. Charmond and, to a slightly lesser extent, Fitzpiers. The ironic name "Felice" hints at her pleasurable, leisure-loving *modus vivendi*, one that dreads contact "with anything painful" (p. 239). Mrs. Charmond, "always with a mien of listlessness," murmurs to Grace: " 'I am the most inactive woman when I am here,' she said. 'I think sometimes I was born to live and do nothing' " (p. 64). Fitzpiers, who too "did not study economy when pleasure was in question" (p. 183), always finds Mrs. Charmond "reclining on a sofa" (p. 199), indulging "in idle sentiments" (p. 205), and arousing for him an "indefinite idle impossible passion" (p. 207). In a marvellously inverted sentence,

[12] Lord David Cecil remarks: "Only those like Marty, who have planted trees year after year for their daily bread, have achieved that intimacy with such activities which enables them to perceive therein their profounder imaginative significance" (*Hardy the Novelist*, 2d ed. [London: Constable, 1965], p. 77). I cannot however agree with Peter J. Casagrande ("The Shifted 'Centre of Altruism' in *The Woodlanders*"). To say that "Marty is a monstrosity of humanity, crushed into frustration and bitter spitefulness by the woodbines of economic necessity and unrequited love" or that she is "blindly destructive" (p. 116) seriously miscalculates the novel's tone and moral vision in an effort to make characters analogous to trees. The destructive monstrosities, Hardy often suggests, are Fitzpiers and Mrs. Charmond, frustrated by idleness and uncontrolled passions (see below). Although I sometimes disagree with his detailed analysis of *The Woodlanders*, Casagrande has very perceptive things to say about the structural similarities between *Under the Greenwood Tree, The Woodlanders*, and *Return of the Native*.

[13] Ian Gregor arrives at a different view: "Hardy juxtaposes past and present in such a way that we don't think in terms of . . . an opposition between 'love' and 'work' " (p. 289).

loaded with artifice, Hardy remarks that, while holding her cigarette, Mrs. Charmond "idly breathed from her delicately curled lips a thin stream of smoke towards the ceiling" (p. 194). Even Fitzpiers contemplates a distant scene in an "idle way" (p. 208). Stripped of purposive direction, Fitzpiers enjoys "too many hobbies" to reach professional eminence, reading books of "emotion and passion as often as . . . science" (pp. 127–28). Pastoral leisure, condemned as it is by the implied author, unlocks the characters' idle indulgence, which then breaks loose to destroy the simplicity and tranquillity of the innocent pastoral characters. Idleness in turn fertilizes those emotions that eventually blossom into consuming passions. Fearing "his own rashness," Fitzpiers "allowed himself to be carried forward on a wave of his desire" (p. 160). When he initiates the "impassioned enterprise" of paying Grace Melbury a social call, he senses "that he was casting a die by impulse which he might not have thrown by judgment" (p. 168). Mrs. Charmond, Byronic rather than pastoral, is "capriciously passionate" (p. 221), like Trollope's Madeline Neroni in *Barchester Towers*. Acting always "on impulse," she possesses a heart "passionately and imprudently warm" (p. 44). Hintock bottles up her emotions, and neither she nor Fitzpiers can outgrow "the foolish impulsive passions" of their youth (p. 196). Having no means of ordering their emotions, they enter upon agitated misalliances that plunge them, to use the surgeon's phrase, into "sorrow and sickness of heart at last" (p. 200). Their withdrawal into a lovely place, directed by their idle and passionate natures, propels them downward into a churning vortex in which order—both personal and social —is lost. Fitzpiers, like Arthur Donnithorne, ignores social barriers and allows his professional practice to decline; Mrs. Charmond, in practicing adultery, breaks legal barriers and in the scene of Fitzpiers' rumored death witnesses the crumbling of her self-respect. Throughout the novel these fluctuating passions and shifting alliances find their scenic equivalent in the frequent changes of light intensity—flaring matches, swinging lanterns, fleeting shadows, moving candles, dying fires, dawn turning to day and day to dusk—thus explaining in part Hardy's unusual concern with light.

Despite the moral hiatus between purpose and work on the one hand, and idle leisure and romance on the other, Hardy does connect both admired and unadmired characters by using romantic love and physical setting as connective agents. In the seventeenth century, Fontenelle theorized that pastoral results from a marriage between love and idleness; love, that is, prevents leisure from turning to sloth, and enlivens *otium*.[14] Hardy will tolerate love in the pastoral world (provided it is

14 "Of Pastoral," trans. Motteux (London, 1695), p. 282; quoted by Rosenmeyer, p. 77.

chaste) but not idleness. The result is that the idle, whimsical characters intrude unnaturally into the *locus amoenus* and violate its purity. The motif of intrusion, producing imaginatively a reaction of fear and anxiety, dominates the novel and requires us to look briefly at the U-shaped curve of the action it originates.

As intruders, both Fitzpiers and Mrs. Charmond (and to a much lesser extent Grace) hail from urban climes. Edred Fitzpiers, "of late years a town man" (p. 120), comes to the secluded village as a surgeon reportedly in league with the devil (p. 10). Having chosen the shady woodland hamlet arbitrarily, he had quit the urban world on a mere impulse, "in a passion for isolation, induced by a fit of Achillean moodiness after an imagined slight" (p. 202). Not long afterward, Grace Melbury, daughter of a prosperous Hintock timber merchant, returns home, her education complete. Fashionable and refined, though "not ambitious" (p. 203), Grace has acquired a "veneer of artificiality" (p. 213) that quite appeals to Fitzpiers and that provides a welcome contrast to the "crude rusticity" of Hintock (p. 119), although unlike Arthur Donnithorne, Fitzpiers hesitates but a moment to seduce Suke Damson, a lusty village plum. Quickly wooing Grace from Giles, to whom her father had promised her many years before, Fitzpiers manipulates Grace into his wife only a few months before he encounters the sophisticated widow, Mrs. Felice Charmond, a woman with a mysterious past, "a charmer in her time," a one-time actress "who has smiled where she has not loved, and loved where she has not married" (p. 235). To the surgeon's joy, she returns his passion with fervor. In their "erratic abandonment to doubtful joys" (p. 326), they make easy conquests of each other and, without sanctions, elope to the continent, where they had met earlier. Fitzpiers, stationed at the center of romantic complications, thus conquers a woman from each level of society: rural, rural/ urban, urban. As Hardy portrays them, the two intruders invade Little Hintock like an army, leave with the spoils, and cause others to leave— Giles, Suke and Tim, Grace. We never see a conflict among the villagers that has not its roots in urban culture or (much more frequently) the aliens. Thus, in modifying pastoral, Hardy has not only shifted sympathy from the disguised rustics of tradition to actual rustics of his observation, but he has illustrated that the novel's moral hierarchy is inversely related to class structure: the characters who command the narrator's admiration are those without property or rank. Hardy makes no attempt, as pastoralists often have and as Lawrence does in *Lady Chatterley's Lover*, to remove barriers between classes. Instead, his deep sympathy for country people encourages what Lawrence in his study of Hardy calls "moral antagonism" toward the aristocrat.

The kind of relationship that a character establishes between himself and his physical setting serves as Hardy's usual method of judging a character's moral worth—a narrow test rigorously applied. If the intruders with their idle passions disturb the emotional calm of the pastoral world, the narrator retaliates by concretely demonstrating how that world, by exposing their alien natures, rejects them. Consistently and with skillful art, Hardy pairs the aliens and then contrasts them openly, without subtlety, to their pastoral surroundings. Unlike Connie and Mellors, they enter the pastoral haven not to be reoriented by its simplicity and charm but to disturb its texture of tranquil daily life. Much of Hardy's careful pairing of the aliens depends for its effect upon the city-country contrast that is a touchstone of pastoral literature. The persistent contrast of the modern pair and the traditional life they endanger allows Hardy to clarify his moral vision through the use of negative definition and to heighten dramatic tension by using the pair as foils. If both are worldly, both excite the woodlanders' interest with the mystery of their lives: Mrs. Charmond "liked mystery in her life" (p. 202), and Fitzpiers' appeal grew out of the "mystery" of his life (p. 210). Fitzpiers, likened to a tropical plant in a hedgerow, "had nothing in common with the life around" (p. 54). Mrs. Charmond, bored by the region, proved "a piquant contrast to her neighbours" (p. 66). Both of them emancipated, she smokes cigarettes and he holds "irreverent" views—alerting the reader to their moral nature. Both of them dishonest amid "honest people" (p. 231), Fitzpiers—a bit of an actor himself—delivers a "theatrical . . . effusion" to Grace, concluding: " 'Never. . . . Never could I deceive you' " (p. 136). Not to be outdone, Mrs. Charmond, alarmed by Grace's knowledge of her affair with Fitzpiers, denies the attachment "with insistent untruth" (p. 246). If Giles is "the fruit-god and the wood-god in alternation," Fitzpiers is demonic. Calling the surgeon a villain (p. 263), Melbury explains how "the devil tempted him in the person of Fitzpiers, and he broke his virtuous vow" (p. 234). Thus: "What could he and his simple Grace do to countervail the passions of those two sophisticated beings—versed in the world's ways, armed with every apparatus for victory?" (p. 222). The acknowledged power of these two beings masters their integrity and dissipates the simplicity of the bower.

Alien not to the woodlanders alone, Fitzpiers and Mrs. Charmond —like the gentleman from South Carolina—are alien to their setting as well, which in typically pastoral fashion refuses to harmonize with their unnatural natures. For them, lacking as they do Wordsworthian memories of their present environment, Little Hintock and its woods are lonely and monotonous. Hintock House, for example, reveals its unfitness "for modern lives" like Mrs. Charmond's (p. 62). Fitzpiers "hated the solitary midnight woodland" (p. 120), and his mate in passion, because she hates solitude (p. 63), also "disliked the woods" (p. 241). If the tricks of the weather "prevented any sense of wearisomeness" in the natives of Hintock (p. 130), Fitzpiers requires some romantic diversion "to relieve the monotony of his days" (p. 138). Because they fail to harmonize with their setting, nature does not excite their interest, but tricks them instead. Fitzpiers, "ever unwitting in horseflesh," mistakes his horse because of the gloom (p. 259); and shortly thereafter, Blossom unseats this "second-rate" equestrian (p. 265). Both Mrs. Charmond and Grace lose their sense of direction (physical *and* moral) in the "umbrageous surroundings" of the wood (p. 247). In like surroundings, Fitzpiers experiences "a sudden uneasiness" at the contrast of nature's "great undertakings" and his own idleness (pp. 139–40).[15] Nature exerts a moral force, as it does when Troy plants flowers on Fanny's grave. This kind of oppression arises from lack of sympathy with one's environment: Mrs. Charmond must, for example, counteract "the fine old English gloom" of Hintock House (p. 258). Fitzpiers, already "oppressed" by Hintock (p. 119), suffers an "indescribable oppressiveness" near the end of his wedding journey and later feels "doomed" to Hintock (pp. 186, 261). This place "oppresses me," Mrs. Charmond cries to Grace (p. 64). Although Grace "never got any happiness outside Hintock" (p. 230), Fitzpiers wants to "get away from this place for ever" (p. 191). The failure of the invaders to appreciate the woods and the woodlanders confirms their antipastoral function, which is heightened in *The Woodlanders* nearly to obsession. The invaders' inability to sympathize genuinely with whatever, natural or human, lies outside the confines of the self corrodes their humanity, and the negative landscape descriptions beautifully reflect the corrosive texture of their minds.

These quotations document the antipastoral pattern of disharmony and intrusion that persistently counterpoints the pastoral pattern of happiness, tranquillity, harmony with nature, and spiritual love. The intruders permit Hardy to make explicit the conservative moral vision that controls the novel: the man who allows license (or, departure from Christian codes) to guide his actions lives *immorally*; the man who comprehends nature, rejects ambition, embraces altruism, and favors reticence lives *morally*. In using his villains to represent a vision of immorality, Hardy encounters the problem that Lawrence faced with Clifford Chatterley: how to prevent the novel from becoming morally schematic and therefore weakening its reality. I do not think that Hardy,

15 But contrast strangely: "Fitzpiers dreamed and mused till his consciousness seemed to occupy the whole space of the woodland round, so little was there of jarring sight or sound to hinder perfect mental unity with the sentiment of the place" (p. 145).

like Lawrence, entirely surmounts this difficulty. Because he allots much space to Mrs. Charmond and Fitzpiers, so that their villainy becomes exaggerated, his indictment of their idle passion and their devotion to pleasure loses, finally, some of its force. There are two reasons for this critical imbalance: whereas the reticence of Marty, Giles, and Grace tends to deny life, the passion of Mrs. Charmond and Fitzpiers asserts life; it becomes, finally, more attractive to the reader than perhaps it should if we are to remain persuaded by the novel's moral vision. More troublesome, I think, is the treatment accorded the characters who exemplify moral and immoral visions. Unlike Sergeant Troy, Felice Charmond and Fitzpiers indulge their passions with no worse effects than the characters who refuse indulgence. Chastity and honor, while praised by the narrator, merit punishment; virtue enjoys no clear sustained value.[16] The unchaste and dishonorable, while censured, are punished with no more severity; although Fitzpiers promises to pass through "a long state of probation" (p. 351), his dishonorable character, the narrator implies, will endure. Now, it will be objected that in this Hardy simply gives us a picture of an unschematized reality, or that he admits no inherent moral system to order human life—that the Unfulfilled Intention manifests itself indifferently. But values that a reader is persuaded to accept at the start of a novel lose their power and their sense of moral precision when they are compromised, to the extent that Hardy allows, by an opposing scale of values. Hardy's art, fascinating but also disturbing in its lack of moral coherence between plot strands, does not provide the intellectual subtleties we relish in George Eliot or Conrad. To say so is not to criticize but to try to seize upon the novel's distinctive features.

Earlier I said that Hardy's moral vision was conservative and traditional rather than innovative; and, with the exception noted, his vision is consistent with the pastoral vision. But like Sidney or Spenser or Marvell, Hardy had little fear of innovation in pastoral and, without reluctance, mixed genres—readily fusing pastoral themes with realistic techniques. His conception of the pastoral novel permitted substantial innovation in his focus on Grace as a bridge character between rural and urban, and in his use of the principle of *division* as the template for the narrative.

Although Grace functions as the valence of the novel, tautly joining city to country, Hardy provides her until the end of the novel with clear moral direction. When she returns "from the world to Little Hintock"

---

[16] Matchett nicely observes: "Of what avail were Giles's goodness and the good things he did?" (p. 260).

(p. 54), she had "fallen from the good old Hintock ways" to become "well-nigh an alien" (pp. 47, 50). Like Cyril in *The White Peacock*, Grace, longing for simplicity and even physical labor, upbraids her father: " 'I wish you had never, never thought of educating me. I wish I worked in the woods like Marty South! I hate genteel life, and I want to be no better than she!' " (p. 229). Despite Grace's cultured refinement, she emerges like Bathsheba Everdene as young and naive, a girl deceived by alcoholic sophistication. Fitzpiers acts upon her "like a dram, exciting her" (p. 164) and produces "intoxication" in her brain (p. 169), metamorphosing her into a wasp "which had drunk itself . . . tipsy" (p. 186). Juxtaposed to Mrs. Charmond, Grace becomes a "simple school-girl" (p. 246). Her schooling and her susceptible nature, however, divide her loyalties and deflect the "natural course" (p. 221) of her love for Giles. Directed toward simplicity by her varied experience of both rural and urban and then (when she returns) of her experience of rural-from-urban perspective, Grace at last finds virtue only in the hearts of "unvarnished men." Her discovery of virtue, "her widening perceptions of what was great and little in life" (p. 227), hastens her progress from refined accomplishment and acquired tastes to simplicity. This progression reaches its climax when she recognizes Giles as Autumn's brother: "Her heart rose from its late sadness like a released bough; her senses revelled in the sudden lapse back to Nature unadorned. The consciousness of having to be genteel because of her husband's profession, the veneer of artificiality which she had acquired at the fashionable schools, were thrown off, and she became the crude country girl of her latent early instincts" (p. 213). Hardy traces the trajectory of pastoral innocence on the path toward knowledge and culture; he then reverses directions in order to observe the truncation of the movement. The cultural process or trajectory brings not insight, as it does in Austen or Dickens or Henry James, but regret. Virtually every journey away from Hintock ends in failure: Grace's repeated journeys to a fashionable school, Melbury's to London, Fitzpiers' and Mrs. Charmond's to Germany. An adequate guide to conduct must, the novel suggests, emerge from innocence, instinct, "nature"; it is "nature" that "had striven to join together" Grace and Giles (p. 258). In *The Woodlanders* knowledge warps consciousness, deflects or weakens moral impulses. The implied tragedy of the novel is not, I believe, Giles's death but Grace's inability to return to her native Hintock. Like Cyril Beardsall or Clym Yeobright, Grace possesses firm rural roots; but her return to pastoral contentment is diseased by what Lawrence calls in *The White Peacock* "the torture of strange, complex modern life," a torture Grace must ultimately face. By dissecting the "pastoral" collision between two differing sets of values, Hardy can, by castigating one set, heighten the significance of the other, even though we sense clearly the power of sophistication over innocence. More important, he can use a single main character, of "modern nerves" and "primitive feelings" (p. 306), as the vehicle to express his pastoral theme of art versus nature. Grace's characterization, then, defines Hardy's theme; and the varied *directions* of her characterization do much artistically to define value in the novel.

One other innovation that illustrates Hardy's altered conception of the pastoral form is his insistence on division—physical, social, emotional—as the principle basic to the novel's texture and theme. It is well known that the book is divided between early conception (1874) and late execution (1885–87), and divided again between pastoral and realism. But, that the principle of division controls theme, characterization, quality of diction, and representation of physical objects has not been recognized. The sharp central division between *rus* and *urbem*, which Hardy insists on, easily subsumes other kinds of division. Both the book's moral vision and its theme of art versus nature or sensual versus spiritual love depend on the city-country contrast for their sustained effectiveness. From a social standpoint, Grace and her father are both divided between rural and urban affinities. From a romantic or emotional standpoint, characters are nicely split between one lover and another, as we have seen: Grace between Giles and Fitzpiers; Fitzpiers between Suke and Grace and Mrs. Charmond; and Suke between Tim and Fitzpiers. Melbury is socially divided between Fitzpiers and Giles, Marty is separated from Giles by Grace and by death, Giles is exiled from his ancestral homeplace, John South is tortured by a tree he loves. Nature herself divides her work between displays of beauty and revelations of cruelty or unfulfilled intentions. These assorted divisions, while they sustain the plot and give significance to the theme, produce tension rather than pastoral stasis. Similarly, what the bark-rippers do to the branches of the trees or what the surgeon does to John South's brain or what nature does to itself when the ivy strangles a sapling, the characters do to each other.

These larger conceptual and philosophical divisions are mirrored, with sharp accuracy, in quality of diction and in representation of physical objects. Accusing her father of driving Giles from her door, Grace says, " 'You do things that divide us more than we should naturally be divided' " (p. 270). Fitzpiers to Grace: " 'A parting is unavoidable, as you are sure to be on his side in this division' " (p. 275). Giles felt sure that his old friend Melbury would repair the "error of dividing two whom nature had striven to join together" (p. 285). And for Tim Tangs, the scheme of emigration "was dividing him from his father" (p. 359). The principle of division, moreover, holds true physically as well as emotionally. Insistently the novel uses paths, roads, stiles, gates, walls, gloom, fog, and foliage screens as typical physical objects or conditions. Holly bushes "divided the coppice from the road" (p. 70). The grassy ride was "screened on either hand by nut-bushes" (p. 215). A railing "divided . . . the house from the open park." Characters disappear "amid the gloom of the lawn" (p. 259). The quadrangle of Melbury's house, "divided from the shady lane by an ivy-covered wall, was entered by two white gates" (p. 256). If the honeysuckle formed "a tangled screen" (p. 156), Grace was "screened and roofed in from the outer world of wind by a network of boughs" (p. 242). The physical barriers and linguistic choices functionally extend the divided emotions of the characters. That setting, character, and theme are so fully intertwined helps to define the novel as pastoral, however much the negative implications of barriers and imagery and divided emotions qualify its pastoral texture.[17]

One reason Hardy is attracted to pastoral is that his imagination is intensely visual and therefore extremely sensitive to the setting in which his characters live and work. Not only are most of his novels *seen* by the narrator; his characters are shown *observing* most of the time. He lets us see characters or events, or lets us see *with* his characters, much more frequently than he lets us share their thoughts. A few random pages will illustrate—those in which Hardy introduces us to Fitzpiers' abode (pp. 117–19). We find a long architectural (and therefore visual) description of the house in which an orchard "could be seen" over the roof of the house or in which a swing-gate is "visible" from the parlor "window." Inside, Fitzpiers stands "looking out," then "notices" Suke grasp the gate "without looking," then "recognized" Marty, and then Grace's "appearance." As Grace "looked" at the gate, Fitzpiers "looked for his hat," "glancing again out of the window," then "watched" her out of sight, "recognizing" her unlikeness to the others he had "seen" in Hintock. The novel's setting, like the *locus amoenus* of pastoral, is evoked in a similar manner, dominated by visual perceptions and images. Although its penchant for music and romance is well known, pastoral has an equal fondness for landscape, which is visually apprehended by most pastoralists. In *The Woodlanders* Hardy eliminates the resounding melodies of pastoral—they are too mellow for a modern pastoral novel —and substitutes for them a visual harmony of light and shade, of shape and size and proportion and color, painting with the dark hues

17 George S. Fayen remarks acutely: "Experience in *The Woodlanders* takes shape as an intertwined, matted profusion of human desires and natural impulses that are deflected and distorted; every move seems impeded by something resistant and contentious" (p. 90). See also Ian Gregor's interesting essay on *Jude the Obscure* in *Imagined Worlds*, ed. Maynard Mack and Ian Gregor (London: Methuen, 1968), pp. 244–45, for further analysis of Hardy's use of dividers.

of Millet's *The Gleaners* rather than with the tones of sunny peace and benevolent order typical of a Constable landscape.

Hardy's skillful integration of landscape and character, found universally in pastoral, constitutes the novel's major strength. Landscape in pastoral both reflects and projects a character's emotions. Vergil's *Eclogues* or Marvell's "Mower" poems classically illustrate this correspondence, in which outer and inner worlds provide images of each other. Although the last section of the novel, from Grace's escape to the conclusion, limps regrettably, the pastoral correspondence between landscape and mind is in this section very successfully developed. When Grace retreats from Fitzpiers to Giles's hut beyond the boundaries of Mrs. Charmond's estate, the autumn rains have begun. Already sick, Giles, his altruism and chivalry at a peak, moves from his hut to a rough shelter of hurdles fifty yards away. In so doing he can avoid impropriety and offer Grace the better shelter. Critics have then usually suggested that nature helps to kill Giles by chilling him and thus hastening his death. In fact, the polarization of figurative language supports this contention. Hardy's conception of nature made figuratively like man has, generally, a strongly *negative* resonance: puddles are like corpses (p. 325), stumps like black teeth (p. 320), rain like blood (p. 317), roots like claws (p. 219), fungi like lungs (p. 56). His conception of man made figuratively like nature, though less frequent, consistently carries neutral or positive resonance: Giles is faunlike (p. 297) and like Autumn's brother (p. 213), Grace is like a queen bee and a tipsy wasp (pp. 221, 186), her heart like a bough (p. 213), her husband like a tropical plant (p. 54), and Marty like a great bird (p. 140). This pattern of polarized figures reinforces the "downward" movement of man to nature, which is sanctioned by the favorable "man-is-like-nature" strand of imagery. Although Marty sustains Giles's work, the favored *direction* of the figurative relationship between man and nature cannot be used to argue for the perpetuation of human life, but only for the perpetuation of nature's life. In this respect the novel's imaginative consistency, pulling always groundward, is remarkable.[18]

Hardy follows Giles's removal to the shelter with a description of a night storm, more grotesque than the famous description of the storm in *Far from the Madding Crowd*; the description images Grace's fear:

The wind grew more violent, and as the storm went on it was difficult to believe that no opaque body, but only an invisible colourless thing, was trampling and climbing over the roof, making branches creak, springing

[18] My view differs from that of Casagrande, who finds little polarization in the imagery and, upon this premise, "a monistic view of man and nature" in the novel (pp. 113–14).

out of the trees upon the chimney, popping its head into the flue, and shriek-
ing and blaspheming at every corner of the walls. . . . Sometimes a bough
from an adjoining tree was swayed so low as to smite the roof in the manner of a gigantic hand smiting the mouth of an adversary, to be followed
by a trickle of rain, as blood from the wound. To all this weather Giles must
be more or less exposed; how much, she did not know. [P. 317].

As both are dying, Nature's wound becomes Giles's wound. While the
storm shrieks, Giles repeatedly coughs, ill with fever. When Grace looks
out of the hut for Giles, the trees, signaling, brandish "their arms"
wildly (p. 318). Giles's reply floated to her "upon the weather *as
though a part of it*" (p. 319; my italics); human and natural thus
merge. As Giles's clock (representing human time) stops inside his hut
(p. 320), natural time has also run out: scattered about the hut were
"dead boughs" (p. 320). When the wind ceases and the rain begins its
"steady dripping" (p. 321), Giles begins his "low mutterings"—"an
endless monologue, *like that we sometimes hear from inanimate nature*"
(p. 322; my italics). Internal and external perfectly correspond, then
are explicitly compared. If the evening sun made "the wet trunks shine"
and threw ruddy splotches on the leaves (p. 321), Giles in correspond-
ing fashion reveals, that same evening, eyes of "burning brightness" and
a face "flushed to an unnatural crimson" (p. 322). Night, blind with
the dark, becomes Giles, his senses opaque, unable to recognize Grace
"in his semi-conscious state" (p. 323). When Grace manages to get
Giles inside the hut and then at last to sleep, his mutterings having come
to an end, "there [was] now no rain" (p. 325), no equivalent sound
from nature. Instead, puddles formed by the rain "had a cold corpse-
eyed luminousness" (p. 326). Shortly afterward, Giles dies (p. 330).
The autumn death of nature and the death of Giles occur simultaneously
(he is twice called "Autumn's brother"). True to pastoral tradition, the
landscape has, elegiacally, reflected and projected Giles's condition. The
two layers of description, human and natural, run parallel in such a
way that the metaphorical resonance at times becomes richly allegorical.

   Before we examine the pastoral elegy which aptly closes the novel,
something more should be said about the hut to which Giles and Grace
retreat. As we saw in *Adam Bede*, the hut or cabin in the wood away
from the village forms the center of the *locus amoenus*, the place in
which the characters—Hetty and Arthur in this case—become reoriented to reality. In *Lady Chatterley's Lover* the hut, at the center of the
locus amoenus, serves a like function, permitting Connie and Mellors
to renew their perspective through the regenerative medium of sexuality.
Replacing the cave of pastoral tradition, a secluded hut, then, carries
potential relevance to pastoral. Hardy's use of so similar a hut in *The
Woodlanders* demonstrates yet another way in which the novel attempts

to adapt pastoral motifs to realistic fiction. But where the abodes in *Adam Bede* and *Lady Chatterley* are places of regeneration, the hut in *The Woodlanders* is a chamber of sickness and death, a place of degeneration that encourages not sexual fulfillment but a full savoring by Grace and Marty of abortive, disappointed love. In all three novels, a man and a woman escape frustrating circumstances (both Giles and Grace have escaped from urban intruders) by retreating to a hut located at a short distance from a manor house. But where sexual freedom engenders the sequence of actions of Hetty and Arthur or Connie and Mellors, strict propriety restrains the actions of Grace and Giles. " 'Can it be that cruel propriety is killing the dearest heart that ever woman clasped to her own!' " (p. 322), Grace cries at last. Yet two pages later, Hardy calls our attention to the parallel between Mrs. Charmond nursing the injured Fitzpiers and the present scene portraying Grace's devotion to Giles; mechanically similar as the scenes are, says Hardy, they are "yet infinite in spiritual difference" (p. 324). Thus he nicely underlines the pastoral theme of sensual versus spiritual love, a distinction that Hardy, unlike George Eliot or Lawrence, forcefully insists on.[19] At Giles's hut, license becomes prudence, and sensuality rises to spirituality; the first is expressive, the second however repressive. Hardy has with some bitterness inverted a convention of pastoral romance.

The novel closes, after a lengthy denouement, with a muted pastoral elegy, spoken by Marty, that has inspired the admiration of the novel's commentators (e.g., Cecil, pp. 103–4). If nature's lamentation does not form part of Marty's elegy, something certainly akin to lamentation occurs a little earlier and reinforces the pastoral harmony between character and setting. As Grace and her father walk away from the hut after Giles has died, "the chilling tone of the sky was reflected in her cold, wet face. The whole wood seemed to be a house of death, pervaded by loss to its uttermost length and breadth. Winterborne was gone, and the copses seemed to show the want of him" (p. 336). If the sky finds its image in Grace's chilled features, Giles's death finds its reflection in the grieving wood. But Hardy heightens still more the pastoral intimacy between dead hero and nature. During their walk home, Grace and her father had seen "but one living thing on their way, a squirrel, which did not run up its tree, but, dropping the sweet chestnut which it carried, cried chut-chut-chut and stamped with its hind-legs on the ground" (p. 338). Hardy shows a frequent fondness for using animals to comment on human folly (earlier a bird complains sarcastically as Fitzpiers and Suke make love on the moonlit hay). His use of the squirrel implies

[19] Casagrande's view is the opposite of mine: "The entire episode at One Chimney Hut is made to parallel—to Giles' discredit—an earlier scene at Hintock House in which Felice lovingly renders aid to Fitzpiers after his fall from a horse" (p. 122).

the criticism of Grace that as narrator he refrains from expressing. As in traditional pastoral—in Theocritus' *Idyll* 1 or briefly in *Idyll* 7, for example—Hardy allows nature to alter her course because of the death of the pastoral hero: the squirrel, which would normally head for the safety of the tree, stops to complain of Giles's death. The participation of a sympathetic nature, though separated from Marty's elegy, is properly a part of it.

The elegy is preceded by the periodic visits of Marty and Grace to Winterborne's grave. The visits form the processions of mourners, one of the conventions of the pastoral elegy. Like those who lament the death of the gamekeeper in *The White Peacock*, the mourners lay flowers on the grave. Marty and Grace follow their weekly ritual "for the purpose of putting snowdrops, primroses, and other vernal flowers thereon as they came" (p. 354) until Grace, at last, rediscovers "the arms of another man than Giles" (p. 379) and is accused by the narrator of neglect, the accusation being still another convention of the pastoral elegy. Marty alone remains loyal: "whenever I get up I'll think of 'ee, and whenever I lie down I'll think of 'ee again. Whenever I plant the young larches I'll think that none can plant as you planted; and whenever I split a gad, and whenever I turn the cider wring, I'll say none could do it like you. If ever I forget your name let me forget home and heaven! . . . But no, no, my love, I never can forget 'ee; for you was a good man, and did good things!" (p. 380).[20] Remarkable here is Hardy's use of two more conventions of the pastoral elegy—the praise of the dead hero and the consolation of the aggrieved friend. Like the rites of praise that Menalcas in Vergil's *Eclogue* 5 promises to the dead hero Daphnis, Marty also promises a ritual of remembrance and praise. The ritual, suggested stylistically by the use of anaphora, will keep burning the memory of the sylvan hero she loved, at the same time that it offers her a consolation.[21] Using anaphora also, Menalcas sings: "Long as boars love heights and fish love streams, / long as cicadas sip at the dew, / Long as bees suck thyme—will you remain / praised and famed, our yearly vows receiving" (ll. 75–78). Marty's vow expresses her

[20] A similar passage occurs in the "Lament for Bion," attributed to Moschus, in which the loyal Galatea mourns the death of Bion, then carries on his work in the fields: "She looked upon you more gladly than upon the sea. And lo! now the waves are forgotten while she sits upon the lone lone sands, but your cows she tends for you still" (*The Greek Bucolic Poets*, 2d ed., tr. J. M. Edmonds, Loeb Classical Library [1912; rpt. Cambridge: Harvard Univ. Press, 1928], p. 449).

[21] Cf. Rosenmeyer: "The keynote in a pastoral lament is the sounding of life in death, not death in life" (p. 226). Renato Poggioli remarks: ". . . the pastoral of friendship finds its highest expression in the funeral elegy, which is but a shepherd's lament for a friend 'dead ere his prime' " ("The Oaten Flute," *Harvard Library Bulletin*, 11 [1957], 164).

commitment in a more personal way: "If ever I forget your name let me forget home and heaven!" In a view more pagan than Christian—a view true to the pastoral vision—death is absorbed into the continuing cycle of planting and harvesting, the seasonal duties themselves serving as reminders of Giles's goodness and deeds; Giles is finally integrated into the larger sphere of animal and vegetable life.

If Hardy lingers awhile inside the hut, it is to renew the conflict between Grace and Fitzpiers, not to sentimentalize the death of Giles. In fact, although Hardy's sacrifice of his hero on the altar of propriety has in it the sting of social criticism, Giles's death is muted, the narrator is detached, the tragic implications are unnoted. Rosenmeyer (p. 112) has commented that in the pastoral lyric the peace and gentleness and simplicity of the bower have the effect of muting the pathos of death. Hardy's elegiac close unfolds from similar assumptions: the quiet seclusion of the graveyard, the intimation (both earlier and at the close) of cycles larger than a single life, compress grief into its proper perspective. If immortality is passed over, yet the simple and homely elegy murmured by Marty succeeds in assuaging sorrow and revealing to man his place in the universe.

The Woodlanders, for all its realism, is, I hope I have shown, more purely and more fully pastoral than has heretofore been allowed. Persuasively I think, Hardy adapts conventions and patterns of classical and Renaissance pastoral—the motif of dispossession, the rejected swain, pastoral setting fused with pastoral heroes, the intruder motif, the retreat to a hut, and the pastoral elegy at the close—and modernizes them with gloomy hues of brown and black, often staining their polite surfaces with futility and despair. Still, if the novel leaves behind it the heady stale fragrance of cut flowers on a grave, it leaves also the thick smells of oozing cider and rich harvests. What *The Woodlanders* lacks in scrupulous proportioning of thematic lines, it gains in Hardy's imaginative and successful integration of setting and character. What it lacks in dramatic power, it gains in its perception of the historical forces that juxtapose present with past, and rural with urban, and in its ability to suggest both historical and ahistorical perspectives. Hardy evokes a sense of the timeless world of pastoral, the world of Marty and Giles, as much as he does the emerging modernity of Grace and Fitzpiers. If too many scenes are sketched rather than developed, the delineation of emotional conflict must be judged full and successful. Although pastoral *otium* has been sacrificed to the demands of Hesiodic realism, the sacrifice allows Hardy to wed to his pastoral vision an unflinching, yet unobtrusive, moral vision. Most important, Hardy reveals, in his love of pastoral forms and attitudes, a surprising measure of continuity with the pastoral tradition, even though that tradition has undergone alteration in Hardy's hands. If *The Woodlanders* maintains a twilight atmosphere of change and stoical regret, D. H. Lawrence's *The White Peacock* unfolds under a bright morning or early afternoon sun. Though both develop the same broad themes of rural change, with intruders and dispossession and talk of emigration, Lawrence's novel treats younger, more vital, more joyous characters within the context of a pastoral valley. Copses give way to open fields, regret to nostalgia, stoicism to delight, listlessness to exuberance, elegy to idyll. We turn from a novel steeped in Vergil to one brisk with Theocritus.

The White Peacock

"Fit for Old Theocritus"

MORE FULLY than either Thomas Hardy or George Eliot, D. H. Lawrence discovered early the dual nature of his experience: his profound and permanent attachment to the English countryside, and his immersion in industrialized town life. Born in 1885, when Hardy was at work on *The Woodlanders*, Lawrence spent his early days in Eastwood, a small mining town in Nottinghamshire where farms and coal pits lay juxtaposed and where industrialization was firmly entrenched. In fact, financial need required him to work in a Nottingham factory for several months in 1901. But as the antidote to this experience, he discovered in himself a magnetic attraction to the life and scenery at the Haggs farm, where the Chambers family were admired tenants; and he used the family as a model for the Saxtons in *The White Peacock*, although they, like Tim and Suke Tangs, emigrated to a distant land and so illustrate forcefully the depopulation process that profoundly disturbed Hardy. From 1901 to 1908 Lawrence very frequently walked or cycled to the Haggs farm, two miles from Eastwood, where he was virtually adopted as a son, helping Alan Chambers with the farm work, teaching songs and games to the family, and reading to them in the evening. The impact on Lawrence's imagination of both the family and their farm cannot be underestimated. Much later, the second version of *Lady Chatterley's Lover* ends with Connie and Parkin looking ruefully on the "Haggs Farm . . . and the mill-ponds at Felley, lying so still, abandoned." In 1928, the year he published *Lady Chatterley's Lover*, Lawrence wrote to a member of the Chambers family: "Whatever I forget, I shall never forget the Haggs—I loved it so. I loved to come to you all, it was really a new life began in me there."[1] Connie Chatterley, too, often takes walks into a lovely wood and discovers "a new life" begin in her there. But in 1908, at age twenty-three, Lawrence like Hardy and George Eliot before him migrated to London, where he taught in an elementary school. Although he came to like his fellow teachers and occasionally his teaching, his first reaction to London was

---

[1] Harry T. Moore, ed., *The Collected Letters of D. H. Lawrence* (New York: Viking, 1962), II, 1100.

"full of the anguish of the loss of the old life."[2] Lawrence declared to a friend: "I'll not endure it. I'd rather work on a farm."[3] But three years later, tuberculosis relieved him of the need to stay in London, and the publication of *The White Peacock* and some stories and poems assured him of a literary career. In 1912 he left for Germany with a married woman, just as George Eliot earlier had fled to Germany with George Henry Lewes. An exile now, Lawrence would return to England only for visits. Thus the pressures of Lawrence's experience played a decisive part in directing him toward the pastoral genre: the spread of factories and mines whose ugliness compelled him to revel in the Haggs farm and the beauty of the countryside; his exposure to London and to the enforced routine he despised; and the models of pastoral literature that hung before him like threads of light—Theocritus, Vergil, Milton, *As You Like It*, and especially the novels of George Eliot and Hardy.

Lawrence almost surely had *The White Peacock* in mind when he wrote to Sydney Pawling in 1910, calling one of his novels "a decorated idyll running to seed in realism."[4] Lawrence's remark accurately describes his first novel, *The White Peacock*. Rewritten several times, it was published finally in 1911 when Joyce and Proust were initiating the modern novel and when a temporary equilibrium had settled over Georgian England. Yet its roots lie deep in nineteenth-century fiction. Graham Hough points out that in the major sections of the novel "Lawrence approaches most nearly to George Eliot or Hardy—to the traditional novel of English provincial life."[5] When Lawrence began to write *The White Peacock*, he seems to have had George Eliot and *The Mill on the Floss* particularly in mind.[6] Like *Sons and Lovers* (1913) or *The Rainbow* (1915), *The White Peacock* is a transitional novel between the nineteenth and twentieth centuries, between traditional and modern; what makes it distinctive is that it begins as a nineteenth-

[2] Edward Nehls, ed., *D. H. Lawrence: A Composite Biography* (Madison: Univ. of Wisconsin Press, 1959), III, 611.

[3] Harry T. Moore, *The Intelligent Heart*, 2d ed. (New York: Grove, 1962), p. 111.

[4] *Collected Letters of D. H. Lawrence*, I, 67.

[5] *The Dark Sun: A Study of D. H. Lawrence* (London: Gerald Duckworth, 1956), p. 27.

[6] We have Lawrence's statement to Jessie Chambers that when he was ready to write a novel, it was with George Eliot's novels in mind: " 'The usual plan is to take two couples and develop their relationships,' he said. 'Most of George Eliot's are on that plan' " (E. T. [Jessie Chambers], *D. H. Lawrence: A Personal Record*, 2d ed. [London: Frank Cass, 1965], p. 103).

century novel but ends on a dissonant, twentieth-century chord.

The link between *The White Peacock* and the early pastoral novels of George Eliot and Hardy is stronger than we might at first imagine.[7] All the novels examined in this study reveal the same structural pattern, the same kind of human conflict: a young woman living in the country is forced to choose between two dissimilar suitors, one rural and one urban. In each novel the motivation for much of the action lies in the conflict that this double attraction ignites in the lives of the characters. In *The White Peacock* Lettie Beardsall, cultured and lovely, must choose between Leslie Tempest, son of a wealthy industrialist, and George Saxton, a farmer's son. The conflict, which follows the vagaries of courtship and culminates both in Lettie's marriage to Leslie and in George's decline, forms the essence of the plot. In Hardy's pastoral novels, Fancy Day in *Under the Greenwood Tree*, Bathsheba Everdene in *Far from the Madding Crowd*, and Grace Melbury in *The Wood-landers* face exactly the same kind of choice. Hetty Sorrel in *Adam Bede* must choose between Arthur Donnithorne and Adam Bede, and the pattern of *Silas Marner* is only slightly different: Eppie chooses not between two lovers, but between two "worlds"—one humble, one proud and wealthy. In *Lady Chatterley's Lover*, Connie Chatterley chooses between her husband, Sir Clifford, and his gamekeeper, Mellors. These fictional conflicts between urban and rural connect the novels and represent, moreover, the actual class conflict at the center of much nineteenth-century social history—the conflict between the working class and the nobility or landed gentry. The fictional pattern has most significance if we see it within this broad context of an historical reality that the novels reflect.

Despite its impressive link with the structural pattern revealed in the pastoral novels of George Eliot and Hardy, one comes to study *The White Peacock* apologetically, for it is frequently dismissed by its critics. Dr. Leavis calls it "painfully callow," an "extremely immature novel"; and Keith Sagar argues that as a novel in its own right, "*The White Peacock* is hardly worth attention."[8] As a novel, it is easily dismissed

[7] W. J. Keith, however, has argued that "in the case of *The White Peacock*, comparison with Hardy is more a hindrance than help" ("D. H. Lawrence's *The White Peacock*: An Essay in Criticism," *University of Toronto Quarterly*, 37 [1968], 231). But see now Richard Swigg, *Lawrence, Hardy, and American Literature* (London: Oxford Univ. Press, 1972).

[8] F. R. Leavis, *D. H. Lawrence: Novelist* (1955; rpt. Harmondsworth: Penguin, 1964), p. 6; Sagar, *The Art of D. H. Lawrence* (Cambridge: Univ. Press, 1966), p. 9. In *D. H. Lawrence: The Failure and the Triumph of Art* (1960; rpt. Bloomington: Indiana Univ. Press, 1964), p. xi, Eliseo Vivas adds: "His first two novels I have not examined at all. The work of a talented beginner, they can have only biographical interest." George H. Ford makes perhaps a fairer assessment of the

because it lacks formal perfection. But to reject it too quickly, we shall see, is to miss much that is worthwhile, for the novel is still readable and still alive and absorbing as a work of the imagination. It is not a great novel; it survives as a collection of striking parts rather than as an aesthetically coherent whole. But it will seem most successful to us if we follow Lawrence's suggestion and view it not as a realistic or naturalistic novel, but as a mutation of pastoral.

Mark Schorer has already noticed the pastoral element in *The White Peacock*: "The background of ... *The White Peacock*, is a slow cultural convulsion ... in which the ancient pastoralism of the yeoman way of life yields to the new mechanization of the industrial way of life."[9] George H. Ford has similarly written that in the novel "the action seems less important than the loving evocation of a pastoral setting,—the brooks, hayfields, and wild flowers which the characters observe in their walks."[10] Yet other critics differ sharply. W. J. Keith has recently argued that the predominant tone of the novel is one of frustration and disillusion.[11] But this argument denies a large portion of our actual experience of *The White Peacock*, for the naturalistic portions of the novel do not create the dominant impression that the novel makes on the reader's mind. Keith's remarks, like those of Julian Moynahan, account for only one aspect of the novel, its realism. The long, lyrical, very frequent passages of farm life and landscape description at the heart of the novel are slighted.

Now the realism of the novel is to be neither disputed nor denied: bees, mice, and rabbits are sportingly (though not maliciously) killed; an injured cat is of necessity drowned; wild dogs kill the squire's sheep; the characters gradually become disillusioned; and the world *beyond* idyllic Nethermere is bleak. The bulk of such realism, however, is concentrated in the walking trips outside the valley of Nethermere and in the final chapters and does not provide the novel with its central focus.[12]

---

novel's merit: "It is, however, worth discussing like an early Shakespearian play or Hardy novel, both for its charm in its own right and for its interest as forecasting Lawrence's characteristic preoccupations as a writer of fiction" (*Double Measure* [New York: Holt, Rinehart, & Winston, 1965], p. 48).

9 "Introduction" to *Lady Chatterley's Lover*, Modern Library Edition (New York: Random House, n.d.), pp. ix–x.

10 *Double Measure*, p. 47.

11 "*The White Peacock*: An Essay in Criticism," p. 240. For Julian Moynahan, *The White Peacock* "depicts in a series of loosely repetitive episodes the spiritual ruin or actual physical destruction of several male characters" (*The Deed of Life* [Princeton: Princeton Univ. Press, 1963], p. 5).

12 Claude M. Sinzelle remarks: "The paradox of *The White Peacock* is that, though the treatment of the human plot is pessimistic, the general impression left is one of brightness and hope. . . . This prevailing impression of brightness is not easy

On the other hand, the novel is not pure idyll, either, but, as suggested, is best discussed as a mutation of the pastoral genre. It is not "a giddy little pastoral—fit for old Theocritus," as one character says. Instead, it is a modified or modern pastoral novel characterized by its lyrical landscapes, its circumscribed pastoral valley, its pointed contrast between city and country modes of life, its tensions between rural and urban values, its full representation of a pastoral picnic, its inverted pastoral conclusion, and its nostalgic backward look to the valley that once functioned for the characters as a Golden Age.

What makes the novel complex for the critic are the many impulses at work in the novel. These impulses are numerous because the novel mixes lyrical, elegiac, and harshly realistic elements. In particular, the novel has posed a critical problem in that it manifests two strong but opposing tendencies: a tendency toward romanticism and a tendency toward naturalism. Recent critics have concentrated mainly on the naturalistic strain. This essay, however, while fully recognizing the novel's realism, sets out deliberately to discuss the romantic-idyllic-pastoral strain, which seems frankly to make the dominant impression.

What emerges in a study of the novel as a pastoral (or rather modified pastoral) novel is a matrix of four attitudes toward rural life, four different expressions of the pastoral impulse: a tinge of antipastoral reflected in the occasionally harsh passages about rural life; a modified or realistic pastoral, close to Hardy's, that is reflected in the often idyllic portrait of life at Strelley Mill farm; a portrait of the Beardsall family— Mrs. Beardsall, Lettie, and the shadowy narrator, Cyril—who live in a remote rural setting and who enjoy not regular agricultural labor but the fruits of culture, the beauty of nature, and freedom from any necessary work; and, last, a parody of a traditional pastoral picnic, artificial and self-consciously humorous, which depicts cultured urbanites affecting dialect and pretending to be Theocritean rustics. These attitudes reflect the various pressures of Lawrence's early experience—his reading of naturalistic fiction such as *Jude the Obscure*, his direct observation of the Chambers family at the Haggs farm, his feeling of social inferiority, causing him to shift the Beardsalls from working to middle class, and his sensitivity to the literature of the pastoral tradition. To account for the complexity and the disparate impulses in the novel and to illuminate the varied treatment given to rural life, we should consider each of the four expressions of pastoral.

---

to account for, but it permeates subtly every description, and it is the out-of-doors scenes which impress the mind most in *The White Peacock*" (*The Geographical Background of the Early Works of D. H. Lawrence* [Paris: Didier, 1964], p. 57).

The antipastoral impulse is by far the least fully developed and does not emerge very clearly until the novel has, in Lawrence's words, "run to seed in realism." We have an early glimpse of sordid rural life in the brief picture of the gamekeeper's family living in disorder. Much later, when the family has moved to Selsby, the couple who replaces them—a "mouse-voiced" shrew and her "mouse-voiced man"—are cleverly caricatured by Lawrence. Near the end of the novel, Cyril and Emily return to Nethermere to visit Strelley Mill farm and find the house occupied "by a labourer and his wife, strangers from the north." They possess none of the Saxtons' charm: "He was tall, very thin, and silent, strangely suggesting kinship with the rats of the place. She was small and very active, like some ragged domestic fowl run wild" (p. 291).[13] The charm of the Saxtons has soured. Yet such a description can occur only in the final chapters, when the pastoral world has dissolved and when the novel has ripened into realism.

The pastoral region of the novel is the small, magnificent, rather isolated valley of Nethermere; and the largest portion of the novel evokes, through description of landscape and character, the pastoral atmosphere that permeates the first two of the three main sections of the novel. The valley is a pastoral hollow of happiness, full of youthful glamour: "I thought of the time when my friend should not follow the harrow on our own snug valley side, and when Lettie's room next mine should be closed to hide its emptiness, not its joy. My heart clung passionately to the hollow which held us all" (p. 74). Like George Eliot's Raveloe and like Hardy's Mellstock or Little Hintock, the valley is secluded and enclosed, a variety of *locus amoenus*; inside, a multitude of birds and wild flowers live in pristine freshness. As Robin Magowan writes of nineteenth-century pastoral narrative, the pastoral haven becomes a felt experience "through the sensual concreteness with which its details are presented. Presented with sufficient pictorial skill, these details form the image of a world rich and satisfying, the perfect complement in space to the lives of the pastoral characters."[14] So it is with the snug hollow that harbors the two families at the center of the novel, the Saxtons who live at Strelley Mill farm and the Beardsalls who occupy Woodside nearby.

Lawrence sees the Saxtons nostalgically, as living an admirable life; yet he also sees that their life has a realistic side, and thus he does not

[13] Parenthetical page numbers in my text refer to D. H. Lawrence, *The White Peacock*, Crosscurrents / Modern Fiction Edition (Carbondale: Southern Illinois Univ. Press, 1966). Inconsistencies have been silently corrected in the following lines of the novel: 54.35, 171.12, 177.38, 250.21, 250.41, 251.27.

[14] "Fromentin and Jewett: Pastoral Narrative in the Nineteenth Century," *Comparative Literature*, 16 (1964), 334.

oversimplify it, creating a modified version of pastoral. Often enough, realistic details rupture the pastoral atmosphere of cowslips and violets. The squire allows rabbits to invade the Saxtons' pasture lands and to crop their grass. External urban forces, such as industrialism and education, invade the stability of the pastoral valley. Even the hooters from the nearby mines can be heard. And occasionally George himself, virile and "of handsome physique"—the center of narrative interest—is discontented with the sameness of his life. It is George who provides the focus of the transition from country to town, which is part of the novel's theme of the dissolution of human character when its roots in the ancient rhythms of agriculture are cut by aspiration for the world beyond.

A September harvest spent with George at Strelley Mill farm evokes the nostalgic lyricism that is so notable a strength in the novel. Cyril, the narrator (his name is an anagram of *lyric*), works through the quiet autumn mornings, sharing his knowledge of books with George; this particular autumn "fruited the first crop of intimacy between us":

We tramped down to dinner with only the clinging warmth of the sunshine for a coat. In this still, enfolding weather a quiet companionship is very grateful. Autumn creeps through everything. The little damsons in the pudding taste of September, and are fragrant with memory. The voices of those at table are softer and more reminiscent than at haytime.

Afternoon is all warm and golden. Oat sheaves are lighter; they whisper to each other as they freely embrace. The long, stout stubble tinkles as the foot brushes over it; the scent of the straw is sweet. When the poor, bleached sheaves are lifted out of the hedge, a spray of nodding wild raspberries is disclosed, with belated berries ready to drop; among the damp grass lush blackberries may be discovered. Then one notices that the last bell hangs from the ragged spire of fox-glove. The talk is of people, an odd book; of one's hopes—and the future. . . . The mist steals over the face of the warm afternoon. The tying-up is all finished, and it only remains to rear up the fallen bundles into shocks. The sun sinks into a golden glow in the west. The gold turns to red, the red darkens, like a fire burning low, the sun disappears behind the bank of milky mist, purple like the pale bloom on blue plums, and we put on our coats and go home. [Pp. 66–67]

The concrete, metaphorical language of this striking passage approaches the concentration and evocation of poetry in its marked rhythm and alliteration and consonance. The work of the harvesters is not wearisome but pleasant. The labor of the farm is apprehended lyrically so that the emphasis falls on the beauty and fulfillment that accompany the harvest work. The passage maintains the easy, wistful rhythm of the September harvest. Its mood is one of bounty and fullness, aroused by the heavy pull of adjectival words and phrases, yet saved from languor by the opposing pull of vivid verbs and striking figures. Especially notable is the use of personification to suggest that inanimate nature is as active and engaging as the human harvesters. Since personification integrates man and nature by causing nature to assume human qualities, man and nature seem equal. The artistic success of the passage lies in its rich variety, with sentences evoking a response from all five senses.

The climax of the hymn to farm life comes in a well-known chapter, "A Poem of Friendship," famous—like Vergil's second eclogue—for its unguarded expression of homoerotic love. Both Lawrence and Vergil skillfully use a pastoral landscape to absorb passion that cannot be openly expressed. But they approach the love from opposite temporal perspectives: whereas Vergil portrays the yearning for an idyll, Lawrence portrays the idyll coming to a close. When his vacation from college begins, Cyril yearns to help George gather in the hay for the last time before the Saxtons leave Nethermere. In excitement, "I rose the first morning very early, before the sun was well up. The clear sound of challenging cocks could be heard along the valley. In the bottoms, over the water and over the lush wet grass, the night mist still stood white and substantial. As I passed along the edge of the meadow the cow-parsnip was as tall as I, frothing up to the top of the hedge, putting the faded hawthorn to a wan blush. Little, early birds—I had not heard the lark—fluttered in and out of the foamy meadow-sea, plunging under the surf of flowers washed high in one corner, swinging out again, dashing past the crimson sorrel cresset" (p. 243). Surrounding him everywhere on his path, the flowers and birds create an aptly lyrical mood.[15] After a quick swim in the pond, Cyril and George

went together down to the fields, he to mow the island of grass he had left standing the previous evening, I to sharpen the machine knife, to mow out the hedge-bottoms with the scythe, and to rake the swaths from the way of the machine when the unmown grass was reduced to a triangle. The cool, moist fragrance of the morning, the intentional stillness of everything, of the tall bluish trees, of the wet, frank flowers, of the trustful moths folded and unfolded in the fallen swaths, was a perfect medium of sympathy. The horses moved with a still dignity, obeying his commands. When they were harnessed, and the machine oiled, still he was loth to mar the perfect morning, but stood looking down the valley.

"I shan't mow these fields any more," he said, and the fallen, silvered

15 Thomas G. Rosenmeyer believes that the inventory, or serial listing, is the "single most effective and congenial literary device in the pastoral lyric" (*The Green Cabinet* [Berkeley and Los Angeles: Univ. of California Press, 1969], p. 258).

swaths flickered back his regret, and the faint scent of the limes was wistful. . . .

"But merely to have mown them is worth having lived for," he said, looking at me.

. . . . .

Later, when the morning was hot, and the honeysuckle had ceased to breathe, and all the other scents were moving in the air about us, when all the field was down, when I had seen the last trembling ecstasy of the hare-bells, trembling to fall; when the thick clump of purple vetch had sunk; when the green swaths were settling, and the silver swaths were glistening and glittering as the sun came along them, in the hot ripe morning we worked together turning the hay, tipping over the yesterday's swaths with our forks, and bringing yesterday's fresh, hidden flowers into the death of sunlight.

It was then that we talked of the past, and speculated on the future. As the day grew older, and less wistful, we forgot everything, and worked on, singing, and sometimes I would recite him verses as we went, and sometimes I would tell him about books. Life was full of glamour for us both. [Pp. 245–47]

In the first paragraph, work and beauty blend into unison as Cyril and George, like the paired harvesters in *Idyll* 10, labor in the lush fields. The vision of man in harmony with his natural environment has always been a prime attraction of the pastoral genre; and here, as in all pastoral, we find "a scene and some means for expressing man's accord with it."[16] Since the human sphere is in sympathy with the natural world, the morning is perfect. This "perfect morning" then mirrors the idea in a preceding paragraph that "our love was perfect for a moment," so that the human and the natural mirror and interpenetrate each other. The relationship between Cyril and George and the relationship between Cyril and nature are both conceived in lyrical terms. George and nature both elicit a rapturous affection from the narrator, although the relations between the opposite sexes are fraught with the usual romantic conflicts. Thus to the narrator Cyril, George is more closely identified with nature than the other characters, not simply because we often see him working on the farm, but because at a deeper level of the narrator's consciousness George is conceived of and then presented to the reader in the same imaginative terms as nature is—with the same images, the same sympathy, the same pure feeling. Because human and natural are perceived and described in the same terms, they seem in accord.

Throughout this and other passages, the details are primarily visual.

---

[16] Walter R. Davis, *A Map of Arcadia* (New Haven: Yale Univ. Press, 1965), p. 28.

As in the novels of both George Eliot and Hardy, the eye dominates the book, recording the look of landscape and characters and catching the movement of eyes and limbs with as much precision as it catches the fluttering of a cowslip, the shape of a lark's nest, or the scent of honeysuckle. The love of rural life is created not through summary but through evocation, through poetic language that creates in the reader the feeling and atmosphere of country life. The poetic quality is evident particularly in the onomatopoeic effects and in the rhythm. Especially effective in the penultimate paragraph is the way in which the prose rhythms, the building up of anaphoric *when* clauses and the heavy use of gerunds and participles, capture the rolling physical movement of turning the hay, or the way in which the scents of flowers create exquisite sensuousness. The artistic achievement of *The White Peacock* lies as much in the sensuous apprehension of the natural world as it does in the creation and interaction of the characters.

Living also in the valley are the Beardsalls, different from the Saxtons because they are financially independent and place a high value on culture. Their dialogue is in its way as stylized as that in *Under the Greenwood Tree.* Since they uphold the urban values of culture and sophistication, they are not the "realistic" pastoral figures that we have found in novels of George Eliot and Hardy or that we see in the Saxtons; instead, they fall between the Saxtons and the artificial figures of traditional pastoral, who savored only leisure and music and love. The Beardsalls' frequent allusions to literature, painting, music, and foreign languages sometimes suggest the artificiality of traditional pastoral— largely, one suspects, because Lawrence transposed his own family, in fiction, from the mining town of Eastwood into a middle-class country setting. The Beardsalls do not of course don the disguise of a farmer, nor do they pretend to be rural laborers and then speak as courtiers. But their basic attitudes often resemble those we encounter in traditional pastoral—particularly the praise of rural life from an urban-committed point of view.

Lettie and Cyril frequently admire the rural life at Strelley Mill farm. With admiration, Lettie says to George when he pauses in his mowing: " 'You are picturesque . . . quite fit for an Idyll' " (p. 54). Then he shows her how to bind the grain:

"I wish I could work here," she said, looking away at the standing corn, and the dim blue woods. He followed her look, and laughed quietly, with indulgent resignation.

"I do!" she said emphatically.

"You feel so fine," he said, pushing his hand through his open shirt front, and gently rubbing the muscles of his side. "It's a pleasure to work or to stand still. It's a pleasure to yourself—your own physique." [P. 55]

Cyril's attitude is similar to Lettie's: "On the other side of the valley I could see a pair of horses nod slowly across the fallow. A man's voice called to them now and again with a resonance that filled me with longing to follow my horses over the fallow, in the still, lonely valley, full of sunshine and eternal forgetfulness" (pp. 172–73). Cyril's desire to leave the cultured life is an expression of the pastoral impulse in one who lives already in pastoral Nethermere. Lettie and Cyril want to become like George, but they are already committed to a life that is essentially urban in outlook, and thus cannot transform their desires into action.

The creation of a pastoral world is complicated, then, by characters living in a pastoral world but ultimately adhering to the cultured views of the urban world. The pastoral world is complicated also by the dissatisfaction and unrest that the culture of Lettie and Cyril brings to George, a figure fully immersed in rural life. George says to Lettie: " 'things will never be the same—You have awakened my life—I imagine things that I couldn't have done' " (p. 130). And to Cyril: " 'But you see, you and Lettie have made me conscious' " (p. 260). In this respect Cyril and Lettie function, paradoxically, as antipastoral figures. Although Cyril and Lettie inhabit a beautiful pastoral world ("We had lived between the woods and the water all our lives") and although they are free from responsibility, like traditional pastoral figures, they also create unrest with their cultural values. They inhabit a pastoral world, but their allegiance to its values is only partial. They praise, often ecstatically, the world and life of Nethermere, yet with their sophistication they place this world and its life in the perspective of the urban world. It is such a perspective that classical and Renaissance pastoral had always accomplished.

Pastoral narrative has been called an art of perspective. In *The White Peacock* perspective is achieved by placing the valley of Nethermere in the larger context of cultured urban life: the sophisticated allusions to literature, art, and music suggest a framework through which to see the simple rural beauty of Nethermere and the simplicity of life at Strelley Mill farm. Because Lawrence lets us see both sets of values, he shows us the strengths of both "urban" and "rural" and so uses, as often in pastoral, one way of life as a premise for criticizing the other. Only after we have a firm sense of this perspective do we see that the novel is prorural and antiurban, even anticultural, in its denouement and conclusion. Like Grace Melbury in *The Woodlanders*, the characters are led down the road of disillusion toward sophistication. They see then (as we do) the past through the perspective of the present.

In addition to Strelley Mill farm, what the narrator remembers through this lens of the present is the diversion and adventure in the pastoral valley. The young people of Nethermere amuse themselves with parties and frequent walks into the rapturously beautiful countryside around Woodside and Strelley Mill farm, where they go "wandering round the fields finding flowers and birds' nests," sensitive to the beauty around them, laughing, teasing, and discovering afresh the wonder of human and natural life. The writing in such passages is vivid, idyllic, and unusually metaphorical. The sordidness that the characters occasionally find in or beyond the valley—the life of the gamekeeper's family, for instance—only heightens by contrast the beauty they find. The lush texture of the landscape is often rapturously evoked, weaving a verbal arabesque; and the evocation of landscape, in its pictorialism and in its suggestion of nature's independent life, helps to place Lawrence alongside Hardy in the first rank of novelists who write of rural life.

A major part of the evocation of landscape consists of detailed descriptions of flowers: primroses, violets, cowslips, forget-me-nots, snowdrops, dog-mercury, wood-anemones, bluebells. In addition to promoting the lyricism characteristic of pastoral, flowers gradually assume a symbolic value. They are a concrete and objective manifestation, a symbol, of the quality of life in the Nethermere valley. The emphasis on flowers, moreover, suggests a yearning for beauty that intensifies the pastoral escape from the ugliness and squalor of the surrounding industrialism. Though occasionally set pieces, the evocations of flowers nurture the pastoral quality that is the source of the novel's charm.[17]

Similar to our awareness of flowers is our awareness of allusions to the innocence and beauty of the Garden of Eden. Pastoral and Eden

---

17 Although it forms a digression from the central thread of the novel, an outgrowth of the novel's emphasis on flowers is the pastoral elegy for Annable, the gamekeeper. In the pastoral mode, grief conventionally expresses itself in the form of a pastoral elegy, employing among its many characteristics a personal expression of sorrow, a procession of mourners, the pathetic fallacy, flower symbolism, and a joyous consolation. These all occur in the pastoral elegy found in *The White Peacock* (pp. 171–72), where the natural world—especially birds and flowers—laments the death of the gamekeeper. In nature's lamentation over a human death, the funeral procession bears a significant relation to the pastoral of tradition. Renato Poggioli thinks, in fact, that the pathetic fallacy may be a variant of the pastoral fallacy ("The Oaten Flute," *Harvard Library Bulletin*, 11 [1957], 184). Because Lawrence's elegy is written in prose and because it does not follow closely the conventions of the pastoral elegy, it should be considered a variation of the traditional form.

share a father-son relationship; the concept of the Garden of Eden is a later Christian version of the pastoral myth of the Golden Age, when innocence, leisure, and contentment blossomed freely. The implication throughout *The White Peacock* is that Nethermere is a kind of Eden out of which the characters are gradually lured. Even in winter, Edenic overtones appear in the landscape description: "On the second Saturday before Christmas the world was transformed; tall, silver and pearl-grey trees rose pale against a dim-blue sky, like trees in some rare, pale Paradise; the whole woodland was as if petrified in marble and silver and snow" (p. 102). In other passages the Edenic overtones are explicit. When the group wanders into a field of yellow cowslips, Lettie draws near to George, surprised:

> "Ah!" she said. "I thought I was all alone in the world—such a splendid world—it was so nice."
> "Like Eve in a meadow in Eden—and Adam's shadow somewhere on the grass," said I. [P. 228]

The quotation comes from a chapter entitled "The Fascination of the Forbidden Apple" (referring to the fact that both Lettie and George are fascinated by each other but forbidden to each other by Lettie's engagement to Leslie Tempest). This chapter title echoes an earlier one, "Dangling the Apple"—both alluding clearly to the Christian myth. At one point, George says of Lettie: " 'She is offering me the apple like Eve' " (p. 105). These quotations show that the association of Eden and Nethermere was in Lawrence's mind when he wrote the novel. The specific cause of the Fall remains obscure, but one suspects that it has much to do with Lettie's luring George out of Nethermere because he picks the apple of temptation that she dangles. The allusions to Eden are significant; we understand the characters better if we see that they trespass beyond their Eden and are in effect cast out, in the same way that Adam and Eve were expelled from Paradise. In the final chapters of the novel, perhaps the most significantly repeated world is *exile*. The characters, except for Emily, feel that they have been expelled from their pastoral paradise. The numerous short excursions that they take outside Nethermere—excursions that reveal ugliness—serve as warnings. Once the characters have trespassed too far beyond Nethermere and have stayed too long, they cannot return, as the final chapters prove. The novel, though far more than mere allegory, nonetheless makes vivid use of the myth of the Fall. If the parallels are imperfect, they are yet strong enough to show Lawrence's indebtedness in the novel to the Christian myth of Eden and to the earlier pastoral myth of the Golden Age. Like George Eliot in *Adam Bede*, Lawrence attempts to

Christianize the pastoral. He introduces into the pastoral haven two different forms of corruption—the traditional pastoral form of time and ambition as enemies of pastoral innocence, and the Christian form, less clearly treated, of original sin. Thus Lawrence reveals his awareness of the richness of literary tradition, yet some imprecision in his handling of character motivation and analysis.

The final expression of the pastoral impulse in *The White Peacock* is found in the chapter called "Pastorals and Peonies," which closes Part 2 of the novel. This chapter, describing a picnic, is a mock pastoral—a parody of the *Idylls* of Theocritus. Leslie Tempest, Lettie's fiancé, asks Mr. Saxton if a few of his guests might picnic one afternoon in a choice spot in the Strelley hayfields. The wedding guests, it turns out, are sophisticated, intelligent, refined urbanites who long to escape for a few hours into the pastoral world of Nethermere. Thus we have a simulated, conventional situation of traditional pastoral, one of the characters even affecting speech thought to be country dialect, then pretending to be a Theocritean shepherd. The chapter may have been suggested by Theocritus' *Idyll* 7, "The Harvest Home," in which three urban friends dressed as herdsmen join a harvest feast in the country, then sit on piles of leaves and straw, eat pears and apples and plums, and drink wine. The details of the singing contest and the allusions to the pastoral figures of Theocritus probably derive both from *Idyll* 6, a country singing match between Damoetas and Daphnis, and from *Idyll* 8, a second match in which Daphnis and Menalcas contest for a shepherd's pipe; the allusions to Amaryllis and the ripening apples probably refer to *Idyll* 3, although the names Daphnis and Amaryllis occur together in Vergil's *Eclogue* 8.

The group wants to help, not to hinder, in the haymaking, so Mr. Saxton gives them light hayforks and they begin "just tipping at the swaths." They soon tire of the work:

"Ain't it flippin' 'ot?" drawled Cresswell, who had just taken his M. A. degree in classics: "This bloomin' stuff's dry enough—come an' flop on it."
He gathered a cushion of hay, which Louie Denys carefully appropriated, arranging first her beautiful dress, that fitted close to her shape. . . .
Cresswell twisted his clean-cut mouth in a little smile, saying:
"Lord, a giddy little pastoral—fit for old Theocritus, ain't it, Miss Denys?"
"Why do you talk to me about those classic people—I daren't even say their names. What would he say about us?"
He laughed, winking his blue eyes:
"He'd make old Daphnis there,"—pointing to Leslie—"sing a match

with me, Damoetas—contesting the merits of our various shepherdesses—begin Daphnis, sing up for Amaryllis, I mean Nais, damn 'em, they were for ever getting mixed up with their nymphs."

"I say, Mr. Cresswell, your language! Consider whom you're damning," said Miss Denys, leaning over and tapping his head with her silk glove.

"You say any giddy thing in a pastoral," he replied, taking the edge of her skirt, and lying back on it, looking up at her as she leaned over him. "Strike up, Daphnis, something about honey or white cheese—or else the early apples that'll be ripe in a week's time."

"I'm sure the apples you showed me are ever so little and green," interrupted Miss Denys; "they will never be ripe in a week—ugh, sour!"

He smiled up at her in his whimsical way:

"Hear that, Tempest—'Ugh, sour!'—not much! Oh, love us, haven't you got a start yet?—isn't there aught to sing about, you blunt-faced kid?"

"I'll hear you first—I'm no judge of honey and cheese."

"An' darn little apples—takes a woman to judge them; don't it, Miss Denys?"

"I don't know," she said, stroking his soft hair from his forehead, with her hand whereon rings were sparkling.

"'My love is not white, my hair is not yellow, like honey dropping through the sunlight—my love is brown, and sweet, and ready for the lips of love.' Go on, Tempest—strike up, old cowherd. Who's that tuning his pipe? —oh, that fellow [George] sharpening his scythe! It's enough to make your back ache to look at him working—go an' stop him, somebody."

"Yes, let us go and fetch him," said Miss D'Arcy. "I'm sure he doesn't know what a happy pastoral state he's in—let us go and fetch him." [Pp. 250–51]

Miss D'Arcy approaches George:

"They are spinning idylls up there. I don't care for idylls, do you? Oh, you don't know what a classical pastoral person you are—but there, I don't suppose you suffer from idyllic love—" she laughed, "—one doesn't see the silly little god fluttering about in our hayfields, does one? Do you find much time to sport with Amaryllis in the shade?—I'm sure it's a shame they banished Phyllis from the fields—"

He laughed and went on with his work. She smiled a little, too, thinking she had made a great impression. [P. 252]

Wandering about, the group picks flowers and talks until teatime, when a manservant comes with the teabasket. Seated on tufts of hay, with "the man-servant waiting on all," the pastoral picnickers, like the picnickers in the seventh idyll, savor the delights of "grapes and peaches, and strawberries, in a beautifully carved oak tray," while "the talk bubbled and frothed over all the cups" (pp. 253–54). Soon, they leave Strelley Mill farm.

The scene is entertaining in an artificial way, and our view of the whole is well expressed in George's initial reaction to the picnickers: "George at first swore warmly; then he began to appreciate the affair as a joke" (p. 248). It is true, as Dr. Leavis (p. 6) has said, that much of the novel is literary and conventional in style and treatment. But we will be less critical of the scene if we view it as mock pastoral rather than as a realistic portrayal of urban picnickers or as an attempt to be merely elegant. Like most scenes of traditional pastoral, this one lacks verisimilitude: we do not regard it as believable or convincing in its own right. If we look at the scene in this way, we can accept the artificiality of the picnic as falling within the boundaries of conventional pastoral poetry, though here, of course, Lawrence mocks the convention at the same time that he uses it as a model for inspiration. Like Theocritus in *Idyll* 7, Lawrence presents a kind of jesting masquerade in the pastoral picnic and wishes us to recognize friends of his own circle (the Pagans) behind the clever disguises.

The picnic is an interlude in the evocation of farm life and shows the city-dweller's view of the farm. What makes the pastoral picnic difficult to analyze is the prominence in the scene of divergent views of rural life. Along with the polished Arcadians relishing flowers and munching on fruit from an oak tray, we find George scything the hay, his hands calloused. In the garden of voluptuous peonies stands a calf sucking on George's finger; nearby are what Miss D'Arcy calls "smelly" cows, and, as Freddy Cresswell points out, with his "whimsical affectation of vulgarity," " 'the stink o' live beef ain't salubrious' " (p. 254). The scene is still more complex because the picnickers are both admired and satirized—satirized for their affectation yet admired for their superior culture and refinement. Yet because there is no suggestion that they think of rural life as superior to urban life, the scene does not represent pure traditional pastoral, but a mock variation of it.

The picnic chapter is like another mock variation of pastoral, namely *As You Like It*. In fact, a surprising correlation exists between the three levels of pastoral life in Lawrence's scene and the three levels of pastoral life that Shakespeare dramatizes in *As You Like It*. The counterparts of Shakespeare's Arcadians, Silvius and Phebe, are the group of wedding guests from the city. The exiled followers of the Duke, courtly but less artificial than the refined Arcadians, find counterparts in Cyril and Lettie—characters who share their urban outlook but who have a particular fondness for rural life and who vocally prefer their rural setting. Last, the counterpart of Shakespeare's real peasants William and Audrey is of course George, who is described more realistically in this scene than earlier in the novel. Although the characters stand in a different relation to each other, both Rosalind and Lettie are beloved by characters who represent two opposing worlds. Lawrence uses the same pastoral situation as did Shakespeare in his pastoral play. But more significant is the fact that both writers express similar attitudes toward their conventional pastoral characters and regard them as lovely and refined, but insubstantial and unreal—as elegant decorations rather than vital men and women. It is possible that the play was, in addition to the pastoral poems of Theocritus, a direct influence on the picnic chapter.[18]

The picnic scene, with its urban elements, prepares us to leave the rural-pastoral world for the ugly industrial world. With the pastoral picnic, we move in terms of aesthetic distance from rural to urban; the placement of this increased distancing in the final chapter of Part 2 prepares us for change. If this final chapter contrasts real and artificial country experience in the form of the pastoral picnic, Part 3 embodies still another contrast to both these representations of country life.

Part 3 (or more precisely, the last six chapters of the novel) shows an affinity for naturalism. The two contrasting portions of the novel—the first three-quarters and the last quarter—thus pose a problem for reader and critic not only because they are difficult to reconcile, but because they do not cohere as an aesthetic whole. The novel modulates into a minor key when the techniques of romanticism give way to those of naturalism and when George's new town environment appears to control him and to be significant in his decline. The last quarter is rushed, and scenes shift rapidly, as though Lawrence were impatient with the denouement, as though the subject matter were unsuited to his genius and failed to call forth his fullest powers. A letter to Blanche Jennings, written by Lawrence in 1909, reveals that he has rewritten the novel: "I have added a third part, have married Lettie and Leslie and George and Meg, and Emily to a stranger and myself to nobody. O Lord—what a farce."[19] We should not be surprised that the artistic level of the last quarter (when George has left Nethermere) shows a falling off in quality, so that the freshness and vitality of the novel exist mainly in the first three-quarters.

The opening pages of Part 3 are nostalgic and elegiac in tone. After

---

[18] In *The Rainbow*, published four years after *The White Peacock*, Lawrence has high praise for *As You Like It*. Of Ursula's studies, he says: "Most tedious was the close study of English literature. . . . Only in odd streaks did she get a poignant sense of acquisition and enrichment and enlarging from her studies; one afternoon, reading *As You Like It*; once when with her blood, she heard a passage of Latin, and she knew how the blood beat in a Roman's body; so that ever after she felt she knew the Romans by contact" (Phoenix Edition [London: Heinemann, 1955], pp. 333–34). And in "Hymns in a Man's Life" (1928), Lawrence mentions "pieces" of *As You Like It* as one of a few lovely poems "which after all give the ultimate shape to one's life" (*D. H. Lawrence: Selected Literary Criticism*, ed. Anthony Beal, Compass Books [New York: Viking, 1966], p. 6).

[19] *Collected Letters of D. H. Lawrence*, I, 57.

Lettie marries Leslie and they leave for France, "everywhere was a sense of loss, and of change. The long voyage in the quiet home was over; we had crossed the bright sea of our youth, and already Lettie had landed and was travelling to a strange destination in a foreign land. It was time for us all to go, to leave the valley of Nethermere whose waters and whose woods were distilled in the essence of our veins. We were the children of the valley of Nethermere, a small nation with language and blood of our own, and to cast ourselves each one into separate exile was painful to us" (p. 259). The voyage leads from youth to maturity, from the pastoral valley to the world of urban masses and machinery and money.

Soon after Lettie's marriage, George too yearns "to venture into the foreign places of life." The Saxtons, including George, are driven out of Nethermere by the squire's refusal to let them protect their farm from rabbits. But more important, Lettie and Cyril have made George restless. To Lettie, George says, " 'Do you know, I'm going to get pretty rich, so that I can do what I want for a bit. I want to see what it's like, to taste all sides—to taste the towns' " (p. 204). Lettie and Cyril stimulate George to develop "the aspiring mind" so antithetical to pastoral happiness. Earlier, George had been unaware and unconscious, in his "good living and heavy sleeping," that he possessed the ideal pastoral condition of the contented mind. But ambition and what Lawrence later called "prostitution to the bitch-goddess, Success" destroy that innocent contentment. George crosses the borders of the valley of Nethermere "flauntingly, and marched towards the heart of the unknown." Before long he replaces "the glamour of our yesterdays" on the farm, which had come over him "like an intoxicant," with the artificial glamour of alcohol in the world outside Nethermere. Yet George "could not get over the feeling that he was trespassing." When he goes to Nottingham to marry Meg, he is fascinated by the adventure of town life: "He had begun to trespass that day outside his own estates of Nethermere" (p. 271). The suggestion of trespass and of consequent exile from Eden dominates the opening pages of Part 3. As soon as George trespasses, he too is faced with the penalty of exile.

Although coming later to love the town, Cyril suffers most "the sickness of exile" in a London suburb:

For weeks I wandered the streets of the suburb, haunted by the spirit of some part of Nethermere. . . . A strange voice within me rose and called for the hill path; again I could feel the wood waiting for me, calling, and calling, and I crying for the wood, yet the space of many miles was between us. Since I left the valley of home I have not much feared any other loss. The hills of Nethermere had been my walls, and the sky of Nethermere my roof overhead. It seemed almost as if, at home, I might lift my hand to the ceiling of the valley, and touch my own beloved sky, whose familiar clouds came again and again to visit me, whose stars were constant to me, born when I was born, whose sun had been all my father to me. [Pp. 283–84]

The tone of the passage suggests a yearning for the Golden Age, for the recovery of the innocence and happiness found in traditional forms of pastoral. In part, the novel can be regarded as a pastoral of innocence— of innocence characteristic of a world that has not discovered the bitterness of maturity or experience. The pastoral world of the novel is essentially a world of childhood. With maturity, that world vanishes. Yet it is not so much time that breaks up the pastoral world of innocence as it is outside influences, the yearning for money and success. It is because Cyril and George both trespass permanently beyond the limits of the Nethermere valley that they find unhappiness. It was necessary, in view of the novel's outcome, that their search for fulfillment end at the perimeter of Nethermere. The novel is therefore closer than we might have guessed to Hardy's pastoral novels, where generally those who remain within the agricultural boundaries of their home communities are happy, but where those who leave come either to ruin or to despair, as in *The White Peacock* or *The Rainbow*.[20]

Once they depart from Nethermere, the characters find themselves in the "bewildering pageant of modern life" (p. 307). Only Emily, by marrying a young farmer and returning to the rural world, "had escaped from the torture of strange, complex modern life" (p. 349) that the other characters must endure. Because George has been most sharply uprooted from his attachment to the land, he succumbs most quickly to the torture of modern life and deteriorates rapidly into an incurable alcoholic. The uprooted are caught in the vice of urbanization. Thus Lawrence tolls the death bell of the old agricultural order.

When, near the close, Cyril returns to Nethermere from London, he takes what would appear to be a pastoral journey—from city to rural

[20] In a number of ways *The Rainbow* is a rewritten and expanded version of *The White Peacock*, especially of its final chapters. Just as George Saxton marries a woman outside of Nethermere (Meg), so Tom Brangwen marries an outsider when he chooses Lydia Lensky. Cyril, the bachelor who is unable to love fully any character in *The White Peacock*, becomes in *The Rainbow* Uncle Tom, flawed and corrupt, who is equally unable to love and whose marriage to Winifred Inger is only a marriage of convenience. Lettie (strong) and Leslie (weak) become Ursula and Skrebensky: both women defeat the men they attempt to love. And Strelley Mill farm has as its equivalent Marsh farm. In both novels Lawrence focuses on three couples and one outsider. The essential difference is that in *The Rainbow* the couples represent three generations rather than one and are connected by family ties. In both novels, moreover, the dominant impression is one of lyrical intensity: in *The White Peacock* the stimulus for the lyrical intensity is nature; in *The Rainbow*, the emotion of love.

oasis—only to find that Nethermere "had now forgotten me" and that "I was a stranger, an intruder" (p. 334). The journey becomes an inverted pastoral journey in which the happiness that the narrator-journeyer had hoped to recover is destroyed by the return visit: "I had done with the valley of Nethermere. The valley of Nethermere had cast me out many years before, while I had fondly believed it cherished me in memory" (p. 335). The pastoral journey is unsuccessful because the narrator, now fully urbanized by his life in London and Paris, no longer needs the pastoral world. Wishfully he wants to return, but cannot, because both he and Nethermere have changed. Urban culture and his success as a painter have outwardly fulfilled the emotional need that Nethermere once supplied. Like George, once Cyril travels away, trespasses beyond the boundaries of Nethermere, he cannot return to innocence and happiness; experience and success bar the way. But the pastoral journey is unsuccessful for another reason. The sustained decline of British agriculture after 1874 has made the traditional pastoral journey—the retreat from urban complexity to rural simplicity—an impossibility: the pastoral people of Nethermere, the Saxtons, have fled the forces that encroached upon them. The novel shows therefore the decline of an old agricultural way of life. More important, it can be read as an inverted pastoral novel—a modern form of pastoral that, as Renato Poggioli points out, embodies "the bucolic aspiration only to deny it."[21] A picture of beauty and loveliness is created, then destroyed; an idyll is transformed into ugliness. Thus the final pages of *The White Peacock* shatter the illusion of Nethermere that the novel has so patiently built up. What makes it a very modern form of the pastoral novel is its ambiguous and ironic ending.

It is thus with uncertainty that Lawrence modified pastoral The four pastoral strains reflect Lawrence's inadequate knowledge, early in his career, of those generic patterns that would best embody his vision of an innocence forced by time into awareness and exile. In modifying pastoral, *The White Peacock* shows finally the insufficiency of pastoral innocence—not certainly because innocence and morality are discontinuous, as they are in *Adam Bede*, but because innocence lies powerless in the wrench of time. In *Lady Chatterley's Lover* innocence and morality can be reached again only by rejecting "immoral" sophistication and by this means returning to the natural, intuitive freedom of innocence (Lawrence himself called his last novel a "truly moral" book). Perhaps one might say that Lawrence in *Lady Chatterley's Lover* makes a pilgrimage to the world before the Fall which he so skillfully creates in *The White Peacock*. But unlike the later novel, *The White Peacock*

21 "The Oaten Flute," p. 177. Cf. Melville's *Typee* in which a pastoral dream is fabricated, then destroyed.

generally separates pastoral from nonpastoral elements by using temporal rather than thematic contrasts; and in doing so, the novel perhaps weakens the force of both elements. Lawrence in *Lady Chatterley's Lover* approaches the genre with greater awareness of its power and shows that the effective use of pastoral requires, in the manner of the traditional pastoralists, the creation of two separate worlds juxtaposed thematically so that one world provides a means of envisioning the other. Still, just as it is useful to know how Thackeray uses history or how Conrad uses travel accounts or how Joyce uses epic, so a knowledge of Lawrence's use of pastoral motifs, in both his first and his last novel, can seize upon much of the richness that readers of these novels invariably feel.

The White Peacock is, then, a prose mutation of traditional pastoral, characterized by richly sensuous evocations of the natural world, intense concentration on a small, circumscribed valley, nostalgia for this pastoral valley, praise of country life, a re-creation of what was for Lawrence a Golden Age, tension between urban and rural values, the inclusion of a pastoral picnic among the Strelley hayfields, and the inverted pastoral of the final pages. Harsh realism manifests itself largely outside the valley of Nethermere and in the third part, written as an afterthought.[22] For the most part, the valley of Nethermere was "a complete, wonderful little world that held us charmed inhabitants" (p. 291)—however much the disillusion of adulthood may qualify this judgment of the narrator. Graham Hough remarks that "in *The White Peacock* the human failures are almost absorbed in the quivering joy of earth, the vibration of the non-human world that surrounds them" and that, paradoxically, "the prevailing impression it leaves behind is one of tenderness, freshness and young growth."[23] The naturalistic details, such as those surrounding Mr. Beardsall's death, were in Lawrence's words only "fading phrases of the untruth. That yellow blaze of little sunflowers was true, and the shadow from the sun-dial on the warm old almshouses—that was real"; with the heavy afternoon sunlight, "the untruth went out of our veins" (p. 47). Nature, and man amid nature, are the "true" and the "real" in the novel. They are what live in

---

[22] It is indicative of the shift from the nineteenth to the twentieth century that in an early draft of the novel, Lettie married George in the same way that Fancy Day marries Dick Dewy or that Bathsheba Everdene marries Gabriel Oak in Hardy's pastoral novels. Lawrence's revision of this early draft shows him to be much closer to the Hardy of *The Woodlanders*, another novel that was rewritten toward a negative conclusion.

[23] *The Dark Sun*, pp. 53, 31.

the novel with greatest independent life and with greatest impact on the imagination. The harsh realism functions chiefly as an antidote to the charge of sentimentality and is not the primary ingredient. The primary ingredient is the marvelous evocation of the pastoral valley, of its people and its landscape, capturing the music of larks, the scent of violets and ripening corn, or the slow rhythm of the harvest.

The novel is not a masterpiece. It is not internally consistent, and its local failures are frequent: the pretentious dialogue, the gamekeeper digression, the failure to integrate the various conflicts and episodes into a coherent whole, and the unsatisfying final portion. But its lyrical beauty creates a pastoral mood that dominates the novel because of the intensity with which the lyrical passages capturing landscape and human character are executed. Yet this world and its fragile pastoral beauty hover just at the brink of dissolution. A French critic reminds us that we are given in *The White Peacock* a "picture of an agricultural community in its last breath of life, with the acute human problems this dissolution involves."[24] Beyond the pastoral world of Nethermere, the industrial forces of destruction and defeat crowd closer, ushering in the new era: "outside the valley, far away in Derbyshire, away towards Nottingham, on every hand the distant hooters and buzzers of mines and ironworks crowed small on the borders of the night, like so many strange, low voices of cockerels bursting forth at different pitch, with different tone, warning us of the dawn of the New Year" (p. 280). Industrial England blots out agricultural England, and the New Year, leaving the lyrical pastoral world behind, is a harbinger of modern industrialism. If in both *The White Peacock* and *The Woodlanders* we witness an exodus from the land, with attendant unrest and deracination, in *Lady Chatterley's Lover* we return if only temporarily to a *locus amoenus* of rare beauty, a retreat remarkable for its power to revitalize those who enter its mystical domain. Connie and Mellors and Wragby Wood are stylized redrawings of Lettie and George and Nethermere, in colors simpler and more passionate, in scale more compressed, in mood more sanguine, in resonance fuller and more urgent.

[24] Sinzelle, p. 45.

Chapter 9

Lady Chatterley's Lover
"Pure Seclusion"

INSPIRED by Lawrence's last visit to Eastwood, *Lady Chatterley's Lover* shows Lawrence returning to the genre that gave focus to his imagination as early as 1905, when he began work on *The White Peacock* and when his imagination was still deeply absorbed in the Haggs farm. But in the meantime the Great War had flooded Lawrence with waves of revulsion and had drowned his optimism. "The War finished me," he says in a letter: "it was the spear through the side of all sorrows and hopes."[1] The "whole world," he writes, "slides in horror down into the bottomless pit." "I will not live any more in this time. I know what it is. I reject it." Lawrence's disillusion with contemporary life—with war and ugly industrialism and emotional sterility—erupted and became a permanent feature of his post-War fiction, charging it with intense moral stamina. Yet Lawrence's wanderings to Australia, Mexico, or America led him finally back to the country of his youth. After his final visit, in 1926, a sense of weary disillusion fuses with moral indignation in his writing. In his commemorative essay "Return to Bestwood," published in *Phoenix II*, he writes: "The country is the same, but scarred and splashed all over with mines and mining settlements. . . . old villages are smothered in rows of miners' dwellings" (p. 262). Now, with the war behind them, the people "never seem to touch the reality of the country-side" as they did before (p. 258). With contrary feelings yoked together—the yearning for hope but the premonition of doom—Lawrence strikes the chord that reverberates like a pulsebeat through his last novel. He writes of the colliers: "I shrink away from them, and I have an acute nostalgia for them. And now, this last time, I feel a doom over the country, and a shadow of despair over the hearts of men, which leaves me no rest. Because the same doom is over me, wherever I go, and the same despair touches my heart" (p. 264). In sharp recoil from this despairing mood, Lawrence creates his finest pastoral novel, representing the ideal pastoral world of Wragby Wood as a temporary haven whose powerful moral significance cannot however, because of its purity, be transplanted into the real contemporary

---

[1] Harry T. Moore, ed., *The Collected Letters of D. H. Lawrence* (New York: Viking, 1962), I, 309. The two quotations that follow are from I, 424.

world of despair and doom. Mellors, says Lawrence two years after the novel was finished, "still has the warmth of a man, but he is being hunted down, destroyed."[2]

Lady Chatterley's Lover is more than sexual: it is pastoral. D. H. Lawrence wrote to Catherine Carswell in 1922, "I think one must for the moment withdraw from the world, away toward the inner realities that *are* real: and return, maybe, to the world later, when one is quiet and sure."[3] In this letter Lawrence, perhaps unconsciously, struck upon the pastoral pattern that he was to embody imaginatively in *Lady Chatterley's Lover* (1928). Because critical interest in pastoral seemed once to have languished, it is hardly surprising that critics have never attempted to analyze the pastoral patterns and pastoral variants in Lawrence's last novel. The novel has for too long been thought a fictionalized treatise on morality or a guidebook to sexual freedom or a work prophetic of an emancipated society. We should, instead, see the novel in its proper perspective: as a pastoral novel that embodies the attitudes, techniques, and patterns of traditional pastoral romance.

In an important essay, Julian Moynahan comes close to seeing a pastoral pattern in *Lady Chatterley's Lover*; and Harry T. Moore, although he does not develop the idea, suggests that the novel is a romance.[4] David Cavitch comes closer to seeing the relationship of the novel to pastoral when he calls *Lady Chatterley's Lover* "a pastoral romance" and writes that "Connie and Mellors live in the formal scheme of a pastoral idyll."[5] But neither Moynahan nor Moore, nor recent critics such as Cavitch, have identified or discussed the remarkable parallels between Lawrence's novel and pastoral. The present analysis attempts to revise the critical focus on the novel by shifting the em-

---

[2] "A Propos of *Lady Chatterley's Lover*," in *Phoenix II*, ed. Warren Roberts and Harry T. Moore, Viking Compass Edition (New York: Viking, 1970), p. 513.

[3] *Collected Letters of D. H. Lawrence*, II, 687.

[4] Moynahan, "*Lady Chatterley's Lover*: The Deed of Life," *ELH*, 26 (1959), 70–72, 84–88. Moore, "*Lady Chatterley's Lover* as Romance," *A D. H. Lawrence Miscellany* (Carbondale: Southern Illinois Univ. Press, 1959), p. 263.

[5] *D. H. Lawrence and the New World* (New York: Oxford Univ. Press, 1969), pp. 200, 197. But Cavitch errs when he adds that "in this Arden also, there is 'No enemy, but winter and rough weather'" (p. 198); industrialism regularly pierces the lovers' retreat. Some other critics have also mentioned the connection between *Lady Chatterley's Lover* and pastoral. For Barbara Hardy, the novel "uses pastoral in a complex way, taking the intimate relationship with nature not merely as a fertility symbol but as a wider demonstration of activity" (*The Appropriate Form* [London: Athlone Press, 1964], p. 164). For Kingsley Widmer, "Lawrence's major pastoral, of course, is not his early work but *Lady Chatterley's Lover*" (*The Art of Perversity* [Seattle: Univ. of Washington Press, 1962], pp. 120–21).

phasis from an exclusively social or moral or sexual concern to an examination of the novel as a modern continuation of the old pastoral tradition, a tradition that embraces the novel's social or moral or sexual content as part of a more comprehensive and durable vision. As we will see, *Lady Chatterley's Lover* sustains the pastoral tradition by blending the patterns of Renaissance pastoral romance with three variants of traditional pastoral. These patterns of development function both to enrich our understanding of the novel and to show how the pastoral tradition survives in modern fiction, thus revising our estimate of an historical category.

Specifically, in withdrawing from the world into Wragby Wood, Connie and Mellors set out on pastoral journeys. Connie's journey leads her into innocence; Mellors' journey has for its destination, solitude. The two pastoral variants of innocence and solitude then merge at a shrine, or supernatural center, into a pastoral of happiness. Reeducated in the inner pastoral circle and revitalized at the center, the two characters then leave for the world beyond their pastoral retreat. If in *The Rainbow* and *Women in Love* the admired characters make a "journey of the soul" in order to be regenerated,[6] the heroes of *Lady Chatterley's Lover* make physical *and* spiritual journeys in order to be regenerated at the point where their separate journeys coincide. After the heroes' regeneration, the forces of the novel merge into one unified thrust toward sustaining tenderness and sensual awareness. Thus the novel moves in two directions at once: inward to the hut and upward from despair, toward withdrawal and toward elevation. Finally, it moves outward, to sustain its victory.

The journey from the urban world to the rural world is a significant pattern in pastoral works. Such works have regularly featured a journey as a structural means of contrasting two opposite worlds, urban and rural, and thus of stating or implying a criticism of sophisticated or (more recently) industrialized life. We think of *Daphnis and Chloe*, Sannazaro's *Arcadia*, Montemayor's *Diana*, Book VI of *The Faerie Queene*, Sidney's *Arcadia*, Lodge's *Rosalynde*, Greene's *Menaphon* and *Pandosto*, *As You Like It*, *The Winter's Tale*, *The Tempest*, and later, *Silas Marner* and *The Country of the Pointed Firs*. In his book on Sidney's *Arcadia*, Walter R. Davis argues that "the heroes of the Renaissance pastoral romances are always *sojourners* in the Arcadian preserve, never native shepherds."[7] As a result, romance settings are multiple. The

---

[6] Mark Schorer, "Introduction" to D. H. Lawrence, *Lady Chatterley's Lover*, Modern Library Edition (New York: Random House, n.d.), p. xxv.

[7] This paragraph is indebted to Walter R. Davis, *A Map of Arcadia* (New Haven:

pattern created by such multiple settings takes the visual equivalent of "a center with two concentric circles surrounding it, implying a kind of purification of life proceeding inward: from the gross and turbulently naturalistic outer circle, to the refined pastoral inner circle, and then to the pure center of the world." This center, possessing supernatural qualities, may be a shrine; it may be the home of a magician or god; or it may exist without a god, like the cave in Sannazaro's *Arcadia.* The pastoral land, often called "Arcadia" to indicate its artificiality, surrounds the supernatural center and forms the inner pastoral circle. Beyond this pastoral land lies the outer circle of the great world. Unlike the inner circle, the outer circle is urban, complex, and sophisticated—a version of the real world drawn with bold exaggeration.

With its very similar multiple settings, *Lady Chatterley's Lover* parallels the topographical structure of the Renaissance pastoral romance. Outside Wragby Wood sprawl Tevershall and other towns, blighted by industrial ugliness and rendered by Lawrence in sharp naturalistic etchings. Also beyond the wood lie London and Paris, cities that embody a sophisticated form of corruption and sterility. Unlike the city, the pastoral circle in the novel is Wragby Wood, laden with flowers and often described as "lovely"; Moynahan calls it "Lawrence's sacred wood." At what appears to be roughly the center of the wood, an isolated hut represents the supernatural center where the heroes' rebirth and reorientation can occur. Out of this multiple setting arises the city-country contrast essential to all forms of pastoral. This contrast is the main method by which Lawrence conveys not only criticism of the dominant culture, but glorification of a simpler and more natural code of values consisting of sensual consciousness, passion, and tenderness.

More important than the multiple settings, however, is the action of the characters in their search for physical and philosophical reorientation. As the heroes journey toward rebirth, a structure of character changes parallels the topographical structure. In the pastoral romance, writes Davis, "the three parts of the pastoral setting represent a gradual purification toward the center"—from complex to simple to supernatural. "The action of the pastoral romance is simply the progress of the hero through the various areas of the setting: from the outer circle into the inner circle, hence to the center, and out again. Since each circle of the setting encourages a certain kind of activity, this progress is equivalent to entrance into Arcady in pain and turmoil and re-emergence in harmony with oneself." The standard pastoral action consists, then, of "disintegration in the turbulent outer circle, education in the pastoral

Yale Univ. Press, 1965), pp. 34–37. See also his *Idea and Act in Elizabethan Fiction* (Princeton: Princeton Univ. Press, 1969), pp. 56–60.

circle, and rebirth at the sacred center" (Davis, p. 38). This pastoral pattern, common to the major Renaissance romances, provides us with an illuminating way of looking at Lawrence's final novel. The double heroes of the novel journey from the turbulent world to the pastoral world of Wragby Wood, and then on into the supernatural center where, under the direction of the god of tenderness and sexual love, they are reborn. Escaping sterile relationships and industrialization by entering the wood, Connie and Mellors discover peace of mind and together gain the strength necessary to reenter the world. But unlike the heroes of standard pastoral works, they remain in the great outer world only long enough to find a haven more permanent than that provided by Wragby Wood.

Constance Chatterley had enjoyed "an aesthetically unconventional up-bringing" and had mingled with artists and cultured socialists. A member of the "well-to-do intelligentsia," she was also "at once cosmopolitan and provincial" (pp. 4–5).[8] In what Lawrence aptly calls "that outer world of chaos" (p. 9), she was poised and confident. Her sophistication and her assurance attracted Sir Clifford Chatterley, himself a baronet, who was later paralyzed and left impotent. After they marry in 1917 and move to Clifford's estate, Wragby, Lady Chatterley tires of the dismal brownstone house and its frequent guests. Gradually the house, located in a beautiful old park of oak trees, becomes "as dreary as a disused street." Even her affair with Michaelis, their friend, eventually reveals its "hopelessness" and causes her sexual feeling to collapse. A restlessness spreads its roots over her dissatisfaction. "Out of her disconnection, a restlessness was taking possession of her like madness" (p. 21). Unnoticed by Clifford, "a strange, weary yearning, a dissatisfaction had started in her" (p. 53), and she was possessed by "the fear of nothingness" in her life. Escape from this nothingness is her only recourse. The ancient wooded park, "private" and "motionless," offers the escape she yearns for: "She would rush off across the park, and abandon Clifford, and lie prone in the bracken. To get away from the house . . . she must get away from the house and everybody. The wood was her one refuge, her sanctuary" (p. 21). Thus like the heroes of pastoral romance, Connie eases the pain of life in the great outer world by escaping to the wood. Before long, she "went out alone every day now, mostly in the wood, where she was really alone" (p. 72).

Essentially she escapes into a world of pastoral innocence, a world characterized by seclusion, simplicity, natural beauty, and a rejection of

[8] Parenthetical page numbers refer to D. H. Lawrence, *Lady Chatterley's Lover*, Modern Library Edition (New York: Random House, n.d.).

money and power. In his penetrating study "The Oaten Flute," Renato Poggioli distinguishes the variants of pastoral.[9] Of these variants, the three that illuminate *Lady Chatterley's Lover* with clarity and power are the pastoral of innocence, the pastoral of solitude, and, developing from these, the pastoral of happiness. In his discussion of the pastoral of innocence, Poggioli argues that the retreat into a world of innocence is usually temporary, "acting as a pause in the process of living, as a breathing spell from the fever and anguish of being." Since *Lady Chatterley's Lover* is framed by a sophisticated atmosphere—it opens at Wragby and closes with Connie in London reading a letter from Mellors—the withdrawal into Wragby Wood represents a similar pause from agitated modernism. What follows then is the "pastoral oasis." Fixed in both time and space, the pastoral oasis is an interlude that occurs at the proper moment and at the right spot. That is, to the heroes who make the retreat, the ideal *time* for a retreat is the moment when the pressures of sophisticated life grow unbearable; the ideal *place* for rest is a quietly secluded charming spot, and hence we have the *locus amoenus* or "lovely place." The presence of the *locus amoenus* in "an epic or a chivalric poem, in a romance or a tragicomedy, foretells . . . a bucolic episode, which breaks the main action or pattern, suspending for a while the heroic, romantic, or pathetic mood of the whole." In this episode or pastoral oasis, the heroes rest from love or adventure. Poggioli finds pastoral oases in the *Aeneid*, the *Commedia*, the *Furioso*, *Don Quixote*, *As You Like It*, and a beautiful and typical example in "Erminia's stay among the shepherds" in Tasso's *Gerusalemme liberata*, Book VII.

Given the similarity of Connie's retreat to the retreat into innocence of traditional pastoral, it is not at all surprising to find clear parallels—both of action and character—between *Lady Chatterley's Lover* and the most typical of the pastoral oases, that of *Gerusalemme liberata* (1581).[10] These parallels illustrate how closely the pastoral of innocence subsumes Lawrence's novel. Although salient differences can be cited, essentially both Erminia and Connie are pursued, Erminia by a band of Crusaders and Connie by the threat of emotional sterility; and both flee into a wood. Both, frustrated and weeping, are comforted by male figures who have themselves retreated into the *locus amoenus* of the wood. And as the old man is frightened by Erminia's warlike disguise, Mellors similarly fears Connie's rank and her strength of will ("he was powerless to preserve his privacy"): both situations reveal the pastoral fear of power. Both the old man and Mellors value their exceptional peace, their poverty, and their lack of envy. Like Mellors,

9 "The Oaten Flute," *Harvard Library Bulletin*, 11 (1957), 147–84. The quotations that follow are from pp. 154–57.

10 See "The Oaten Flute," pp. 155–57, for fuller discussion of this work.

the old man values particularly his happy innocence since he once lost it by following Ambition's charm into the wicked city, and recovered his innocence only by returning to the wood. Just as Erminia's unhappiness moves the old shepherd to console her, Connie's unhappiness excites feelings of sympathy in Mellors. And if Poggioli is right in saying that "the natural outcome of the pastoral of innocence is the family situation,"[11] as in Tasso's poem, we should note that the physical outcome of the withdrawal of Connie and Mellors into the wood is similarly the conception of a child to be born after the novel closes. Such parallels as these and others tell us much about the tradition in which *Lady Chatterley's Lover* seems impressively to fit. The pastoral imagination creates, as a metaphor of rebirth, a lovely country retreat in order to criticize urbanization, or in order to offer recovery and then change of direction. Lawrence's novel does both.

By escaping into a world of innocence and simplicity, Connie is able to rout her despair and unrest: "She wanted to forget, to forget the world" (p. 94), and so she "fled as much as possible to the wood" (p. 125). From the perspective of the wood, Connie recognizes the lack of meaningful connection inherent in the intellectual refinement of Clifford and his friends. "The mental life! Suddenly she hated it with a rushing fury, the swindle!" (p. 77). "A kind of terror filled her sometimes, a terror of the incipient insanity of the whole civilized species" (p. 123). The wood, on the other hand, appeals directly to her senses; its appeal is emotional and sentient rather than intellectual. Despite a few bare spots where timber had been cut during the war, the wood symbolizes "pure seclusion." She can feel its stillness: "In the wood all was utterly inert and motionless." When she first visits Mellors, the gamekeeper, to take a message from Clifford, the wood exudes a melancholy (reflected later in Mellors) that was "somehow soothing to her, better than the harsh insentience of the outer world. She liked the *inwardness* of the remnant of forest, the unspeaking reticence of the old trees. They seemed a very power of silence, and yet a vital presence" (p. 72). Their silent vitality attracts her because she seeks reaffirmation in some code of positive values, a code as yet undiscovered. At the heart of nature she discovers the vague beginnings of such a code, just as she discovers the code itself at the "heart," or center, of Wragby Wood. In both cases, movement inward promotes rediscovery. It is for this reason that she likes, intuitively, "the *inwardness* of the remnant of forest." The human form of this mysterious natural vitality is, of course, Mellors, who is frequently identified with the forest and described with the same words. Connie's preliminary attraction to the primeval forest pre-

[11] "The Oaten Flute," p. 157.

pares her (and us) for her attraction to a human being who embodies the same qualities that characterize the ancient wood. As the instrument for the discovery of truth in *Lady Chatterley's Lover*, sensual experience replaces the intellect and the developed moral sense of Clifford's world.

Connie's search for a revitalizing code of values intensifies when, one day in early spring, she takes Mrs. Bolton's suggestion to walk to the gamekeeper's cottage in the wood, where the daffodils " 'are the prettiest sight you'd see in a day's march.' " The loveliness of the wood quickens her thoughts. Not only is the wood buried under ineffable silence, but gusts of sunshine also light up the celandines "bright and yellow," and the wood seems pale with "endless little anemones, sprinkling the shaken floor." Caught up in the flowers and the cold gusty wind, "Connie was strangely excited in the wood, and the color flew in her cheeks, and burned blue in her eyes" (p. 94). The withdrawal into a world of natural beauty begins reawakening her sensitive physical responses. This aesthetic perception of nature prepares the way for the aesthetic perception of the human male and then of the sexual experience. Both forms of perception pierce to the most intense and expressive region of sensual experience. Since the keeper is at the moment away from the cottage, she beholds the lovely flowers alone. As she feels nature come alive, she feels herself come alive. Nature awakens her in the same way that it awakens the grieving Lydia Lensky in *The Rainbow*. A pine tree communicates to Connie its "curious life, elastic and powerful, rising up. . . . And then, being so still and alone, she seemed to get into the current of her own proper destiny." Landscape and mind interact. The two kinds of currents, one welling up from the mysterious power of spring and the other welling up from Connie's changing sensibility, are simultaneous—a simultaneity that implies Connie's harmony with natural cycles and thus a connection with the rebirth of spring. Connie's education begins, then, appropriately in the pastoral circle of the wood: "She had been fastened by a rope, and jagging and snarring like a boat at its moorings; now she was loose and adrift" (p. 95).

Her education begun, Connie is ready for the rites of rebirth as soon as she can discover the supernatural center of the pastoral world. Thus, when she goes into the wood the next afternoon and follows the riding to a spring called John's Well, she accidentally finds "a secret little clearing, and a secret little hut made of rustic poles" (p. 96). The clearing is a *locus amoenus*; and the hut, as "a sort of little sanctuary," is dark and mysterious without windows, the appropriate dwelling place of Eros. Surrounding the clearing are old oak trees, "throwing off reckless limbs," and lovely anemones sprinkled over the ground. Within the clearing she discovers Mellors making coops for the pheasants. Per-

haps, thinks Connie, this is, in its unstained innocence, "one of the un-
ravished places" (p. 104).

As suggested earlier, we have here a *locus amoenus*. A lovely place
surrounding the supernatural center yet lying inside the pastoral circle,
it shows Lawrence reworking traditional pastoral materials. The *locus
amoenus*, as a clearly defined *topos* or "region" of nature, developed
from antiquity, became standard in landscape description, and also
formed part of the landscape of pastoral (and erotic) poetry.[12] As defined by Curtius (p. 195), the *locus amoenus* is "a beautiful, shaded
natural site. Its minimum ingredients comprise a tree (or several trees),
a meadow, and a spring or brook." Birdsong, flowers, and a breeze may
be added. In *Lady Chatterley's Lover* we find all these ingredients in or
very near the "secret little clearing" in Wragby Wood: "oak trees," a
"little clearing" sprinkled with anemones and "green anemone ruffs"
(p. 104), a "brilliant" spring nearby, a "windy wood" (p. 96), and
later the "clucking" and "peeping" of the hens and chicks (pp. 127–
28). Only the spring and the hut vary the traditional pattern of the
locus amoenus. The spring is just outside the clearing; and the hut as a
place of retreat and reorientation is a modern variant of the cave or
grotto that we find in early versions of the *locus amoenus*, where a cave
within a lovely place introduces sexual experience. As Evett says, "we
are not surprised to find that almost from the beginning sex and the
locus amoenus are intimately related" (p. 506).[13] The beauty and seclusion of the site stimulate in Connie a deep emotional response which
is expressed sexually. Connie's emotional response is so strong that it
leads her into a state of trance, as though she were within the world of
a dream. Entry into the clearing, into the *locus amoenus*, brings her to
a condition of stasis and awe and rest, where she is overcome with
relief. In *Lady Chatterley's Lover*, as in earlier works, the *locus amoenus*
provides a refuge from death and decay. " 'It is so nice here, so restful,' "
she says to Mellors (p. 99); "she sat in the doorway of the hut in a
dream, utterly unaware of time and of particular circumstances" (p.
98). By dissolving time and memory, the *locus amoenus* approaches
eternity and relieves Connie of the pain of contemplating either past or
future. The intersection of the *locus amoenus* and the present moment
has the mystical power to unfetter the communicant. Inside the hut,
"she lay quite still . . . in a sort of dream" (p. 130). Pastoral *otium* remains undisturbed. When the emotional response is (in accord with

---

[12] See E. R. Curtius, *European Literature and the Latin Middle Ages*, tr. Willard R. Trask (Princeton: Princeton Univ. Press, 1953), pp. 192–200.

[13] See David Evett's excellent essay, " 'Paradice's Only Map': The *Topos* of the
Locus Amoenus and the Structure of Marvell's *Upon Appleton House*," *PMLA*, 85
(1970), 504–13.

tradition) transferred from lovely place to sexual act, both she and Mellors enter a realm of "pure peace" (pp. 130, 141) so that in *Lady Chatterley's Lover* the *locus amoenus* provides refuge from pain, encourages the sexual expression of emotion, and initiates the process of reorientation for Connie and Mellors.

In typical pastoral form, Mellors, like Lady Chatterley, has also retreated from "that outer world of chaos" into the wood. Reared in Tevershall, the village juxtaposed to Wragby, Oliver Mellors had married unhappily. So he had joined the army in 1915 and had been sent to India. When released, about a year before he meets Connie, he decides to withdraw into Wragby Wood, to return to "his native place." Like withdrawn courtiers of traditional pastoral, who were stung by sophistication, Mellors even returns to speaking local dialect. He withdraws from society because he has suffered from his human and particularly his sexual contacts: " 'But I wanted to have nothing to do with any woman any more,' " he tells Connie later. " 'I wanted to keep to myself: keep my privacy and my decency' " (p. 230). But Mellors withdraws too because he loathes industrialized society, "which he knew by instinct to be a malevolent, partly-insane beast" (p. 134).

Mellors, however, does not retreat into a pastoral of innocence, as Lady Chatterley does, but into a pastoral of solitude. That is, he withdraws not so much into a world of natural beauty and simplicity as he does into a world of aloofness and isolation from human contact. If Connie yearns for Mellors to "make her a world" and if she is happiest when they are "together in a world of their own" (pp. 240–41), Mellors relishes the solitude and darkness and seclusion of the wood because it allows him to be "private and withdrawn" (p. 133). Connie withdraws largely from ugly industrialization and sterility and, to some extent, from the sexuality of men like Michaelis. Mellors, on the other hand, withdraws largely from women with overpowering wills and, to a lesser extent, from an industrialized and economic society. It is true that their withdrawals are in some ways similar, but to treat their withdrawals separately allows us to focus clearly and precisely on the essential elements in each character's personality.

Although Poggioli fails to distinguish clearly between the pastorals of solitude, melancholy, and self, the pastoral of solitude nonetheless clearly combines self-love and misanthropy. Emphasizing withdrawal, the pastoral of solitude "rejects man's love for woman."[14] Like Lady Chatterley or like Marcela in *Don Quixote*, who rejects all suitors and

---

14 "The Pastoral of the Self," *Daedalus*, 88 (1959), 693, 697.

goes into the fields to tend sheep, Mellors retreats into the secluded, motionless wood of Wragby. As in most variants of pastoral, he retreats in search of a peace of mind and an unspoiled privacy not available beyond the wood. When Mellors first emerges as a major character, we find that Lawrence continually characterizes him as lonely, withdrawing, and alone. To Connie, his body is "like a lonely pistil of an invisible flower!" (p. 94). He is "inwardly alone" (p. 73). Thus Mellors, in retreating to the secluded wood, gradually becomes *like* the wood—silent and strong and vital, yet similarly scarred—showing again the interaction of landscape and mind in the pastoral novel. When Connie chances to discover the secret clearing and the rustic hut, Mellors, true to his nature, hardens himself against her: "He resented the intrusion, he cherished his solitude as his only and last freedom in life" (pp. 96–97). Connie represents "a trespass on his privacy, and a dangerous one! A woman! He had reached the point where all he wanted on earth was to be alone. . . . Especially he did not want to come into contact with a woman again. He feared it; for he had a big wound from old contacts. He felt if he could not be alone, and if he could not be left alone, he would die. His recoil away from the outer world was complete; his last refuge was this wood; to hide himself there!" (pp. 97–98). In his mistrust of human relationships, Mellors represents perfectly the pastoral of solitude. The words *recoil, refuge, hide,* and the insistent repetition of *privacy* and *alone* define his intense shrinking from human society. Even his brown dog, like its master, surveys a world that is "untrustworthy." As Connie gazes on Mellors at work outside the hut, "the same solitary aloneness she had seen in him naked, she now saw in him clothed: solitary and intent, like an animal that works alone, but also brooding, like a soul that recoils away, away from all human contact. Silently, patiently, he was recoiling away from her even now" (p. 98). "He dreaded, with a repulsion almost of death, any further close human contact" (p. 99). "He wanted to keep his own privacy" (p. 126). But why a recoil so deliberate, so adamant? Mellors retreats to the wood in order to escape the insistent and assertive "female will"; he recoils from the passionless and selfish sexual love he experienced in the chaotic world outside the wood. Alone, however, he can skirt temptation. Alone, he can allow his work to absorb his energies, and he can commune intimately with nature. Alone, he can create his own equilibrium. For companionship he has his dog and his pheasants, who wish not to assert their will but to be given protection. Thus his craving for solitude provides a means of blending with the wood, of assuming its stillness and of mirroring its motionless serenity. "He loved the darkness [of the wood] and folded himself into it." His home in the wood offers "a

silence he loved" (pp. 134–35). The equilibrium he achieves is both
with himself and with his environment, both internal and external.

But with Lady Chatterley's entrance into the secret clearing—into
the physical equivalent of his inner security—sexual desire, kindling "a
little thin tongue of fire," startles and begins to stir both characters. With
the awakening of physical desire, the two variants of pastoral that we
have examined merge. The pastoral of innocence and the pastoral of
solitude unite to breed a third pastoral variant, the pastoral of happiness.

The pastoral of happiness, best illustrated in literature by Tasso's pastoral drama *Aminta* (1580), defines happiness as the consummation
of erotic desire. The pastoral of happiness, says Poggioli, "is conceived
as an absolute acceptance of the law of instinct, with no sense of guilt
nor any regard for its consequences."[15] Thus when they become lovers,
Mellors, like Connie, is troubled by "no sense of wrong or sin; he was
troubled by no conscience in that respect. He knew that conscience was
chiefly fear of society, or fear of oneself" (p. 134). Poggioli contends
that one of the tasks of seventeenth-century European writers was, by
developing neglected pastoral variants, to free the pastoral from the
emphasis on passion and sex which had been the focus of the Italians.[16]
With much justice, we might say that it was the task of *Lady Chatterley's
Lover* to introduce passion and sex into the modern pastoral novel,
especially since nineteenth-century pastoral novels such as *Adam Bede*
or *Under the Greenwood Tree* or *Far from the Madding Crowd* had, instead of creating a pastoral of happiness, evoked nostalgic memories of
the countryside, discovering afresh a *locus amoenus*.

Now, in *Lady Chatterley's Lover* two things occur simultaneously:
the pastoral of happiness begins with the rising passion between male
and female, at the same time that Connie and Mellors move, as in pastoral romance, toward the supernatural center of the pastoral world. In
other words, having left the outer world of chaos and having come into
the inner pastoral circle and now into the "secret clearing," both characters are ready to enter the supernatural center. This center is the rustic
hut located in the middle of the pastoral circle and within the *locus
amoenus*. Since it is in the hut (and later in the gamekeeper's cottage)
that Connie and Mellors are reoriented, it is therefore at the supernatural
center that the pastoral of happiness reaches its climax and that the
lovers are gradually fulfilled.

Thus as spring advances and as "the green things on earth seemed to

15 "The Oaten Flute," pp. 157, 159.
16 "The Pastoral of the Self," p. 686.

hum with greenness," Mellors' veneer of resistance to Connie's presence gradually wears thin; and the beginnings of the pastoral of happiness reveal themselves, appropriately, amid the awakening beauty of the season. On one lovely sunny day, when bluebells and primroses and violets fill the wood, Connie comes—as she came every day now—to see the pheasant hens sitting on their eggs: "they were the only things in the world that warmed her heart" (p. 126). Their "hot, brooding female bodies," fluffed on their eggs, stir her to feel acutely "the agony of her own female forlornness. It was becoming unbearable" (p. 127). The pulse of natural processes affects her profoundly, and in Mellors' presence she recognizes her unfulfilled need to create new life, to be like the hens. Her anguished tears quickly excite Mellors' deep tenderness: "His heart melted suddenly, like a drop of fire, and he put out his hand and laid his fingers on her knee" and then on her loins "in the blind instinctive caress" (p. 129). Inside the rustic hut, Mellors makes love to her. The feelings of tenderness aroused by the pheasant hens are carried to fulfillment once the barriers against women, erected by Mellors, have been dissolved.

In the hut Mellors and Connie, like the heroes of pastoral romance, are irrevocably awakened and revitalized by their sexual union. " 'Now I've begun again,' " says Mellors, aware that reinvolvement will eventually create "a new cycle of pain and doom." " 'Begun what?' " she asked." " 'Life.' " " 'Life!' she re-echoed, with a queer thrill" (p. 132). The god-like power of sexual love, vital and alive inside the hut, transforms their level of awareness from apathy to reinvolvement, from disconnection to connection. In the case of Mellors, "She had connected him up again, when he had wanted to be alone" (pp. 132–33). The consummation of their love changes Connie too: "and she was born: a woman. . . . And now in her heart the queer wonder of him was awakened. . . . Beauty! What beauty! a sudden little flame of new awareness went through her" (p. 197). In *Lady Chatterley's Lover* "the experience of love is delivered . . . as religious in itself."[17] Connie and Mellors are reawakened to the possibilities of life. She scarcely understood "the beauty he found in her, through touch upon her living secret body, almost the ecstasy of beauty" (p. 141). In the first version of the novel, "she had burst as if from a chrysalis shell, and she had emerged a new creature." Reawakened by "the touch of tenderness," they gradually commit themselves to sustaining this tender beauty in whatever ways they can. The divine power at work in the hut redirects and then combines the destinies of the two heroes. After Connie visits Mellors again, she recognizes that "another self was alive in her, burning molten and

[17] Mark Spilka, *The Love Ethic of D. H. Lawrence* (Bloomington: Indiana Univ. Press, 1955), p. 191.

soft in her womb and bowels, and with this self she adored him. She adored him till her knees were weak as she walked. In her womb and bowels she was flowing and alive now and vulnerable, and helpless in adoration of him as the most naive woman.—It feels like a child, she said to herself; it feels like a child in me.—And so it did, as if her womb, that had always been shut, had opened and filled with new life, almost a burden, yet lovely" (p. 152). Like the ecstasy of beauty that Mellors finds in her body, she discovers "another self," a lovely "new life," totally divorced from the corrupt world of Sir Clifford.

It is fitting to note here Lawrence's skillful and ironic handling of the relationship between Clifford and Mrs. Bolton, a manipulation that counterpoints perfectly the affair between Connie and the gamekeeper. While Connie and Mellors are receiving their education in the pastoral circle, Clifford is educating Mrs. Bolton ("Yes, he was educating her" [p. 111]), and she in turn educates him by her "tricks" into asserting himself in the industrial world. While Connie and Mellors are reborn at the supernatural center, Clifford also changes under Mrs. Bolton's direction: "And he seemed verily to be re-born" (p. 121). But Clifford and Mrs. Bolton, acting as foils, are reborn not into tenderness and blood consciousness but into corruption and perversion: "And they drew into a closer physical intimacy, an intimacy of perversity" (p. 331). The two relationships illustrate the two separate forces that control both couples. In the case of Clifford and Mrs. Bolton, the dominant force is centrifugal, drawing their lives into a pattern of regression, into "a childish position that was really perverse" (p. 331). In the case of Connie and Mellors, the dominant force is centripetal, pushing them outward into new consciousness and culminating in the conception of their child and in their search for a farm on which to live in the future.

But before Connie and Mellors can form a permanent relationship, they must test the strength of their emotional ties. Before she leaves on a brief visit to Venice, a visit that will test their relationship and allow Mellors to initiate divorce proceedings, Connie and Mellors spend a final night together, a "night of sensual passion" which completes the change that had been brought about by their meetings at the hut. They are entirely transformed. For Connie, this night of "reckless, shameless sensuality shook her to her foundations, stripped her to the very last, and made a different woman of her" (p. 280). For Mellors, the transformation requires that he pledge Connie as his mate and so immerse himself once more in "a battle against the money, and the machine" (p. 316). His new-found strength, the product of his reattachment to a woman, allows him to wage the battle with confidence and to fight the insensate world from which he had earlier withdrawn. Connected and revitalized, Mellors and Connie find, however, that their new security is threatened by forces outside the pastoral world—Mellors' vicious wife Bertha Coutts, Clifford, the ugly industrial noises which puncture the solitude of the wood—and so Connie and Mellors must depart from their paradise. Transformed, however, they are ready to emerge from the inner pastoral circle, so that their action parallels again the standard action of pastoral romance, where the hero, now strengthened and renewed, returns to the great outer world. Thus the novel's movement, in following a pastoral pattern, progresses essentially from the outer chaotic world, to Wragby, to the gamekeeper's cottage, and into the gamekeeper's hut. Then it moves back to the gamekeeper's cottage, back to Wragby, then to London, and finally (perhaps) to a farm. The pastoral pattern is altered only by their anticipated final move. Of Connie and Mellors, Lawrence writes: "Mellors went into the country and got work on a farm. The idea was, he should get his divorce, if possible, whether Connie got hers or not. And for six months he should work at farming, so that eventually he and Connie could have some small farm of their own, into which he could put his energy" (p. 339). Yet even in their departure from the wood, they shun the elements that pastoral has always labeled as corruptors of happiness: sophistication and the pursuit of money. " 'Let's live for summat else,' " Mellors pleads with Connie. " 'Let's not live ter make money, neither for us-selves nor for anybody else. . . . Bit by bit, let's drop the whole industrial life, an' go back' " (pp. 247–48). To the pastoral rejection of money, Lawrence adds the modern equivalent of the courtly sophistication of traditional pastoral—namely, an indictment of advanced technology and of the failure of instinct to assert itself against the will. In doing so, Lawrence successfully updates the content, though not the form, of pastoral. His novel reflects a traditional kind of escape from a modern kind of evil—industrial society, or what he calls "the insentient iron world . . . of mechanized greed" (p. 134). Heartened by their pastoral interlude, by their temporary escape from the demands of modern life, Connie and Mellors will try to live beyond the temptations of wealth and power by humbling themselves before the great altars of: the natural life, peace and love, "inner intuitive knowledge," tenderness, and "the life of the human body." They will combat industrialization and greed with the new perspective they have, together, achieved. In so doing, they will become a model for the regeneration of an effete and sterile society.

For some readers, D. H. Lawrence offers alternate values to those held by the twentieth century; for other readers, he offers practical advice on living one's life as a courageous retreat from the "ghastly world of smoke and iron!" (p. 240). However, the problem with interpreting the novel as a guide to conduct is one that Poggioli was quick to see: "the few men who earnestly heeded the pastoral call found in no time that country life is at best a purgatory, and that real shepherds are even less innocent and happy than city-dwellers and courtiers."[18] What this means is that the pastoral is most effective when it remains an interlude. To sustain the interlude is to invite life's realities to intrude their knotty uncertainties. Perhaps it is significant that Lawrence concluded *Lady Chatterley's Lover* before he was required to face the problem of how to sustain into ordinary reality the pastoral interlude he had created. To complete the pastoral pattern of retreat-reorientation-return, Lawrence might have carried the action a step further and resolved fully the conflicts of the novel. He would have shown that the lovers, newly strengthened, return not to an unindustrialized Canada but to the chaotic world they left. Traditionally the pastoral pattern represents not simply an escape, but an escape that leads to a return. Although he would have blunted his criticism of industrialism by returning the lovers permanently to London or Tevershall, it is true that the lovers do not use the perspective they achieve in the same way that traditional pastoral used perspective. Instead, Connie and Mellors, by freeing themselves totally from sterile industrialism, vary and weaken the traditional pattern because they escape, rather than face, modern industrial society. The significance of their relationship is not conveyed to the civilized world. The pastoral pattern demands that the experience in Wragby Wood give the lovers sensual satisfaction, and also the wisdom and courage to live in the world as it is. Significant modern pastoral, it can be argued, should deal finally with the modern world. Thus the patterns of the genre enlarge our understanding of Lawrence's intention at the same time that they reveal the novel's weakness, its confusion of interlude and completed pattern. What matters is not Lawrence's failure to imitate the pastoral pattern per se, but the fact that observance of the pattern would have achieved for the novel greater universality and would have embodied a fundamental pattern of human regeneration, a pattern that represents a standard response to adult reality.

Yet it is equally important to argue that Lawrence modified pastoral because of the pressures of his civilization. Traditionally, Arcadia has always encouraged the removal of class barriers. With the aid of disguises,[19] Arcadia's leveling tendencies open the lines of communication among those in retreat and allow aristocracy and rustics to intermingle. Thus *Lady Chatterley's Lover* opens with a latticework of class distinctions and then strips these away as the characters discover their true

---

18 "The Oaten Flute," p. 147.

19 The use of disguises at once shows clear continuity with the tradition but also a modification of it. Romance heroes masked themselves in order to go into the pastoral world and purify themselves incognito, whereas Connie and Mellors *unmask*, as they enter the pastoral world, in order to discover their true selves: they

identities: Mellors has rejected Clifford's "English" in favor of dialect, Connie will abandon her rank. But after Connie and Mellors have been transformed, reentry into a *class* society would violate the regeneration they have earned since they (unlike their creator) perceive the world as too fully fallen to allow them to convey to others the significance of their relationship and since, too, they refuse—with the reader's approval—to burden themselves with masks once again in order to bear the weight of industrialization and sterility. The lovers do not return to society because Lawrence's faith in the modern world has been severely damaged: his despair has no parallel in the cultural attitudes which formed pastoralists of earlier centuries. Lawrence's modification of traditional patterns, then, also gauges the failure of modern culture to sustain the confidence of a major creative artist.

Thus the use of pastoral patterns and pastoral variants enriches the novel because they show that we can place the novel in the context of a traditional literary genre and because they help us to understand Lawrence's reasons for using the motifs of that genre. The novel's continuity with a tradition illustrates the recurrence of a widely used pattern of emotional or spiritual adjustment and thus reveals a valuable new dimension in this complex work. As important, the novel shows how the patterns of a traditional genre help Lawrence to express his response to industrialization and its impact on modern man, and then to battle these forces imaginatively. If, in examining the standard patterns of traditional pastoral, we see the novel in the perspective of a traditional literary genre, our discovery of three pastoral variants—the pastorals of innocence, solitude, and happiness—shows that Lawrence succeeded in restoring tenderness and passion and sensual beauty to the throne of the pastoral vision. The discovery of these various pastoral parallels in *Lady Chatterley's Lover* does not reveal Lawrence borrowing directly from earlier writers of pastoral, but it does illustrate that pastoral forms and the pastoral ideal are alive in modern literature, more alive and active than we have been likely to think.

---

strip themselves of their culture's values and then of their garments in order to purify themselves spiritually. Lawrence reverses the masking process and thus modifies the tradition because Connie and Mellors enter a pastoral world *without* shepherds or their equivalent: modern industrialization has shrunk and depopulated the world of refuge.

Chapter 10

Conclusion

IN THESE CHAPTERS I have grouped together the important pastoral novels of three major writers working within a period in which the pastoral impulse manifests itself. I have examined seven novels as pastoral or, more nearly, as a modified form of pastoral. I have looked at the relationship between these novels and traditional pastoral and have considered the way in which these novels use pastoral techniques, attitudes, and forms. In particular I have supported the thesis that a pastoral novel appeared beyond the eighteenth-century date conventionally ascribed to the death of traditional pastoral. In order to define this subgenre of the novel, I have needed, because of the diversity of critical responses to pastoral, to formulate a definition of the pastoral novel as the subgenre of the novel which recreates country life by using elements and techniques of traditional pastoral—principally, contrasts between city and country; the examination of rural life from both urban and rural viewpoints; the implied withdrawal from complexity to simplicity; intense nostalgia for the past and consequent criticism of modern life; and the creation of a circumscribed and remote pastoral world. This circumscribed pastoral world reveals harmony between man and nature, idyllic contentment, and a sympathetic realism which combines both idealization and realism and in which country life, stripped of its coarsest features, is made palatable to urban society. Each of the novels does not necessarily reveal all of the specified characteristics (though several do), but those novels that reveal most of the characteristics have been discussed.

But, one may be tempted to ask, why study these novels? Why should the modern student or the general reader turn to the pastoral novels of George Eliot or Hardy or Lawrence? A study of these novels has been important, generically, in order to see how these writers modify a very old but vital tradition and to see how these fictions give expression to a fundamental impulse that has been poured into imaginative forms by earlier writers. To consider the art is to discover how these novels have endured aesthetically and how we can read them with fuller awareness of both their imaginative coherence and their distinctive effects. Apart from their genre, however, these novels reveal man's fundamental need for an organic community at a time when indus-

trialism, scientific skepticism, war, and a loss of tradition increasingly
weaken the ties among fellow men. The need for community continues
to pose a fundamental problem, though more acute now and less easy
to solve. The novels raise questions about a capitalist society and, if
only by implication, offer the pastoral community as an alternative to
technocracy.

Although we read these seven novels both for their art and for their
contemporary significance, they will have most resonance for us if we
can see them in their literary perspective, if we can place them within
the stream of attitudes that have, rather like a meandering brook than
a swift current, flowed down from earlier writers working in or near
the pastoral genre. From Vergil onward, the standard pattern recom-
mended to prospective writers was to embark on their craft by writing
pastorals. The mold was cast by Vergil, who graduated from the *Eclogues* to the epic form of the *Aeneid.* Spenser, following Vergil, tried
his hand at *The Shepheardes Calender* before he attempted the heroic
genre in *The Faerie Queene,* where he "now enforst a far unfitter taske, /
For trumpets sterne to chaunge mine Oaten reeds, / And sing of Knights
and Ladies gentle deeds" (I.1.3–5). Milton too followed the pattern:
Lycidas emerged long before *Paradise Lost.* And Pope wrote his *Pastorals* as a technical preface to his major work. A century later, in *Sleep
and Poetry,* Keats recalls this tradition:

> First the realm I'll pass
> Of Flora, and old Pan: sleep in the grass
> Feed upon apples red, and strawberries,
> And choose each pleasure that my fancy sees.
>
> [ll. 101–4]

Although he'll create a lovely tale of human life, yet

> . . . can I ever bid these joys farewell?
> Yes, I must pass them for a nobler life,
> Where I may find the agonies, the strife
> Of human hearts.
>
> [ll. 122–25]

In the same way, Wordsworth turned from "Michael" to the *Ecclesiastical Sonnets,* Blake from the *Songs* to *Jerusalem,* Arnold from "Thyrsis"
to a double collection of *Essays in Criticism,* Frost from regionalism and
pastoral to a poetry of ideas.

George Eliot, Hardy, and Lawrence can all be set within the same
traditional pattern, although certainly they were led to experiment with
pastoral as much by the pressures of their experience and by the era in
which they wrote as by the apprenticeship pattern. All of them wrote

their pastoral novels early in their writing careers (the exception is *Lady Chatterley's Lover*, which returns to earlier themes), then turned away from the rural world as a pastoral world. *Adam Bede* and *The White Peacock* are first novels, and *Under the Greenwood Tree* is Hardy's first novel about rural life. In *The Mill on the Floss*, however, George Eliot begins gradually to shift to the life of the town; and *Silas Marner*, published a year later, is atavistic, moving toward *Adam Bede* rather than *Middlemarch*. Hardy, starting with *Under the Greenwood Tree*, travels toward the bleak landscape of *Tess* and *Jude* and then turns off the road of rural fiction entirely in order to focus on poetry; in *The Dynasts* he turns, like Vergil and Spenser, to the epic. If in *The White Peacock* Lawrence begins with "a decorated idyll," he soon enough takes up modern, urban, industrial life in the second half of *The Rainbow* and in *Women in Love*, where Birkin says to Ursula, " 'One is tired of the life that belongs to death—our kind of life,' " where Gerald cries in anger: " 'Sometimes I think it is a curse to be alive.' "[1] All three novelists move beyond their early rural fiction.

The explanation is generic, psychological, and historical. As the quotations from Keats and Spenser suggest, pastoral tends toward the idyllic rather than the heroic and so may appear to have less relevance than other genres to a writer and his readers. Although the pastoral novel may of course anchor itself in nostalgia, that nostalgia has relevance in projecting a viable human community against which to measure our own technocratic society. As a source of fiction, moreover, memories of the rural past may indeed be unable to sustain a creative lifetime; they may, like a well, have limited depth. But they have the capacity to sustain an *era* of writers who confront personally, with sensitivity and perception, the threats to civilization that issue from an age of transition. Thus rapid change gives strength to the pastoral novel but at the same time circumscribes its power, is its own enemy. Why? The reason is primarily psychological. These three novelists made a gradual exit from pastoral because they found themselves either buffeted or uprooted by urban influences. Their urban contact not only produced the standard situation for the writing of pastoral (an urban yearning for the rural past), but their urban experiences also compelled fictional treatment once a reaction to industrialism and a love of country life had been registered in the form of pastoral fiction. That is, once the early novels were written and the yearning for the rural past exorcised, these writers began to concentrate on interpreting a distinctly modern milieu. Acceptance followed reaction. Hardy, it is true, used his urban experience in most of his novels; but in *Jude* he clearly moves toward the deraci-

---

[1] *Women in Love*, Phoenix Edition (London: Heinemann, 1956), pp. 178, 200.

nation that he saw around him. Alone, Lawrence returned at the end of his life to the pastoral mode, and then only once.

The social and economic conditions of the period 1859 to the Great War, in which all but one of the novels appeared, also explains the shift from pastoral to nonpastoral material. That the rural world was ailing, "A tattered coat upon a stick," is a documented fact; tenant farmers and laborers were migrating constantly, at the rate of thousands each year, to lucrative jobs in factory towns; and after 1873 Britain's agricultural stability shattered, the result of cheap grain from America, cheap beef from Argentina, and a series of bad harvests in Britain.[2] Perhaps the rural world gradually grew to lack the substance, vitality, interest, and variety necessary to sustain a major writer for his entire creative life. John Holloway suggests that if we view Hardy's novels as part of the eclipse of the old rhythmic order of rural England, we will see that the earlier way of life "did not possess the inner resources upon which to make a real fight for its existence. The old order was not just a less powerful mode of life than the new, but ultimately helpless before it through inner defect."[3] The new order generated more power because its materialism proved to have magnetic appeal. However, as *The Woodlanders* or *The White Peacock* or *Lady Chatterley's Lover* illustrate, the defect of the old rural order was not *inner* but imported from without. The urban and industrial invasions in these three novels injure the vitality of a pastoral world that would surely have survived had it remained undisturbed. Whether we look inside or outside the world of fiction, these invasions illustrate once again that time is the major enemy of pastoral whenever the pastoralist chooses to write, or to chronicle fictional events, over a period of time: pastoral as a mode tries to *fix* the moment of beauty and peace.

With Lawrence, of course, the Great War also fueled the turn from idyll to industrialism; and the shift, though evident as early as *The White Peacock*, is pointedly dramatized by the mood of despair in *Women in Love*. Lawrence's characters, initially rooted in the early novels, begin to move from one house or one area to another, escaping

2 See Douglas Brown, *Thomas Hardy*, 2d ed. (London: Longmans, 1961), pp. 30–42; W. H. B. Court, *British Economic History: 1870–1914* (Cambridge: Univ. Press, 1965), pp. 33–77; R. C. K. Ensor, *England: 1870–1914* (Oxford: Clarendon Press, 1936), pp. 110–21, 284–86, 511–13; R. E. P. Ernle, *English Farming: Past and Present*, 6th ed. (Chicago: Quadrangle Books, 1961), pp. 377–92, 507; H. Rider Haggard, *Rural England* (London: Longmans, 1902), pp. 536–76; Thomas Hardy, "The Dorsetshire Labourer," in *Life and Art*, ed. Ernest Brennecke, Jr. (1925; rpt. New York: Haskell House, 1966), pp. 20–47.

3 "Thomas Hardy's Major Fiction," in *From Jane Austen to Joseph Conrad*, ed. Robert C. Rathburn and Martin Steinmann, Jr. (Minneapolis: Univ. of Minnesota Press, 1958), p. 235.

what Birkin calls the "horrible tyranny of a fixed milieu" (p. 348). "This war served as a prologue to an age," write George A. Panichas, "particularly to that modern spirit of discontent."[4] In the words of Vera Brittain, "Mankind was never the same again after 1914, any more than it was ever the same again after the Crucifixion. Only those who recall, however dimly, the vanishing sunset splendor of the final Victorian years can estimate in their personal histories the quality of the transformation which the events of 1914 created."[5]

The war, speeding the cultural transformations already evident at the turn of the century, perhaps put an end to the pastoral novel. In 1912, George Bourne remarked: "in another ten years' time there will be not much left of the traditional life whose crumbling away I have been witnessing during the twenty years that are gone."[6] Thus a study of the survival of the pastoral genre is also a study of its demise. The assumptions of a postwar society have not proved congenial to pastoral literature. The tension between rural and urban no longer appears attractive to modern writers, as it did to Thackeray in *Vanity Fair* or Dickens in *Great Expectations*, where city and country plots alternate like the swings of a pendulum; and World War I introduced a sense of cultural collapse that swept away a dependence on the past, on tradition, and on community values. Ford Madox Ford's *Parade's End* (1924–28) illustrates the winnowing of the community, the increasing interest in the self detached from others and from the past. Whereas the pastoral novel pulls the reins of progress in the opposite direction, toward attachment and rootedness and tradition, the condition of flux has now been accepted as normal to twentieth-century existence. In fiction, the technique of stream-of-consciousness, in *Ulysses* or *The Waves*, captures the intense absorption in flux and in the self; and themes of estrangement, violence, evil, and failed heroism have become common in novels as different as Graham Greene's *The Power and the Glory* (1940), Anthony Burgess' *A Clockwork Orange* (1962), or Doris Lessing's *The Four-Gated City* (1969). Graham Greene has written that violence satisfies "the moral craving for a just and reasonable expression of human nature left without belief."[7] Thus, despite some exceptions, the growth of the city as the controlling landscape of modern fiction has meant that pastoral as I have defined it is no longer a truly viable mode of literary expression for major writers.

What remains, then, as a total impression of the seven novels we

[4] "Introduction" to *Promise of Greatness: The War of 1914–1918*, ed. George A. Panichas (New York: John Day, 1968), p. xxxiii.

[5] "War Service in Perspective," ibid., pp. 369–70.

[6] *Change in the Village* (1912; rpt. London: Gerald Duckworth, 1955), p. 11.

[7] *Collected Essays* (New York: Viking, 1969), p. 448.

have studied is that they are a major reassertion of pastoral. To say that they sound the major echo of a minor literary genre is in no way to say that they are an inconsiderable literary achievement. It may well be true that as a group these novels do not achieve the highest reaches of art, do not present a full panorama of society, do not embody the noblest expressions of what it is to be human, do not probe deeply into the arcane regions of human complexity. They should not be ranked with *Middlemarch, War and Peace, Madame Bovary, Tom Jones, The Brothers Karamazov, Moby Dick,* or *Ulysses*; and we should err to call them the great monuments to civilization. Yet if we follow Lord David Cecil's advice, and judge the novels on the basis of what they accomplish within their limited range, we can admire them sensitively and fully. These novels represent a significant and distinct achievement. They provide an index of the transition from rural to urban-industrial modes of life, utilizing the dialectic between opposed methods of organizing human lives and of making them intelligible. At the same time, illustrating concretely the significance of an agricultural society, they bear insight into the meaning of a rural environment and of a traditionally ordered society for those who make up the community. They offer a perspective on the rapid historical changes of the period; and in reviving a moribund literary genre, the pastoral novel proves that genre's elasticity. The grafting of pastoral and the novel, by encouraging a new kind of growth, helped save the genre from a withered end; the addition of realism to pastoral was water to deep but thirsty roots.

Aesthetically the pastoral novel offers distinctive and very real pleasures: a taste of the poetry of rural life, a created world of imaginative coherence and vitality, and (most difficult to enjoy) charm. Twentieth-century readers, trained to like stoicism over sentiment and immediacy over nostalgia, usually prefer *Roderick Random* to *The Vicar of Wakefield, La Terre* to *Under the Greenwood Tree, The Time Machine* or *The War of the Worlds* to *Silas Marner, The Odd Women* to *Cranford* or *Cousin Phillis*. Yet the latter possess virtues the former do not: charm, delicate humor, nostalgia, harmonious interaction between man and his natural environment, and a muted form of social criticism. It is a matter *au fond* of whether explicit confrontation with contemporary experience, or withdrawal that affords perspective, generates great art. Surely both do, assessing reality by different but equally valid and successful artistic methods, both exploring the collision of actuality with the writer's dream of actuality.

Many observers believe that World War I initiated the decadence of our civilization by replacing tradition, religion, authority, and culture with scientific and technological progress. Looking back objectively, recognizing its weaknesses, Edmund Blunden remarks of the rural tradition that "still, something lacks in all ways since the tradition was so heavily impaired."[8] One might think, then, as our industrial state ripens into a technocracy and demands nearly total urbanization, that the pastoral novels of George Eliot, Hardy, and Lawrence will appear as remote and artificial as allegorical pastoral appears to us today. This will likely happen. The rebellion against a technocratic society, against its depersonalization and its materialism, has of course begun, with rural communes sprouting in large numbers, filled with persons in retreat from complexity, wealth, and power, and in search of simplicity, harmony, and the reintegration of the self with nature and society. Several recent American novels in fact illustrate this pattern of retreat and discovery: Saul Bellow's *Henderson, the Rain King* (1959), Ken Kesey's *One Flew over the Cuckoo's Nest* (1962), Richard Brautigan's *Trout Fishing in America* (1967), and James Dickey's *Deliverance* (1970). But the flight into rural innocence is scarcely possible any longer. The pastoral process—here, perhaps, primitivism—does not promise to reveal the moral value of a small community of persons living next to the land, sharing the burdens of labor and the hours of leisure. In truth, considerable distance separates the contemporary commune from the rural communities created in the seven pastoral novels we have studied. The basis of a traditional rural culture lies in centuries of accumulated experience; though akin to the pastoral community in its democratic sentiments and its rejection of money and progress, the commune registers a relatively short-lived reaction to disillusion, war, and a credential society. Moreover, such a retreat may prove to lack literary vitality because it has its roots in urban rather than rural experience. But the fact that those who seek escape are mostly the young, weighted with *ennui*, suggests that some may return to urban society heartened by their interlude and prepared to convey, in artistic form and to civilized society, the significance of the pastoral retreat. Although the city now dominates our contemporary culture, pastoral literature may indeed emerge in the decades ahead if the tension between rural and urban can be felt once again as a stimulus to the creative imagination.

[8] "The Rural Tradition," *Edmund Blunden: A Selection of His Poetry and Prose*, ed. Kenneth Hopkins (London: Rupert Hart-Davis, 1950), p. 44.